SPENCER KIMBALL'S RECORD COLLECTION

SPENCER KIMBALL'S RECORD COLLECTION

ESSAYS ON MORMON MUSIC

MICHAEL HICKS

SIGNATURE BOOKS | 2020 | SALT LAKE CITY

"Elder Price Superstar" and "Spencer Kimball's Record Collection" first appeared in *Dialogue: A Journal of Mormon Thought*.

Different versions or substantial portions of three other essays first appeared in these periodicals: "How the Church Left Emma Smith and Why You Should Care," in *Journal of the Book of Mormon and Other Restoration Scripture*; "Ministering Minstrels," in *Utah Historical Quarterly;* and "How to Make and Unmake a Mormon Hymnbook," in *A Firm Foundation: Church Organization and Administration* (BYU Religious Studies Center).

All photographs are courtesy of the author.

Cover design by Jason Francis.

FIRST EDITION | 2020

LIBRARY OF CONGRESS CATALOGING-IN-PUBLICATION DATA

Names: Hicks, Michael, 1956– author.

Title: Spencer Kimball's record collection: essays on Mormon music / Michael Hicks.

Description: First edition. | Salt Lake City : Signature Books, 2020. | Includes index. | Summary: "At times jubilant, at times elegiac, this set of ten essays by music historian Michael Hicks navigates topics that range from the inner musical life of Joseph Smith to the Mormon love of blackface musicals, from endless wrangling over hymnbooks to the compiling of Mormon folk and exotica albums in the 1960s. It also offers a brief memoir of what happened to LDS Church President Spencer Kimball's record collection and a lengthy, brooding piece on the elegant strife it takes to write about Mormon musical history in the first place. There are surprises and provocations, of course, alongside judicious sifting of sources and weighing of evidence. The prose is fresh, the research smart, and the result a welcome mixture of the careful and the carefree from Mormonism's best-known scholar of musical life"—provided by publisher.

Identifiers: LCCN 2020025707 (print) | LCCN 2020025708 (ebook) | ISBN 9781560852865 (paperback) | ISBN 9781560853855 (ebook)

Subjects: LCSH: Church music—Mormon Church. | Church music—Church of Jesus Christ of Latter-day Saints. | Mormon Church—Hymns—History and criticism. | Hymns, English—United States—History and criticism. | Mormons—United States—Music—History and criticism.

Classification: LCC ML3174 .H52 2020 (print) | LCC ML3174 (ebook) | DDC 781.71/93—dc23

LC record available at https://lccn.loc.gov/2020025707
LC ebook record available at https://lccn.loc.gov/2020025708

CONTENTS

Preface vii

Abbreviations x

I

1 Joseph Smith's Favorite Songs (or Not) 3

2 How the Church Left Emma Smith and Why You Should Care 25

3 Tracking "The Spirit of God" 53

4 Ministering Minstrels 73

II

5 The *Mormon Pioneers'* Trek East 103

6 People of the (Other) Book 129

7 How to Make and Unmake a Mormon Hymnbook 155

III

8 Elder Price Superstar 177

9 Spencer Kimball's Record Collection 187

10 Making Book on the Tabernacle Choir . . . 197

Index 221

PREFACE

I wrote the title essay as a stretched-out journal entry for a journal that doesn't exist. I kept journals for decades, off and on, bound books brimming with confessions, self-analysis, travelogues, movie reviews, and weather reports—all the typical journal fare of an ex-hippie who often regrets the "ex." Now shoved to the back of a closet, those journals are freighted with mood swings and doctrinal noodling, but light on social events, which I shunned, and relationships, which mostly amounted to footnotes to Dickinson's line "the soul selects its own society, then shuts the door." But the events that triggered my title—i.e., being handed a prophet's vinyl "plates," as if I were some shaggy-headed suburban Moroni—escaped my now-defunct journal-keeping. Yet those events midwifed onto the planet the name of this book, a handpicked anthology of shorter pieces I've written on music in Mormondom.

I picked a few old essays, rewrote some, and wrote new ones, then arranged them into something like a row of stained-glass windows, each self-contained, but, all told, making an odd narrative of tableaux. They fall into three sections. The first roams through the nineteenth century's popular songs, hymns, and musical theatre. The second wanders into the twentieth century with the stories behind two record albums, followed by some lifting of the curtain of Mormon hymnbook-making near the century's end. The third collects ad hoc slices of criticism and memoir, from Broadway to Spencer Kimball's shelves to, in the end, a lip-chewing account of the making of the two other books in my Mormon music trilogy.

You see, I do consider this book the third in a set that began in 1989 with the publication of *Mormonism and Music: A History* and continued in 2015 with *The Mormon Tabernacle Choir: A Biography.* To create this new one, I didn't just brush the leftovers of the other books into a pail and call it good. Selecting the stories to include, exclude, or write from scratch for this one proved no small task, yet one far head-scratchier and juicier than whatever doggedness shaped the other books. Most of these essays still have the academic ring to them, however breezy and streamlined the prose might try to be. But I'd like to think they offer a nice journey from, let's say, the front door to the back. I grew up hearing Jesus's line, "In my Father's house are many mansions." I hope this book can be like that: one house, but each room bigger in some way than it looks from the outside. Because in each we get to linger, try out the furniture, stoke a fire, have a drink, and, well, turn on some music.

Better than a journal, I'd say.

The line between "Renaissance man" and "clever dilettante" is a hair's breadth. I've been introduced many times as the former but am much more the latter. Mostly, I think of myself as a plate spinner. You know the routine: spinning plates on top of wooden dowels, one after another, reaching up as needed to keep them all rotating and balanced. It's a circus act I first saw on Ed Sullivan's show (and last saw on YouTube). That's been my whole career, awkwardly but insistently reaching up to keep all these plates of different sizes and weights spinning: writing poetry, singing political folk songs, playing loungey piano, penning comic ditties, composing avant-garde chamber music, sketching portraits and cartoons, analyzing offbeat music for academic journals, and, oh yeah, writing books on music history, from 1960s rock to legit experimental composers to, as you see, music among the Mormons. My favorite literary character as a child was Curious George. He unwittingly became my mentor. One reckless curiosity to the next.

Just when the odd destiny of being a Mormon musical historian settled on me, I have no idea. Nevertheless, I have steered much of my recent life into it. In its wake, I've trailed no clouds of glory, just wisps of interest. I've had help, of course. Most of the culprits are footnoted within each chapter. Certain archives proved foundational, notably the triangle of (1) the Church History Library of the Church of Jesus Christ of Latter-day Saints, (2) the Harold B. Lee Library at Brigham Young University, and (3) the J. Willard Marriott Library at the University of Utah. After forty-something years in the trade, I've also amassed a sizable archive of notes, photocopies, transcriptions, recordings, and photographs. But the well still runs dry, and I have to trek up to the rivers of documents those other libraries provide.

Beyond informants, I didn't have many readers along the way. Just "encouragers," a species that may be the most vital of all, the people who said, "Do this, please, it'll be good." How to acknowledge, or in some cases even remember, all of them? Jeremy Grimshaw springs first to mind. Brian Harker next. Dozens of Facebook friends. And I have to mention Laurie Matheson of University of Illinois Press. A longtime encourager, she yellow-lighted the idea of this book when she heard it, which made me first slow down then slam my foot on the gas. Which led me to Signature Books, whose birth I witnessed decades ago and whose maturing canon of literature has delighted me ever since. I feel honored to take a place in their line and hope this book returns the favor to their august readership.

I hope you will learn things here that will tantalize you. But more than that, I hope you'll enjoy the tour, not just of topics and images, but of tone, angles of vision, and even high-class gossip from the artsy backrooms of Mormonism.

ABBREVIATIONS

BYUS	*Brigham Young University Studies*
CHL	Church History Library, the Church of Jesus Christ of Latter-day Saints, Salt Lake City, Utah
DN	*Deseret News*
HBLL	L. Tom Perry Special Collections, Harold B. Lee Library, Brigham Young University, Provo, Utah
IE	*Improvement Era*
JD	*Journal of Discourses by Brigham Young, His Two Counsellors, the Twelve Apostles, and Others,* 26 vols. (Liverpool and London: various publishers, 1854–86)
MS	*Latter-day Saints' Millennial Star*
SLT	*Salt Lake Tribune*

I

1 JOSEPH SMITH'S FAVORITE SONGS (OR NOT)

The Book of Mormon entered the world in the heyday of "binder's volumes," batches of sheet music sewn together between hard covers as keepsakes. Young men and women, skilled as pianists or singers, collected personal favorites, had them bound, and treasured them for what they captured of their owners' lives. Binder's volumes bundled people's aural pleasures, whose moods and lyrics bespoke the social and emotional lives of those who selected them. The descendants of binder's volumes, of course, are "mix tapes," digital playlists, and so forth, anthologies that contain their compilers' favorite songs, each with private meanings or memories attached.[1]

Now, imagine that Joseph Smith had compiled a binder's volume. What would it contain? And what would those contents reveal about his vision of himself?

We do know songs that surrounded him, of course. As one would expect, most of these are hymns. Joseph's brother William recalls that his family often sang the evening hymn "The Day Is Past and Gone" when he and Joseph were young.[2] The Zion's Camp soldiers that Joseph led to Missouri sang "Hark, Listen to the Trumpeters," which one soldier referred to as "our favorite song."[3] Some hymns appear to have been more popular than others in Mormon meetings of the 1830s: "Glorious Things of Thee Are Spoken," "Adam-ondi-Ahman," and "The Spirit of God

1. For a good discussion of these volumes, see Mark Slobin, "An Ethnomusicological View of Emily McKissick," in Mark Slobin et al., *Emily's Songbook: Music in 1850s Albany* (Middleton, Wisconsin: A–R Editions, 2011), 3–5.

2. See Michael Hicks, *Mormonism and Music: A History* (Urbana: University of Illinois Press, 1989), 4.

3. See "William Cahoon Autobiography," in Stella Shurtleff and Brent Farrington Cahoon, eds., *Reynolds Cahoon and His Stalwart Sons* (Salt Lake City: Paragon Press, 1960), 81–82.

Like a Fire Is Burning," to name three.[4] Joseph not only had all of these in his ears, he also seemed moved by some in particular. Wandle Mace recalled that after some congregational singing of "Glorious Things of Thee Are Spoken" in 1839, "Joseph was overcome" and "it was with difficulty that he controlled his emotions."[5] Eunice B. Snow recalled that while visiting Joseph when she was very young—about seventy years earlier than her statement—"we would sing his favorite hymns: 'When Joseph His Brethren Beheld,' 'Redeemer of Israel,' 'The Spirit of God,' and several others. He would become so inspired with the spirit of the music that he would clap his hands and shout hosanna to the Lord."[6]

Secular songs also filled the air around him. New song texts on broadsides or in newspapers in early nineteenth-century America often appeared with the annotation of another song to which the new one should be sung. Just so, in early Mormon publications we find references to "The Indian Hunter," "Nae Luck Around the House," and "Auld Lang Syne."[7] Smith likely had heard all of these.

But what Smith heard does not tell us what he preferred to hear. For that, we have one main source, the person George A. Smith called "the bosom friend and companion of the Prophet Joseph": Benjamin Johnson.[8] The prophet had spent many days at Johnson's house in Ramus, Illinois, days that included question and answer sessions later recorded in the Doctrine and Covenants. Johnson's 1903 memoir *My Life's Review* paints a vivid portrait of those times. But Johnson's letter to George Gibbs that same year provides the only putative inventory of Joseph's favorite songs.[9]

4. See Michael Hicks, "What Hymns Early Mormons Sang and How They Sang Them," BYUS 47 (2008): 95–118.

5. Wandle Mace, Autobiography, typescript in HBLL. Available online at www.boap.org/LDS/Early-Saints/WMace.html (accessed June 27, 2019).

6. In Mark L. McConkie, ed. *Remembering Joseph: Personal Recollections of Those Who Knew the Prophet Joseph Smith* (Salt Lake City: Deseret Book Co., 2003), 40–41.

7. See Michael Hicks, "Poetic Borrowing in Early Mormonism," *Dialogue: A Journal of Mormon Thought* 18 (Spring 1985): 47–55, and "Joseph Smith, W. W. Phelps, and the Poetic Paraphrase of 'The Vision,'" *Journal of Mormon History* 20 (Fall 1994): 63–84.

8. Quoted in E. Dale LeBaron, "Benjamin Franklin Johnson in Nauvoo: Friend, Confidant, and Defender of the Prophet," BYUS 32, 1, 2 (1992): 180.

9. Dean R. Zimmermann, *I Knew the Prophets: An Analysis of the Letter of Benjamin F. Johnson to George F. Gibbs, Reporting Doctrinal Views of Joseph and Brigham*

In describing the lighter side of Joseph, Johnson writes: "Jokes, rebuses, matching couplets in rhymes, etc., were not uncommon. But to call for the singing of one or more of his favorite songs was more frequent. Of those, 'Wife, Children and Friends,' 'Battle of River Raisin,' 'Soldiers' Tear,' 'Soldier's Dream' and 'Last Rose of Summer,' were most common."

The list has its drawbacks. The list came more than half a century after Smith's death. How much did Johnson's memory filter the list through his own tastes? And Johnson only mentions songs. Did Smith ever request instrumental dance tunes or even classical pieces? The list is, at best, a bank shot into Joseph's listening heart. Still, it is an impressive start. I consider it Johnson's table of contents to Joseph Smith's imaginary binder's volume. These songs, in order, form a nice suite I'd like to examine movement by movement.

• • •

The first song, "Wife, Children, and Friends," introduces the two great themes that dominate all the songs: family and soldierhood. The title phrase itself had appeared in English literature and oratory for decades. Johnson cites it (in quotes) at least once in his letter to George Gibbs, without overt reference to the song, and also says that Joseph's personal motto was "Wives, Children, and Friends."[10] Whatever its origins, "wife, children, and friends" became the tag line for each verse of a poem by William Robert Spencer, which consists of nine quatrains, each of which has a second line that must rhyme with "friends." At some point the poem was shortened to six stanzas—three pairs. Each pair became a verse of a song that one of Beethoven's publishers assigned to a bouncy Irish tune in a minor key. Beethoven arranged the song in 1814, and it spread promiscuously through parlors in ensuing decades.

Young (Bountiful, Utah: Horizon, 1976), 19. Also www.archive.org/details/BenjaminFJohnsonLetterToGeorgeFGibbs (accessed May 21, 2019).

10. Ibid. The pluralization of "wife" may be just an attempt to make all the terms plural, which they are not in the original song lyric, for consistency's sake. More likely, the pluralization of "wife" better suits Johnson's long discussions of polygamy in Nauvoo.

Opening page of Beethoven's 1814 setting of "Wife, Children, and Friends."

The title phrase itself, of course, echoed Joseph's deepening obsession with family, the accumulation of descendants (and their mothers), the linking of generations into one great fabric of humanity, and the perpetuation of these relationships for time and eternity. The opening verse of the song cites "a kind goddess" as the source for this "blessing," a divine compensation for the pain of mortality. The rhetoric of the lyrics that follow—unlike the other songs that Johnson cites—reflects the hifalutin tone that Joseph (or his ghostwriters) often aped in overtly "literary" works like the well-known Liberty Jail letter. The first verse goes:

When the black lettered list to the gods was presented,
The list of what fate to each mortal intends,
At the long string of ills a kind goddess relented
And slipped in three blessings: wife, children and friends.
In vain surly Pluto maintained he was cheated,
For justice divine could not compass its ends.
The scheme of man's penance he swore was defeated,
For earth became heav'n with wife, children, and friends.

The second verse introduces another theme, that of the noble soldier who yearns for that trinity of blessings with his dying breath.

The soldier whose deeds live immortal in story
Whom duty to far distant latitudes sends
With transport would barter whole ages of glory
For one happy day with wife, children and friends.
Though valor still glows in his life's waning embers,
The death-wounded tar who his colors defends
Drops a tear of regret as he dying remembers
How blessed was his home with wife, children and friends.

The last four lines of the song turn it into a toast:

Let us drink, for my song, growing graver and graver,
To subjects too solemn insensibly tends;
Let us drink, pledge me high: love and virtue shall flavor
The glass which I fill to wife, children, and friends.[11]

---

11. The lyrics vary here and there in punctuation or even verse order. I am using the one found in Sigmund Spaeth, *Read 'em and Weep: The Songs You Forgot to Remember* (New York: Doubleday, Page, 1927), 21–23. A few online performances of the song in Beethoven's setting are available, including this one from the KBYU-FM Joseph Smith bicentennial program entitled *Praise to the Man* (2005): www.youtube.com/watch?v=GO6l0aMGUF8 (accessed May 21, 2019). Mormon apostle Erastus Snow published an eight-quatrain version of "Wife, Children and Friends" under the heading "Poetry" on the back page of his tract *One Year in Scandinavia* (Liverpool, England: F. D. Richards, 1851). He precedes the text with this comment: "Had the author of the following lines known the calling and mission of the Latter-day Saints, he would have, most unquestionably, represented them in his song; as it is, we offer it to our readers, assuring them that we often appropriate it to our own use."

Johnson's second song is by far the most obscure of the lot. Although he refers to it as "Battle of [the] River Raisin," it is doubtless the song "Massacre of the River Raisin" as sung in a gathering at Liberty Jail. I can find no imprints of the words with music. The text, however, appears on a broadside, a photocopy of which is in the Brigham Young University library, where its title is "The Michigan Massacre at the River Raisin." Its opening lines are indeed those recalled by Joseph Smith III as being sung at his father's side in Liberty Jail: "In the Michigan forest, the night winds were high / Fast drifted the snow through the bleak winter sky."[12]

This song stood apart from the other four for its bellicosity. In its thirteen verses of elevated metric verse, the lyrics take a dream-like survey of the massacre, in which Native Americans, egged on by British troops, burned down the buildings that housed prisoners of war and hacked apart those who fled. The language is vivid and raw. Given its rarity, I copy here the complete text:

In the Michigan forest, the night winds were high,
Frost drifted the snow, through the bleak winter sky,
and trees, cliffs and mountain were hoary and cold
And the dark waves of the Raisin, congealed as she roll'd.

The wilderness deepened its horror and gloom,
All nature seemed wrapped in the sheet of the tomb,
While the howl of the tempest and ice greeting serge
With heart chilling notes sang her funeral dirge.

The beasts of the desert had gone to their home,
The wolves ceased to prowl, and the otter to roam;
Nor the hoot of the owl, nor the bald eagle scream,
With omen of ill broke the Wiandott's dream.

The hoops and the yell of the savage were still,
No longer the watch fire was seen on the hill;
The war song and dance round the captive had closed,
And wrapped in this blanket the warrior reposed.

If a moment there were when a soldier might dose,
And dream on his station secure from his foes,

12. See the statement by Joseph Smith III cited in "Succession in the Presidency," *Journal of History* (Lamoni, Iowa) 2, 1:10.

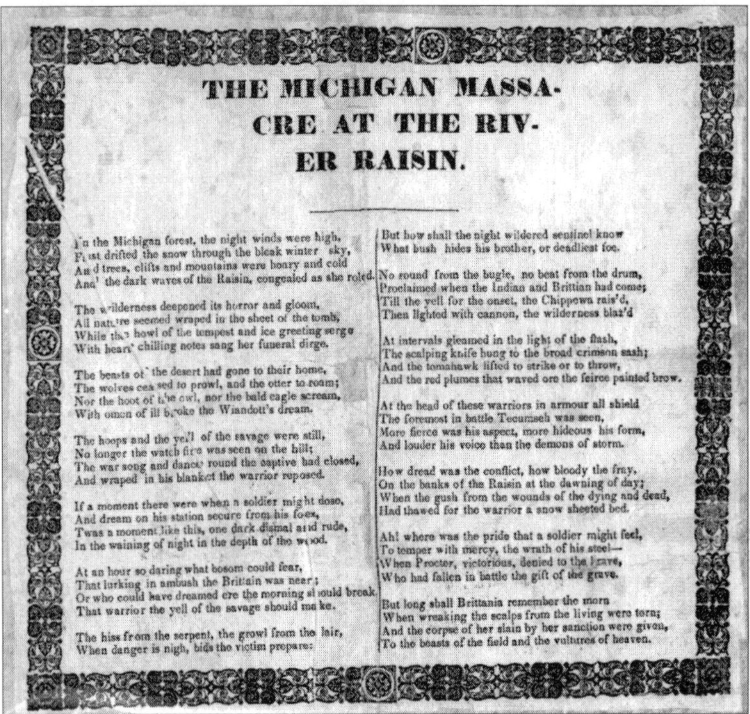

THE MICHIGAN MASSA-
CRE AT THE RIV-
ER RAISIN.

In the Michigan forest, the night winds were high,
Fast drifted the snow through the bleak winter sky,
And trees, clifts and mountains were hoary and cold
And the dark waves of the Raisin, congealed as she roled.

The wilderness deepened its horror and gloom,
All nature seemed wraped in the sheet of the tomb,
While the howl of the tempest and ice greeting serge
With heart chilling notes sang her funeral dirge.

The beasts of the desert had gone to their home,
The wolves ceased to prowl, and the otter to roam;
Nor the hoot of the owl, nor the bald eagle scream,
With omen of ill broke the Wiandott's dream.

The hoops and the yell of the savage were still,
No longer the watch fire was seen on the hill;
The war song and dance round the captive had closed,
And wraped in his blanket the warrior reposed.

If a moment there were when a soldier might doso,
And dream on his station secure from his foes,
Twas a moment like this, one dark dismal and rude,
In the waining of night in the depth of the wood.

At an hour so daring what bosom could fear,
That lurking in ambush the Britain was near;
Or who could have dreamed ere the morning should break
That warrior the yell of the savage should make.

The hiss from the serpent, the growl from the lair,
When danger is nigh, bids the victim prepare:
But how shall the night wildered sentinel know
What bush hides his brother, or deadliest foe.

No sound from the bugle, no beat from the drum,
Proclaimed when the Indian and Brittian had come;
Till the yell for the onset, the Chippewa rais'd,
Then lighted with cannon, the wilderness blaz'd

At intervals gleamed in the light of the flash,
The scalping knife hung to the broad crimson sash;
And the tomahawk lifted to strike or to throw,
And the red plumes that waved ore the feirce painted brow.

At the head of these warriors in armour all shield
The foremost in battle Tecumseh was seen,
More fierce was his aspect, more hideous his form,
And louder his voice than the demons of storm.

How dread was the conflict, how bloody the fray,
On the banks of the Raisin at the dawning of day;
When the gush from the wounds of the dying and dead,
Had thawed for the warrior a snow sheeted bed.

Ah! where was the pride that a soldier might feel,
To temper with mercy, the wrath of his steel—
When Procter, victorious, denied to the brave,
Who had fallen in battle the gift of the grave.

But long shall Brittania remember the morn
When wreaking the scalps from the living were torn;
And the corpse of her slain by her sanction were given,
To the beasts of the field and the vultures of heaven.

Broadside of the lyrics to "The Michigan Massacre at the River Raisin" (a.k.a. "Battle of the River Raisin"), date unknown.

T'was a moment like this, one dark dismal and rude,
In the waning of night in the depth of the wood.

At an hour so daring what bosom could fear,
That lurking in ambush the Brittain was near;
Or who could have dreamed ere the morning should break
That warrior the yell of the savage should make.

The hiss from the serpent, the growl from the lair,
When danger is nigh, bids the victim prepare;
But how shall the night wildered sentinel know
What bush hides his brother, or deadliest foe.

No sound from the bugle, no beat from the drum,
Proclaimed when the Indian and Brittian had come;
Till the yell for the onset, the Chippewa rais'd,
Then lighted with cannon, the wilderness blaz'd

At intervals gleamed in the light of the flash,
The scalping knife hung to the broad crimson sash;
And the tomahawk lifted to strike or to throw,
And the red plumes that waved ore the fierce painted brow.

At the head of these warriors in armour all shield
The foremost in battle Tecumseh was seen,
More fierce was his aspect, more hideous his form
And louder his voice than the demons of storm.

How dread was the conflict, how bloody the fray,
On the banks of the Raisin at the dawning of day;
When the gush from the wounds of the dying and dead,
Had thawed for the warrior a snow sheeted bed.

Ah! where was the pride that a soldier might feel,
To temper with mercy, the wrath of his steel—
When Procter, victorious, denied to the brave,
Who had fallen in battle the gift of the grave.

But long shall Brittania remember the morn
When wreaking the scalps from the living were torn;
And the corpse of her slain by her sanction were given,
To the beasts of the field and the vultures of heaven.

Whatever appeal the song had for Smith, two things stand out in "The Massacre." First, it reminds us how vivid the War of 1812 was in the memories of Smith and his generation. They knew only *this* war firsthand. Second, the song portrays Native Americans in "anti-savages" rhetoric, rather than pro-Indians-as-Israelites rhetoric. One finds both rhetorics in the Book of Mormon, where Nephites and Lamanites, the original two warring factions, are at once the Chosen People and devils. In this song, we see only the latter. "Massacre" offers only resentment—not the hope that Lamanites would be restored to their former glories. At the same time, the song echoes the Book of Mormon in its descriptions of battle scenes: "And it came to pass that many died in the wilderness of their wounds, and were devoured by those beasts, and also the vultures of the air" (Alma 1:97).

"The Soldier's Tear" both is and is not an operatic aria. Many shows in Joseph Smith's day were called "operas," but resembled what we call "musicals," stitched together with songs and dialogue. And "arias" could be any solo songs in such shows. Most of these arias hardly differed from a typical parlor song or even hymn. So "The Soldier's Tear," from Alexander Lee's wonderfully titled "opera" *Music and Prejudice* (1825), fills that bill.[13] It is strophic (meaning that it has multiple verses sung to the same music) and uses the simplest of harmonies with nothing virtuosic (i.e., "operatic") in its melody. It resembles, as much as anything, a common Stephen Foster song. It gained enough popularity to be published over and over in single sheets, plump anthologies, florid arrangements, and even hymn-style four-part harmony.

Of the five songs in Johnson's list, "Soldier's Tear" has the simplest, most direct moral at its end. In the first verse, a soldier stands on a hill preparing to leave for battle. He drinks up the sights and sounds of home and "wipes away a tear." In the second verse a girl—lover? wife? daughter?—kneels at his side, praying. He blesses her in return and "wipes away a tear." In the third verse he leaves the scene—but "do not deem him weak" because of his tears. "Go and watch the foremost ranks in danger's dark career," the final lines exhort: "Be sure the hand most daring there has wiped away a tear."

Songs with a soldier's dream in their titles abound in nineteenth-century America: "The Soldier's Dream," "A Soldier's Dream," "The Soldier's Last Dream," "The Soldier's Dream of Home," "Dream of a Soldier Boy," and even "Soldier's Dream March." Johnson likely referred to some setting of a text by Thomas Moore that was widely printed on broadsides—sometimes alongside "The Soldier's Tear." Unlike "The Soldier's Tear," "The Soldier's Dream" was a well-known poem first, and only later a song. It speaks in the voice of a soldier who, having survived a recent battle, lies down to sleep and dreams of home and family. It ends with a toast to their longevity, then a jarring awakening:

> Then pledged we the wine-cup, and fondly I swore
> From my home and my weeping friends never to part

13. The score: www.archive.org/details/soldierstearsung00leea/page/n5 (accessed May 21, 2019).

My little ones kissed me a thousand times o'er,
And my wife sobb'd aloud in her fulness of heart

"Stay—stay with us!—rest!—thou art weary and worn!"
And fain was their war-broken soldier to stay
But sorrow return'd with the dawning of morn
And the voice in my dreaming ear melted away.

When this poem appears as lyrics with musical notation, the tunes differ widely. One cannot say which Joseph had in mind, or if he even cared. (Among the many settings of the text from 1811 on, one does have a serendipitous relationship to Joseph Smith as a young prodigy: it was composed by a boy of thirteen, Abraham Taylor, whose youth was often remarked upon.) As with "Wife, Children, and Friends," though, Beethoven set Moore's "Soldier's Dream" to music, probably using a tune written by someone else, as he tended to do in his commercial arrangements.

The final song on Johnson's list sets to music another Thomas Moore poem. The text and tune to "The Last Rose of Summer" always appeared together, beginning in 1813, when the song debuted in Moore's own *Irish Melodies*. An apt coda to Johnson's other four, it treats loss, yes, but this time *not* in military terms. The narrator sees a single surviving rose, speaks tenderly to "her," and adopts her as an emblem of loneliness. He will tend her till she, too, passes away, because, the narrator confesses, "So soon may I follow / When friendships decay"—resonating with Joseph Smith's remark on the way to Carthage, "If my life is of no value to my friends, it is of no value to me." The last lines of "Last Rose" crystallize Smith's family-obsessive legacy: "Oh! who would inhabit/ This bleak world alone?"

• • •

If we take these five songs as an imaginary binder's volume for Joseph Smith, what would we construe about him? Three things come to mind.

First, soldier imagery fills four of the five. "Battle of the River Raisin" speaks of a specific time and place. But the other three—"Wife, Children, and Friends," "Soldier's Tear," and "Soldier's Dream"—describe an archetypal soldier, one not tied to any war,

THE SOLDIER'S DREAM.

Our bugles sang truce—for the night-cloud had lower'd,
  And the sentinel stars set their watch in the sky;
And thousands had sunk on the ground overpower'd,
  The weary to sleep, and the wounded to die.

When reposing that night on my pallet of straw,
  By the wolf-scaring fagot that guarded the slain,
At the dead of the night a sweet vision I saw,
  And thrice ere the morning I dreamt it again.

Methought from the battle-field's dreadful array,
  Far, far, I had roam'd on a desolate track;
'Twas autumn, — and sunshine arose on the way
  To the home of my fathers, that welcomed me back

I flew to the pleasant fields traversed so oft
  In life's morning march, when my bosom was young,
I heard my own mountain-goats bleating aloft,
  And knew the sweet strain that the corn-reapers sung.

Then pledged we the wine-cup, and fondly I swore
  From my home and my weeping friends never to part;
My little one kiss'd me a thousand times o'er.
  And my wife sobb'd aloud in her fullness of heart.

Stay. stay with us, — rest, thou art weary and worn;
  And fain was their war-broken soldier to stay;
But sorrow return'd with the dawning of morn,
  And the voice in my dreaming ear melted away

THE SOLDIER'S TEAR.

Upon the hill he turn'd, to take a last fond look,
At the valley and the village church and the cottage by the brook,
He listened to the sound so familiar to his ear,
And the soldier lean'd upon his sword and wip'd away a tear.

Beside yon cottage porch a girl was on her knees,
She held aloft a snowy scarf that flutter'd in the breeze,
She breath'd a prayer for him, a prayer he could not hear,
But he paused, to bless her as she knelt, and wip'd away a tear.

He turned and left the spot, O! do not deem him weak,
For dauntless was the soldier's heart tho' tears were on his cheek.
Go watch the foremost rank in danger's dark career,
Be sure the hand most daring there has wip'd away a tear.

Ten Illustrated Songs on Notepaper, mailed to any Address on receipt of 50 cts. Published by Chas. Magnus, 12 Frankfort St., N. Y.

One of at least three extant broadsides with the "The Soldier's Dream" above "The Soldier's Tear."

but suggestive of every war. This may be the songs' most powerful symbol. Although we scrutinize Joseph as prophet, seer, mayor, counselor, prolific husband, and even gamesman, these songs hint at how seriously he took his role as Lieutenant General of the Nauvoo Legion. He loved the parading, the horsemanship, the inspections, the uniforms and epaulets, even, presumably, the band playing its marches and serenades, all of the accoutrements of the military, though with no real battle front to daunt him. These soldier lyrics reveal a fantasy that may have colored his vision of himself more than we care to notice.

Second, the toasting of alcohol rises to the surface in two of the songs. Indeed, on the basis of its last four lines, music historian Sigmund Spaeth calls "Wife, Children, and Friends," "a most eloquent argument in favor of light wines and beer."[14] Joseph's freedom with the spirits of alcohol has been doted upon, notwithstanding the anti-hard liquor stance of the Word of Wisdom.[15] Here, in Johnson's recollection, two songs confirm that freedom.

Finally, given Smith's aptitude for romance, spiritualized or not, one might expect to see songs of courtship among his favorites. Instead one finds longing for family and home by one who has lost—or is about to lose—both. *Longing*, not "romance" per se, was the foundation of "romanticism" in that era. As E. T. A. Hoffman put it as early as 1813, all true music expresses "the infinite," which means a certain unreachability of fulfillment and, hence, "infinite longing."[16] Such longing sometimes turned into depression or "melancholy," as it was better known at the time. One scholar has cited Abraham Lincoln's fondness for singing "The Soldier's Dream" as evidence of the president's chronic depression.[17] The gloom that Joseph felt, sometimes in the guise of resignation, fills the songs Johnson remembered. The Joseph

14. Spaeth, *Read 'em and Weep*, 22.

15. The most meticulous (and entertaining) treatment of this is LaMar Petersen, *Hearts Made Glad: The Charges of Intemperance against Joseph Smith the Mormon Prophet* (Salt Lake City: LaMar Petersen, 1975).

16. See E. T. A. Hoffmann, "Beethoven's Instrumental Music" (1813), www.scribd.com/document/391728551/E-T-A-Hoffmann-Beethoven-s-instrumental-music-pdf (accessed May 21, 2019).

17. Michael Burlingame, *The Inner World of Abraham Lincoln* (Urbana: University of Illinois Press, 1994), 112.

Smith binder's volume, so far as we can reconstruct it, suggests a man whose sense of impending doom supported attractions both to sedating drink and soldierly bravado, all steeped in the longing for a better world.

• • •

One of the early nineteenth-century's best-known lyric poets in English was James Montgomery. In 1827 he published a 56-line poem entitled "The Stranger and His Friend," which spread like brushfire during the decade that followed. Its narrator (the "friend") meets a "poor, wayfaring" stranger. This stranger is a beleaguered "man of grief." That phrase alerts the clever reader to the big reveal of the poem's ending: the "man of grief" is Jesus in disguise, the messiah whom Isaiah (53:3) deemed "a man of sorrows and well acquainted with grief." In Montgomery's poem, the narrator keeps encountering the stranger in various states of need and in each case satisfies him, protects him, relieves him, even cheers him.

Montgomery had begun writing the poem with what became the fourth verse and then wrote his way backward and forward to the poem's completion. Here is that verse:

'Twas night; the floods were out; it blew
A winter hurricane aloof.
I heard his voice abroad and flew
To bid him welcome to my roof.
I warmed and clothed and cheered my guest
And laid him on my couch to rest,
Then made the earth my bed and seemed
In Eden's garden while I dreamed.

The sixth verse moves to a scene of unjust incarceration:

In pris'n I saw him next, condemned
To meet a traitor's doom at morn.
The tide of lying tongues I stemmed,
And honored him 'mid shame and scorn.
My friendship's utmost zeal to try,
He asked if I for him would die.
The flesh was weak; my blood ran chill,
But my free spirit cried, "I will."

And then, in the next verse, the unmasking, ending with a trope on Jesus's parable in Matthew 25:

Then in a moment to my view
The stranger started from disguise.
The tokens in his hands I knew;
The Savior stood before mine eyes
He spake and my poor name he named,
"Of me thou hast not been ashamed.
These deeds shall thy memorial be;
Fear not, thou didst them unto me."

In 1835, Reverend George Coles composed a modest hymn tune and named it for one of the New York churches in which he sometimes preached: "Duane Street." It caught on. While he may or may not have intended it as a setting for Montgomery's poem, the two quickly became fused: "A Poor Wayfaring Man of Grief" to the tune of "Duane Street" became a hymn whose text appeared in the British hymnbook that Mormon apostles compiled in Manchester, England, in 1840.[18]

Many accounts of Joseph Smith's assassination appeared in the months following June 27, 1844. Only one of these mentions the singing of that song. In *A Correct Account of the Murder of Generals Joseph and Hyrum Smith*, author William Daniels writes that apostle John Taylor, a fellow inmate with Smith, his brother Hyrum, and Willard Richards, had been singing the hymn shortly before the attack on the jail and that, "at the request of Hyrum Smith, it was sung over again."[19] Daniels must have gotten this detail from either John Taylor or Willard Richards, the two survivors of the attack. Richards never made a public statement on the matter. (In his "Joseph Smith Diary," kept during the afternoon of the assassination, he had simply recorded, under the time of "3.15 P.M.," that "Taylor sung 'poor way faring man

18. All of the foregoing background on this poem and song may be found in Michael Hicks, "'Strains Which Will Not Soon Be Allowed to Die ...': 'The Stranger' and Carthage Jail," BYUS 23 (Fall 1983): 389–400.

19. William M. Daniels, *A Correct Account of the Murder of Generals Joseph and Hyrum Smith at Carthage, on the 27th day of June, 1844* (Nauvoo, Illinois: John Taylor, 1844), 10–11.

of grief.'")[20] Taylor spoke publicly about the singing ten years to the day after the "Martyrdom," at a commemorative service held in Salt Lake City. Thomas Bullock, clerk of the service, took down Taylor's account in his peculiar shorthand, and quotes Taylor as saying: "I remember bro Hy requested me to sing a poor wa[y]faring man of grief which I done he requested it the 2nd time."[21] That is, he sang the song twice at Hyrum's asking before the mob stormed the jail. This confirmed Daniels's earlier statement that Hyrum requested the repeat.

When Taylor gave his address, the Historian's Office staff were writing the official church history, largely under the direction of Willard Richards, who had been Joseph's private secretary and historian. Had he lived, Richards could have added his own recollection of the matter to Taylor's. But Richards had died three months before the Taylor tenth anniversary discourse. George A. Smith, cousin to the prophet, was sustained as Church Historian on April 7, 1854, replacing Richards as director of the writing of the history. On March 27, 1856, Smith and Taylor were both called to present a Utah statehood petition to Congress. That left the new Assistant Church Historian, Wilford Woodruff, to supervise the writing of the Martyrdom, at which the narrative of the church history was about to arrive.[22]

Woodruff decided to approach Taylor. On June 30, 1856 he wrote Taylor a passionate plea for a fresh eyewitness account, to be made with "great care and minuteness," and yet with haste—"lose no time in attending to this matter," he wrote. To clarify the "Poor Wayfaring Man of Grief" episode, Woodruff asked Taylor: "was it Joseph or Hyrum that requested you to repeat it?"[23]

Taylor (with George A. Smith) quickly produced a long draft of his recollections of the entire Carthage jailing. Dated August 23,

20. At www.josephsmithpapers.org/paper-summary/appendix-3-willard-richards-journal-excerpt-23-27-June-1844/1 (accessed June 24, 2019).

21. Thomas Bullock Minutes, CHL.

22. Much of the information concerning the writing of the martyrdom history I have taken from Dean C. Jessee, "Return to Carthage: Writing the History of Joseph Smith's Martyrdom," *Journal of Mormon History* 8 (1981):3–19; and Howard C. Searle, "Authorship of the History of Joseph Smith: A Review Essay," BYUS 21 (Winter 1981): 101–22.

23. Historian's Office Letterpress Copybook, 1:315, 320, CHL.

1856, Taylor's manuscript repeats—albeit with slightly convoluted construction—his earlier testimony that he sang the song twice at Hyrum's request: "After a lapse of some time, Brother Hyrum requested me again to sing that song."[24]

Somewhere around this time the Historian's Office prepared its own rough draft of the Martyrdom story. Written by Thomas Bullock, Jonathan Grimshaw, Leo Hawkins, and Robert Campbell, and inscribed in black ink on blue, ruled "legal" sized pages, the draft bears the title: "An Account of the arrest, imprisonment, and martyrdom of President Joseph Smith, and Patriarch Hyrum Smith in Carthage Jail Hancock County, Illinois, as collected from the journals kept at the time by Dr Willard Richards, and the statements published by John Taylor, Messrs Reid and Woods, and John S. Fullmer, and the writings and statements of Dan Jones, Cyrus H. Wheelock, Stephen Markham, and many other persons who were personally acquainted with his transactions." (The subscript, "By George A. Smith," is crossed out in the original ink.) On page 59 of this document appeared the only reference to the song, taken directly from Richards's Joseph Smith Diary: "3¼ … Taylor sang 'A Poor wayfaring man of grief.'" (Inserted into this are directions to include the full text of the song.) Red ink revisions cover this manuscript, among which is an insertion after the line about the song and the subsequent line in the draft: "When he got through, Joseph requested him to sing it again, which he did." The handwriting appears to be similar to that of the original line about the song, except that it is a hurried scrawl, completely lacking the methodical precision of the original black ink draft.[25]

Although George Smith had read the Taylor manuscript as it was being written, Taylor may not have left a final copy of his account with the Historian's Office until *more than a year* after his first draft was written. Wilford Woodruff's journal entry for September 27, 1857, reads: "I called upon Elder Taylor in the Morning to get the History of Joseph which he had written but

24. The statement apparently first appeared in print in Appendix III to Richard F. Burton, *The City of the Saints and Across the Rocky Mountains to California* (London: Longman, Green, Longman, and Roberts, 1861), 652.

25. Early Drafts of the History of the Church, CHL.

He informed me he had left it at the Historians office the evening before." (Subsequent entries, which discuss Woodruff reviewing the manuscript, make it clear that this "History of Joseph" was the Martyrdom account.) Nine days later Woodruff apparently asked Brigham Young about publishing Taylor's full account as part of the official Joseph Smith history, since that account would be the most detailed source for Joseph's final days. But Young discouraged this idea, telling Woodruff to put only "what there was necessary" into "Joseph's History" (the common name then for what we now call the "History of the Church"), and "publish the rest as John Taylors History."[26] Yet the final draft for the official Martyrdom history had already been completed by the clerks of the Historian's Office. They were now writing the "History of Brigham Young." Despite all the care that Woodruff had taken to get every detail accurate, the scribal insertion that Joseph (not Hyrum) had requested the song was set in type and published in the *Deseret News*, November 18, 1857. In time, this first printed version of the official story took its place in the B. H. Roberts collation known as the *History of the Church*.[27]

The "Joseph" error in the Carthage singing episode, however, has not been corrected. Why? Because it is a comforting error. It elevates the song from a fragment of Hyrum Smith's legacy to a sacred relic of "Joseph the Prophet." For this reason the error has not only been left largely intact, it has been nurtured and dressed up by countless writers and speakers from the late nineteenth century to the present.

John Taylor himself may be indirectly to blame for the persistence of the error, because the song would probably not have

26. Scott G. Kenney, ed., *Wilford Woodruff's Journal: 1833–1898*, 9 vols. (Midvale, Utah: Signature Books, 1983), 5:68.

27. This was not the first time the Historian's Office had inadvertently transposed a name in its history of the prophet. In the official account of the coming forth of the Book of Mormon, the manuscript "History of the Church" (and in turn the *Times and Seasons* published version) had said that *Nephi* (not Moroni) was the messenger who appeared to Joseph on the night of September 21, 1823, to tell young Joseph of the book. This erroneous name—an obvious slip of the pen—appeared in the official history and in several sources that copied from it even after several other published accounts had referred to "Moroni" as the messenger' name. The text of the B. H. Roberts edition of the *History of the Church* corrected the name to accord with these other accounts.

survived at all without him keeping it alive. Even though the text remained in the Manchester hymnbook, the hymn was still so little known in 1855 that the *Deseret News* published the words as a poem under the original title, "The Stranger and His Friend," as though they were new to the reader—and with no reference to Carthage.[28] Taylor tried to keep the song alive by singing it in gatherings of church leaders for the rest of his life. In time it became something of a trademark for him, especially after he became president of the church.[29] Sometime after 1880, Ebenezer Beesley had the Tabernacle Choir sing the hymn, but to the tune of the anthem "How Sweet the Hour of Closing Day" (taken from J. R. Thomas's 1866 *Sacred Music*).[30] But Taylor felt the song should be sung to the tune he used at Carthage. So he had Beesley transcribe it from Taylor's own singing, then harmonize it for publication. In roughly this form, though with notable alterations by Beesley, it first appeared in the 1885 *Juvenile Instructor*. A note at the bottom of the page accounts for the song's appearance there and suggests that its connection was still not widely known, at least among the young.

> We publish this hymn as a relic or curiosity, as it is historically connected with the most diabolical tragedy that ever disgraced the American continent—the assassination of the Prophet Joseph Smith and his brother, Hyrum. The circumstances which make it memorable are as follows: In the afternoon of the 27th day of June, 1844 … Elder (now President) Taylor sang this hymn to the tune here set to it. After awhile Hyrum Smith requested him to again sing it … The subsequent occurrences all are no doubt familiar with.[31]

---

28. DN, Nov. 28, 1855.

29. See William Clayton, Diary, Nov. 30, 1845, www.boap.org/LDS/Early-Saints/clayton-diaries (accessed July 29, 2019); also Affidavit of George Earl, Aug. 2, 1949, reprinted in J. Max Anderson, *The Polygamy Story: Fiction and Fact* (Salt Lake City: Publishers Press, 1979), 59.

30. Beesley's notes on this setting are in his copy of Thomas's collection, Ebenezer Beesley Papers, HBLL.

31. *Juvenile Instructor* 20 (Mar. 1, 1885): 79. The hymn—including the explanatory note—first appeared in a book in *The Improvement Association Song Book* (Salt Lake City: Juvenile Instructor Office, 1887). On Taylor's commission to Beesley to transcribe the song, see "A Sketch of the Musical Compositions of Ebenezer Beesley and Conditions which Inspired Him to Compose (written by his son, Frederick)," typescript in Beesley Papers, HBLL. A facsimile of Beesley's transcription of Taylor's sung version of the song appears in Sterling E. Beesley, *Kind Words: The Beginnings of*

Some leaders of the Mutual Improvement Association, though, began to take extreme liberties with the idea that *Joseph* had called for the song. In 1891, for example, H. W. Naisbitt wrote an article for the Association's magazine, *The Contributor*, containing this exuberant version of the facts: "at the request of the Prophet, the late President John Taylor sang those suggestive and touching lines … when the end was reached, at the renewed request of the doomed servant of God, it was repeated again and again."[32] Early in this century, BYU president George Brimhall reportedly told Florence Madsen and Alice Reynolds that the song was "the favorite hymn of the Prophet. … It was sung to him three times before his assassination."[33] Not content even with this exaggeration, Madsen and Reynolds began to teach in their hymnology courses that not only was the song Joseph's favorite, but "by his request [it] was sung to him six times before his assasination."[34] Meanwhile, in 1914 Heber J. Grant wrote that the song was, in fact, *Taylor's* favorite hymn, though still incorrectly cited Taylor's version of the incident, by changing the name "Hyrum" to "The Prophet."[35]

In 1939 the General Music Committee of the church urged George D. Pyper to compile the hymn stories he had written for the *Improvement Era* into the book *Stories of Latter-day Saint Hymns*. This work, as does Spencer Cornwall's revision and expansion of it, *Stories of Our Mormon Hymns* (1961), follows Taylor's account of the repetition faithfully, but still inserts the idea that the hymn was "a favorite song of the Prophet."[36] Cornwall's daughter, historian Carol Cornwall Madsen, continued the trend in an 1975 *Ensign* article called "Our Heritage of Hymns": "At length, Joseph

---

Mormon Melody, A Historical Biography and Anthology of the Life and Works of Ebenezer Beesley, Utah Pioneer Musician (privately published, 1980), 398–99.

32. "Music and Her Sister, Song," *Contributor* 12 (Apr. 1891): 236.

33. Alice Louise Reynolds and Florence Jepperson Madsen, "Hymnology," manuscript, 3 vols., 2:6, HBLL.

34. Ibid., 3:8.

35. Heber J. Grant, "Favorite Hymns," IE 17 (June 1914): 787–88.

36. This statement first appeared in Pyper's essay on the song, "The Story of Our Hymns," IE 39 (June 1936): 356–57. The idea that this was Joseph's favorite hymn was echoed in B. Cecil McGavin, *Nauvoo the Beautiful* (Salt Lake City: Stevens and Wallis, 1946), 130, 136.

broke the silence and asked to hear one of his favorite hymns."[37] By this time, many variants of the Carthage singing episode had appeared in secondary accounts, one source uncritically copying from another and occasionally adding its own twist.

Although secondary accounts often now correctly note that *Hyrum* requested the repeat, the idea that the song was "beloved" of Joseph was included in the first edition of the 1985 LDS hymnbook. In defense of that idea, David Haight of the Quorum of the Twelve, rebutted my own findings by insisting that George Albert Smith, Trustee-in-Trust, had copyrighted Joseph Fielding Smith's *Essentials in Church History*, which quotes (without citation) *History of the Church* that *Joseph* requested the song be repeated at Carthage. To Haight, the copyright of the history by a church president settled the question.[38]

If we leave "Poor Wayfaring Man of Grief" in the hymnbook for sentimental reasons we should tear it out of Joseph Smith's imaginary binder's volume. What it teaches about discipleship remains golden. But what it tells us about Joseph Smith is mostly how much his followers yearn for the right song to put in the book of his heart.

On the one hand the transposition from Hyrum to Joseph was accidental. On the other, inevitable. In Joseph's day, saints venerated the martyrdom of both brothers, almost equally. They formed a pair of witnesses and, per scripture, any lasting testimony requires at least two. But in ensuing decades as Joseph's image grew brighter, Hyrum's faded. And in time it just would not do to have so loftily Christian a song attached to Joseph's right-hand man. Think of a groom versus the best man, or a president versus a vice-president. One will always fall far below the other in narrative weight, regardless of the intrinsic worth of his character. The classic song goes with the classic leader, evidence notwithstanding.

• • •

If I have brooded over song lyrics, I have said little about *music*. That is not just because of problems knowing the right

37. *New Era* 5 (Nov. 1975): 15. For a list of other secondary sources that treat the Carthage singing episode in various ways, see Hicks, "'Strains,'" 396n.

38. David B. Haight, Letter to Michael Hicks, Mar. 24, 1986, in my possession.

tunes. Beyond tunes, what about the arrangements, accompaniment, dynamics, tempi? What Joseph heard in style and detail is impossible to say with surety. The *music* of the Smith binder's volume is too speculative, too dicey as a platform for judgments or interpretations.

The best we can say about it is that Johnson's list leans toward what was known as "sweet music" in its day. In and out of Mormondom, the term connoted Stephen Foster-esque parlor songs. It was the kind of music that Brigham Young endorsed.[39] "Sweet music" was simple, calming, sentimental, gushy, easy on the ear. If we read anything into Johnson's list from a *musical* point of view it might be that, deep down, Joseph Smith craved the soothing effects of sweet music. A gambler at a high stakes spiritual table, he needed music to settle him, free his mind for the next play, the next bet. Would one expect Smith to favor music as radical or daring as his theology or social manipulations were? In an ideal, everything-fits-together-neatly world, perhaps. No doubt, Smith had little access to anything that would challenge him aesthetically. If he did, would he be drawn to it or snub it?

What we find in Smith's imaginary binder's volume is what Marcel Proust talked about in his famous "In Praise of Bad Music." The adjective "bad [*mauvaise*]" is ironic, of course, one that the musical elite would apply to just such music as Smith "called for" the most. But Proust argues for its worth, a sum of value that transcends "mere" aesthetic gauges. Stephen Foster trumps Franz Schubert—or even Beethoven as we normally think of him, the composer of symphonies and sonatas, not writer-arranger of "Wife, Children, and Friends." With that in mind, I hand my conclusion to Proust.

> Detest bad music but do not despise it. As it is played, and especially sung, much more passionately than good music, it has much more than the latter been impregnated, little by little, with man's tears. Hold it therefore in veneration. Its place, nonexistent in the history of art, is immense in the sentimental history of nations. … Before an imagination sympathetic and respectful enough to silence for a moment its

39. See, for example, JD 1:48.

aesthetic scorn, from this dust that flock of souls may rise holding in their beaks the still verdant dream which has given them a foretaste of the other world, and made them rejoice or weep in this one.[40]

40. Marcel Proust, "In Praise of Bad Music," *Pleasures and Days and Other Writings*, ed. F. W. Dupee (New York: Doubleday Anchor, 1967), 117.

2 HOW THE CHURCH LEFT EMMA SMITH AND WHY YOU SHOULD CARE

People often ask me if I think "Amazing Grace" will ever be in our hymnbook. I tell them that it *was* in our hymnbook: Emma Smith's, 1841. Their follow-up is always the same: "Why did they take it out?" The simplest answer is that they took Emma Smith out of the hymnbook. When she snubbed the apostles after Joseph's killing, sure that his mantle lay in her late husband's DNA, the apostles effectively tore up her hymn license and used their own. That formed the Great Divide in Mormon hymnody. One brand headed west, the other stayed in the Midwest.

What's the difference between brands? Character. A hymnbook's *character* seldom comes up when we talk about hymns. We talk about hymns' authorship, derivation, structure, use, and Mormonesque doctrines.[1] We usually overlook a hymnbook's tone, its manner, the "feel" of the words overall. That's only natural. Gauging a hymnbook's character seems sneakily subjective. But it is a way of looking at hymnbooks that was not lost on, say, Sidney Rigdon, that failed contestant in the spiritual brawl over who would succeed the dead Prophet Joseph. Rigdon wrote in the preface to his own 1845 hymnbook that he is "careful to insert compositions which are rather subjects of praise than of prayer or of exhortation. If saints pray let them do it without singing their prayers: and if they exhort let them do so; for the subject matter of prayer and exhortation is never the subject of praise, at the same

1. For two recent examples, see Marilyn J. Crandall, "The Little Gardner Hymnal, 1844: A Study of Its Origins and Contribution to the LDS Musical Canon," BYUS 44 (2005): 137–60; and Mary D. Poulter, "Doctrines of Faith and Hope Found in Emma Smith's 1835 Hymnbook," BYUS 37, 2 (1997–98): 32–56. Recall that all early hymnbooks of the church contained words only. Hence, that is my focus here.

126 PUBLIC WORSHIP.

2 Since with pure and firm affection,
Thou on God hast set thy love,
With the wings of his protection,
He will shield thee from above:
Thou shalt call on him in trouble;
He will hearken, he will save;
Here for grief reward thee double,
Crown with life beyond the grave.

HYMN 118. C. M.

1 Amazing grace! (how sweet the sound,)
That saved a wretch like me!
I once was lost, but now am found,—
Was blind, but now I see.

2 'Twas grace that taught my heart to fear,
And grace my fears reliev'd;
How precious did that grace appear,
The hour I first believ'd!

3 Through many dangers, toils, and snares,
I have already come;
Tis grace has brought me safe thus far,
And grace will lead me home.

PUBLIC WORSHIP. 127

4 The Lord has promis'd good to me,
His word my hope secures;
He will my shield and portion be
As long as life endures.

5 Yes, when this flesh and heart shall fail,
And mortal life shall cease;
I shall possess within the veil,
A life of joy and peace.

6 The earth shall soon dissolve like snow,
The sun forbear to shine;
But God, who call'd me here below
Will be forever mine.

HYMN 119. P. M.

1 Redeemer of Israel,
Our only delight,
On whom for a blessing we call;
Our shadow by day,
And our pillar by night,
Our king, our companion, our all.

2 We know he is coming
To gather his sheep,
And plant them in Zion, in love,
For why in the valley

"Amazing Grace" in Emma Smith's 1841 hymnbook.

time. A subject cannot be a subject of praise until it ceases to be a subject of prayer or of exhortation." And on and on, he harps on how a collection of hymns of praise—i.e., his book—*must* differ from one of prayer or exhortation.[2]

That Rigdon hymnbook was at least the *tenth* in a series of Mormon hymnbooks compiled by this or that Saint since 1835 (see Appendix). Eight of those were small to moderate in length, from seventeen to 155 hymns apiece. But two others stood out, each with more than 300 hymns apiece. Those, like two stone lions at a gateway, stood for the two different characters that vied for dominance from 1840 onward.

• • •

2. S[idney] Rigdon, comp., *A Collection of Sacred Hymns for the Church of Jesus Christ of Latter Day Saints* (Pittsburgh: E[benezer] Robinson, 1845), iv. It is not clear to what hymnbooks he was contrasting his own.

Joseph Smith dictated a revelation in July 1830 that enticed his wife to submit to him mostly by offering her the sole authority over the new church's hymnody. "And it shall be given thee also to make a selection of Sacred Hymns as it shall be given thee which is pleasing unto me to be had in my Church for my Soul delighteth in the song of the heart yea the song of the righteous is a prayer unto me & it shall be answered with a blessing upon their heads."[3] The wording made two things clear: (1) She had the right to choose hymns; and (2) Singing them counted as prayer. We have no list of her selections, just the assortment of texts that began to be published on the back page of the church newspaper, *The Evening and the Morning Star*, beginning in 1832. The problem—indeed the first breach of her authority—was twofold: convert journalist William Phelps owned the press and Joseph's top leaders had ordered that he "correct" and "revise" what she had selected.[4] Whatever authority she had been handed by a revelation had quickly been snapped up by men. Meanwhile, a *book* of hymns lay years away, to be compiled and printed by, literally, God only knew who.

The Book of Mormon was *the* book until another one could catch up, some gathering of new revelations that would, in effect, trump the evangelistic tone and sermonizing of the earlier book. That was the ostentatiously titled *Book of Commandments*, planned for an edition of 10,000, later cut to 3,000—a number which itself was thwarted by mobs in 1833.[5] The follow up, Doctrine and Covenants, complete with often puzzling "lectures on faith" clearly derived from Sidney Rigdon, came off the press in 1835. A hymnbook quickly followed in 1836 (despite its imprint date of 1835).[6] The hymnbook, credited to Emma Smith, contained

3. This is from a transcript of the Book of Commandments holograph copy found here: www.beta.josephsmithpapers.org/paper-summary/revelation-july-1830-c-dc-25/1#full-transcript (accessed June 28, 2019).

4. See Donald Q. Cannon and Lyndon W. Cook, eds., *Far West Record: Minutes of the Church of Jesus Christ of Latter-day Saints, 1830–1844* (Salt Lake City: Deseret Book Co., 1983), 46; Peter Crawley, *A Descriptive Bibliography of the Mormon Church*, 3 vols. (Provo, Utah: Brigham Young University, Religious Studies Center, 1997–2012), 1:59. This source is available online here: www.rsc.byu.edu/out-print/descriptive-bibliography-mormon-church-volume-1 (accessed June 28, 2019).

5. See the history of the book in Crawley, *Descriptive Bibliography,* 1:38–39.

6. The dating issue is treated in ibid., 1:59.

ninety hymns (texts only), mostly borrowed, but many by Phelps and other Latter-day Saints. Given his earlier "correcting" and "revising" assignment, Phelps stamped her book with his own biases and quirks. He altered many of the "selected" hymns to be more group-oriented (e.g., changed from "I" to "we") or more millennial (e.g., in "Joy to the World": the phrase "the Lord is come" changed to "the Lord will come").[7]

We do not know the size of the imprint of that first hymnbook, though it was probably less than that of Doctrine and Covenants (print run also unknown). Whatever the number of copies of Emma's book, circumstantial evidence suggests it was either sold out or in disuse within three years. I say "disuse" because missionaries traveling with books to distribute would have carried copies in the obvious proportions of priority: Book of Mormon, Doctrine and Covenants, and, only last of all, hymnbooks. Even though people would have wanted the Book of Mormon (republished in Kirtland in 1837) and Doctrine and Covenants (1835) more than a hymnbook, Emma's book was in short supply. In 1838 David W. Rogers claimed Jesus had appeared to him in a dream and told him to compile a new Latter-day Saint hymnbook.[8] While the size and title of the book he published implies that it was Emma Smith's original, Rogers is clearly shown on the title page as the compiler.

At the church's October 1839 general conference—by which time another non-Emma hymnbook had also appeared—the leaders resolved "that a new edition of Hymn Books be printed immediately, and that the one published by D. W. Rogers be utterly discarded by the Church." He, in turn, would have to answer to the Nauvoo Stake High Council. When that council met on Rogers's case twenty days later, they voted "that Sister Emma Smith select and publish a hymn-book for the use of the Church, and that Brigham Young be informed of this action and he not publish the hymns taken by him from Commerce [Nauvoo]."

7. The changes are surveyed in my "Poetic Borrowing in Early Mormonism," *Dialogue: A Journal of Mormon Thought* 18, 1 (Spring 1985): 132–42.

8. See the preface to David W. Rogers, *A Collection of Sacred Hymns for the Church of the Latter Day Saints* (New York: C. Vinten Printer, 1838).

They themselves, the council added, should "assist" in publishing Emma's book.[9]

Unfortunately, Joseph had already gone his own way. His 1839 journal mentions that on Monday, Tuesday, and Wednesday, July 8–10, he not only spent most of his time ministering to the sick in the Saints' new gathering place in Illinois, but also "selecting hymns with the 12."[10] When the journal entry was published in the *History of the Church*, the editors expanded the statement to read: "I was with the Twelve selecting hymns, for the purpose of compiling a hymn book."[11] The change may seem subtle. But although the Twelve were about to leave on their mission to the East Coast and Great Britain, the issue of publishing a new *book* of hymns was far from settled. Emma had the authority, and, once again, men were trampling it.

In a letter dated November 22, 1839, Apostle Parley Pratt made clear that he did not expect the Twelve (of which he was a member) to publish their own hymnbook. He was waiting for a new one from Emma: "There is a great call for hymn-books, but none to be had. I wish Sister Smith would add to the old collection such new ones as is best and republish them immediately. If means and facilities are lacking in the west, send it here [New York], and it shall be done nicely for her; and at least one thousand would immediately sell in these parts wholesale and retail." After offering to raise money to publish the Book of Mormon and Doctrine and

9. This is from the oft-cited, oft-reprinted, originally serialized, B. H. Roberts-edited, *History of the Church*, under the date of October 27, 1839. This and all other references to the events cited in this chapter to this source may be found online most easily here: www.boap.org/LDS/History/History_of_the_Church/Vol_IV; or here: www.byustudies.byu.edu/content/volume-4-table-contents (both accessed June 28, 2019). One can find scans of the original holographs of these citations, with transcriptions, under the pertinent dates here: www.josephsmithpapers.org/paper-summary/history-1838-1856-volume-c-1-2-november-1838-31-july-1842/543 (accessed June 28, 2019). No variations of note on these matters appear among the various versions. For a fastidious polemic on how not to cite this source, see www.juvenileinstructor.org/bh-robertss-documentary-history-of-the-church-1903-2011-r-i-p/ (accessed June 28, 2019). Meanwhile, for further discussion of the Rogers hymnbook, see Michael Hicks, *Mormonism and Music: A History* (Urbana: University of Illinois Press, 1989), 23–25.

10. Dean C. Jessee et al., eds. *The Joseph Smith Papers: Journals: Volume 1: 1832–1839* (Salt Lake City: Church Historian's Press, 2008), 348.

11. *History of the Church*, July 8, 1839.

Covenants in the East, Pratt added, "Any hymn book which Sister Smith or the Church will favor us with, shall also be published on similar conditions."[12]

In his letter of reply to Pratt, December 22, 1839, Joseph's brother and protégé, Hyrum Smith, made clear that the Book of Mormon, Doctrine and Covenants, and hymnbook should all be published at Nauvoo and *then*, if non-English versions were needed, the Nauvoo editions could be translated and published elsewhere.[13] The high council, meanwhile, effectively declined Pratt's offer to publish the book in the East, voting on December 29 to print 10,000 copies of Emma's new book "under the inspection of the First Presidency at Nauvoo, so soon as means can be obtained."[14] Within a few days, Hyrum wrote to Joseph, bringing up Pratt's request and urging Joseph to get all three books out "under your immediate inspection. I am afraid some have been induced to tarry and assist Parl[e]y in these undertakings."[15]

The zeal with which the people of Nauvoo tried to protect Emma's authority as the church hymnodist came to a head on April 6, 1840, when Thomas Grover preferred charges against David Rogers (who was not present) "for compiling a hymn-book, and selling it as the one compiled and published by Sister Emma Smith." The next day, though, Rogers was forgiven of his breach.[16]

Ten days later in Manchester, England, a council meeting of seven of the Twelve Apostles voted to appoint its own three-member committee to select hymns, presumably following up on what they had begun with Joseph before leaving on their mission. If there was an unclarity about whether their selection was to be published as a *book*, however, Brigham Young skipped over propriety in favor of pragmatism: "Concerning the hymn-book—when we arrived here, we found the brethren had laid by their old hymn-books,

12. Ibid., Nov. 18, 1839.

13. Hyrum Smith, Letter to Parley P. Pratt, Dec. 22.,1839, www.josephsmithpapers.org/paper-summary/lettervook-2/85#full-transcript (accessed Dec. 24, 2019).

14. *History of the Church*, Dec. 29, 1839.

15. Hyrum Smith, Letter to Joseph Smith and Elias Higbee, Jan. 2, 1840, www.josephsmithpapers.org/paper-summary/letterbook-2/85#full-transcript (accessed Dec. 24, 2019).

16. *History of the Church*, Apr. 6, 1840.

and they wanted new ones: for the Bible, religion, and all is new to them. When I came to learn more about carrying books into the states, or bringing them here, I found the duties were so high that we never should want to bring books from the states." With that justification, Young steamed ahead without any official permission to publish a new British hymnbook. No time to bow to Emma's authority, not to mention the high council's.[17]

Apostles Orson Hyde and John E. Page, puzzled about Joseph's opinion on the hymnbook, wrote him from Ohio on May 1, 1840, about their upcoming mission to Germany. "Should we deem it necessary to publish an edition of Hymn Books in any Country: are we at liberty to do it? The fact is we need such works; and we cannot get them from the Church here; and if we could we could not well carry them with us, in any quantity. ... We did not convers[e] so much upon these literary works as we should have done before we left." Part of the problem, Elders Hyde and Page said, was that "we did not begin to see the greatness of our mission before we left home; our minds were in a nutt shell."[18]

The prophet fired a letter back. "In answer to your inquiries respecting the translation and publication ... I would say that I entirely approve of the same; and give my consent, with the exception of the Hymn Book, as a new edition, containing a greater variety of Hymns, will be shortly published or printed in this place; which, I think will be a standard work." He added that, "As soon as it is printed, you shall have some to you, which you may get translated, and printed in any language you please. Should we not be able to send some to you, and there should be a great call for Hymns where you may be, then I should have no objections to your publishing the present one [i.e., the 1835 edition]. Were you [to do so] I desire the copy rights of the same to be secured in my name."[19]

17. Ibid., Apr. 16, 1840 (punctuation as in original).

18. Orson Hyde and John E. Page, Letter to Joseph Smith, May 1, 1840, www.josephsmithpapers.org/paper-summary/letterbook-2/85#full-transcript (accessed Dec. 24, 2019).

19. Joseph Smith, Letter to Orson Hyde and John E. Page, May 14, 1840, www.josephsmithpapers.org/paper-summary/letterbook-2/85#full-transcript (accessed Dec. 24, 2019).

In the midst of that exchange, on May 7, 1840, Brigham Young wrote to the prophet with a formal request to publish the Book of Mormon and Doctrine and Covenants in England, but not the hymnbook, except perhaps by implication. On May 26 John Taylor arrived in Manchester, and joined the hymnbook committee, though the process they would follow was still unclear to him: it seemed to favor Parley Pratt, as Taylor had written to Willard Richards on May 4, 1840:

> I am preparing hymns for the book but should be pleased of a little explanation on a sentence dropped in your letter. You say, 'He Er [Elder] Young intends to prepare what hymns he can & forward them to Er Pratt.'—Am I to understand that Er Young will prepare what hymns he can & that he wishes me to do the same & forward them to Er Pratt & leave it for Er Pratt to select and compile the same—or that when we have each made our selections we as a committee meet together & select & compile the hymns—This latter was my view that I had formed of it. I should think that it would be necessary for us to meet because we may all of us have made large selections & the question will be which shall be left out & which shall go in, a question that would be easily decided were we all together.[20]

The full committee did meet from May 27–30 and made their collective decisions. By the end of June they had prepared a manuscript for the press with the intent to publish 3,000 copies.[21]

A small note below Young's May 7 letter in Smith's letterbook says that an answer was sent by Lorenzo Snow, authorizing the Twelve to publish books, *including* the hymnbook. Because of the time delay in receiving Young's initial request, though, that reply was not sent until July 19. By then Young had *already* published the apostles' new hymnbook and introduced it at a public meeting in Manchester (July 6, 1840). The congregation at that meeting voted to receive and approve the new book.[22]

When he learned of this, Smith, it seems, wrote a letter to the

20. John Taylor Papers (typescript), bx. 1, bk. 1, Special Collections, J. Willard Marriott Library, University of Utah, Salt Lake City.

21. Elden J. Watson, ed., *Manuscript History of Brigham Young, 1846–1847* (Salt Lake City: J. Watson, 1971), 77–78.

22. *History of the Church*, July 6, 1840.

Twelve scolding them for what they had done. Although the letter seems not to have survived, Brigham Young wrote to his wife about it on November 12: Joseph

> said he had somthings against them, according to whatt I could learn from the letter it was because we did not wright to him upon the subject of printing the hymbook and the Book of Mormon which we should have ben glad to have don if we could, but it did not seeme to be posable, all I have to say about the matter as to my self is I have don all that I could to due good and promote the cause that we are in, I have done the verry best that I knew how, and I think that Br Joseph will tel us all about things when we return home, there was some of his letter Blotted out But I think we understood it by what we could read of the part bloted out, you may read this letter to Br Joseph or not jest as you plese, but tell him at ennyrate to say what he wants me to doe and I will try and doe it the Lord will.[23]

Nevertheless, when Joseph received a copy of the hymnbook, he wrote to the apostles: "In my former epistle I told you my mind respecting the printing of the Book of Mormon, Hymn Book &c &c I have been favored by receiving a Hymn Book from you, and as far as I have examined it I highly approve of it, and think it to be a very valuable Collection."[24] And indeed, as we shall see, the evidence shows that Emma Smith would rely on it in her new compilation.

At the church's general conference on October 4, 1840, Ebenezer Robinson had given an account of the recent publication of the Book of Mormon in Nauvoo and said that arrangements had now been made for printing Emma's new hymnbook. He soon left for Cincinnati to buy paper and other materials for printing and binding. When he returned, he wrote a starkly headlined article—"HYMNS!! HYMNS!!"—for the *Times and Seasons*, of which he was editor. He wrote that he had the physical makings of the hymnbook but now (November 1) needed content for

---

23. Brigham Young, Letter to Mary Ann Angell Young, Nov. 12, 1840, Philip Blair Papers, Special Collections, Marriott Library.

24. Joseph Smith, Letter to Council of the Twelve, Dec. 15, 1840, www.josephsmithpapers.org/paper-summary/letterbook-2/85#full-transcript (accessed Dec. 24, 2019).

> a new selection of Hymns which have so long been desired by the saints, [of which] we contemplate commencing the work immediately; and feeling desirous to have an extensive, and valuable book; it is requested that all those who have been endowed with a poetical genius, whose muse has not been altogether idle, will feel enough interest in a work of this kind, to immediately forward all choice, newly composed, or revised hymns. In designating those who are endowed with a Poetical genius, we do not intend to exclude others; we mean all who have good hymns that will cheer the heart of the righteous man, to send them as soon as practicable, directed to Mrs. Emma Smitth, Nauvoo, Ill. Post Paid.[25]

What must have struck many who read this plea was the lack of any reference to the apostles' hymnbook, of which many must have been aware in a city now swelling with the inflow of British immigrants. Emma herself—via Joseph—must have had one; Brigham Young himself was anxious to know that she did as of January 1841.

On March 15, 1841, the *Times and Seasons* published a notice under the heading "Books." It noted that "The Hymn books are also, just out of the press, and as many will be bound and ready for distribution upon [the occasion of general conference] as possible." They would be "For sale by Prest. J. Smith."[26] Nevertheless, after the recriminations about the propriety of making their own hymnbook in England and the appearance of Emma's new collection in Nauvoo, on April 3, 1841, the apostles voted unanimously to allow Parley Pratt to reprint their hymnbook "if he deems it expedient" and not to alter it in any way—not even to reflect Emma's selections, apparently—only "typographical errors."[27] That decision ensured that there would be *two* official hymnbooks in the church.

What did all this wrangling reveal? First, that even the patriarchy of the highest men's quorum in the church knew they had crossed a line into Emma Smith's domain. And they felt guilty about it, at least for a time. Second, that Joseph needed what the apostles had to offer in the spread of his religious empire more

25. "HYMNS!! HYMNS!!" *Times and Seasons* 1 (Nov. 1, 1840): 204.

26. "Books," *Times and Seasons* 2 (Mar. 15, 1841): 355.

27. *History of the Church*, 4:326.

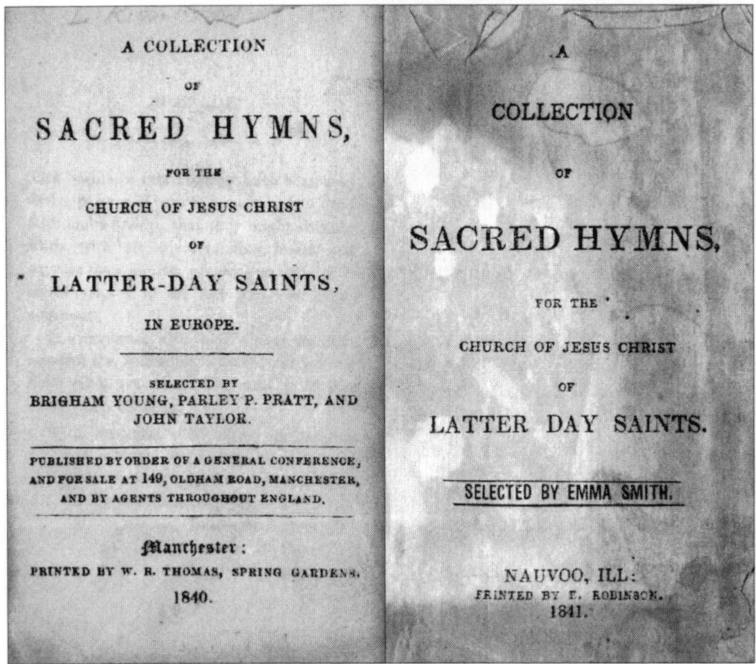

A COLLECTION
OF
SACRED HYMNS,
FOR THE
CHURCH OF JESUS CHRIST
OF
LATTER-DAY SAINTS,
IN EUROPE.

SELECTED BY
BRIGHAM YOUNG, PARLEY P. PRATT, AND
JOHN TAYLOR.

PUBLISHED BY ORDER OF A GENERAL CONFERENCE,
AND FOR SALE AT 149, OLDHAM ROAD, MANCHESTER,
AND BY AGENTS THROUGHOUT ENGLAND.

Manchester:
PRINTED BY W. R. THOMAS, SPRING GARDENS.
1840.

A
COLLECTION
OF
SACRED HYMNS,
FOR THE
CHURCH OF JESUS CHRIST
OF
LATTER DAY SAINTS.

SELECTED BY EMMA SMITH.

NAUVOO, ILL:
PRINTED BY E. ROBINSON.
1841.

Title pages of the two chief Mormon hymnbooks used in the four years before Joseph Smith's death.

than he needed the small circle of trust that surrounded his wife regarding hymns. He was soon about to complicate his marriage in far more treacherous ways. This faux pas could hardly compare.

Joseph had seemed to use hymnody as a bargaining chip from the beginning. He had worked behind the scenes to pick hymns with the apostles for their new book, both faulted and endorsed it after it came out, then pushed Emma's new book into the spotlight of divine imprimatur and treated it as official—despite the claims the apostles' hymnbook had on the minds of British converts, who were fast taking the reins of music in the church. If there was any saving grace of typography it was that the apostles' book explicitly said on its title page—for now—it was a collection of sacred hymns for the Latter-day Saints "In Europe." Emma's had no such constraint. It was "A Collection of Sacred Hymns for the Church of Jesus Christ of Latter Day Saints." Period.

CHARACTER

The character of Emma's new hymnbook would depend largely on what hymns she added. But before looking at those, we should look at what hymns she *deleted.* As to why she deleted them, we should be cautious. One deletes for various reasons. Sometimes a hymnbook compiler's personal preference may be enough to omit hymns that a book once included. Sometimes hymn texts turn out to be awkward, hard to fit to a tune. Sometimes hymns fall into disuse—if nobody wants to sing them, perhaps it is time to delete them to make way for potentially more popular ones. And sometimes the message is off or, in the case of LDS doctrine, has been superseded by new revelation. All such reasons may have led Emma to cut *twelve* hymns from the ninety in her earlier book.

The apostles had also removed four of those in their 1840 book. The reasons seem clear. "There's a Power in the Sun"—too mystical? It refers continually to divinity in nature but mentions God as such only in the last line of each verse ("Oh behold the Lord is nigh"). "Through all the world below" was too overtly trinitarian to remain in the hymnbook. "There Is a Land the Lord Will Bless" (a rewrite of Isaac Watts's "There Is a Land of Pure Delight") often jangled (e.g., "joy" rhymed with "<u>Destroy!</u>" [emphasis in original]). It also seemed obsolete, since it dwelt on the Saints' gathering to Missouri, from which they had been chased out. The fourth hymn deleted from both hymnbooks was "When earth was dressed in beauty," a text that Phelps had written to his wife, Sally, to celebrate their marriage. It was the only hymn in the 1835 book's section marked "On Marriage." Both the hymn and the section were cut from both hymnbooks.

But Emma omitted seven more hymns that the apostles kept. Let me speculate on her motives. The opening line of "God spake the word and time began" seemed at odds with Joseph's increasingly "eternalist" perspective, in which God, though outside of time, did not necessarily create it. "There's a feast of fat things for the righteous preparing," a hymn celebrating the feasts of the poor at Kirtland, may now have seemed a relic.[28] "When restless on

28. See Michael Hicks, "What Hymns Early Mormons Sang and How They Sang Them," BYUS 47, 1 (2008): 100–01.

my bed I lie" was weak, essentially a hymn about insomnia. Two hymns may have been deleted because of metric awkwardness. The boldly millennialistic "Let all the saints their hearts prepare" fit well the apostles' breeding of a people ready for God's kingdom; "The Lord into his garden comes" seems especially attuned to what seem to be Emma's predilections, with its celebration of the individual soul's intimate relationship with Christ. But one would have a hard time fitting a tune to either of those two texts. Sadly, for Emma's deletion of "Jesus the name that charms our fears," I find no plausible rationale.

One deletion Emma uniquely made is telling. Phelps had rewritten Isaac Watts's "He dies, the friend of sinners dies" into "He died, the great Redeemer died." Here are their respective first verses:

Watts

He dies! the Friend of sinners dies!
Lo! Salem's daughters weep around;
A solemn darkness veils the skies,
A sudden trembling shakes the ground.

Phelps

He died; the great Redeemer died,
And Israel's daughters wept around;
A solemn darkness veiled the sky,
A sudden trembling shook the ground.

Phelps, of course, moves the lyric from the vividness of present tense to the past and also discards Jesus as "the Friend of sinners." In restoring Watts's original, Emma reverts to Protestant language and its focus on heavenly grace.

One more case I need to mention is complicated. While Phelps's popular "Redeemer of Israel" remains in the 1841 volume, it is omitted from the index. Thus, if anyone were looking for it by name, it would seem cut from the collection. What does appear in both the book and the index is Joseph Swain's "O Thou in whose presence my soul takes delight," the model for Phelps's "Redeemer of Israel." Swain's hymn is in the first person singular, reflecting on the singer's joy in his Savior:

O thou in whose presence
My soul takes delight,
On whom in affliction I call:
My comfort by day
And my song in the night,
My hope, my salvation, my all!

Where dost Thou at noon-tide
Resort with Thy sheep,
To feed on the pastures of love;
For why in the valley
Of death should I weep,
Or alone in the wilderness rove?

Oh, why should I wander
An alien from Thee,
And cry in the desert for bread?
Thy foes will rejoice
When my sorrows they see,
And smile at the tears I have shed.

Phelps's massive rewrite makes the song a first-person *plural* praise song for the redemption of Zion and her people:

Redeemer of Israel, our only Delight,
On Whom for a blessing we call,
Our Shadow by day, and our Pillar by night,
Our King, our Deliverer, our All!

We know He is coming, to gather His sheep
And lead them to Zion in love;
For why in the valley of death should they weep
Or in the lone wilderness rove?

How long we have wandered as strangers in sin,
And cried in the desert for Thee!
Our foes have rejoiced when our sorrows they've seen,
But Israel will shortly be free

I believe that Emma picked Swain's song in her first harvest of Mormon hymns in the 1830s, then lost it to Phelps's new version when "her" hymnbook came out in 1835. As good as "Redeemer of

Israel" was, she wanted the original back as part of a more privately worshipful collection.

The Manchester book had 108 new hymns that did not appear in Emma's book. Emma's had 141 new hymns that did not appear in the Manchester book. Both books added many hymns by Protestant authors and some by Mormon authors. The Mormon author that looms largest among the new indigenous hymns in both books is one of the apostles who edited the Manchester volume: Parley Pratt, who contributed at least thirty-six new hymns to that book. Pratt's themes mirrored those of his missionary tracts: the Second Coming, the Kingdom of God, the Millennium, the people of God, priesthood, and the apostleship. Emma used one-third of those new Pratt hymns in her collection (and no other new ones by Pratt), including several that have become classics (e.g., "Jesus, Once of Humble Birth," "The Morning Breaks, the Shadows Flee"). But, unlike the apostles' hymnbook, Emma's collection turned more to Protestant authors.

Of the 141 new hymns Emma included that the apostles did not, eighty-three were borrowed from known Protestant sources. At least a dozen more whose sources I cannot find also seem to come from mainstream Protestantism. The church, of course, was still far from creating any fully indigenous hymnody (and still is). And Protestant hymns had a wide range of themes, including many like Pratt's: the Kingdom of God, the Second Coming, and so forth, though not priesthood or apostleship. More often, Protestant hymns dwelt on praise, confession, and the search for comfort. They leaned toward one's personal relationship with Christ or meditations on how he and his atonement affect the lone singer's soul.

I would like to dwell on three themes that tint the character of Emma's collection with a Protestant revivalist air: the cross, the blood of Jesus, and grace. These themes, I should note, form constellations, not conglomerations. That is, there is no overwhelming mass of new hymns with these themes, but notably strong exemplars—points of light from which I infer images of the hymnbook's distinct character.

THE CROSS

In all his published doctrinal writings and addresses, Joseph Smith almost always refers to "the cross" in the literal sense of the object on which Jesus was hung to die.[29] The two exceptions are (a) when he says, "I can go to the cross—I can lay down my life," and (b) when he vaguely alludes to Catholic doctrine thus: "tis not the cross as the Catholics would have it"—a statement whose context is puzzling, but seems a slam on Christian devotion to the cross as a *symbol.*[30] Emma's 1835 hymnbook uses the term as Joseph did, only treating "the cross" in its literal sense or, one time, in this analogy: "If we, like Jesus, bear the cross / Like him despise the shame."[31] That is, "the cross" is the burden of being a follower of Christ.

In her 1841 book, though, she begins to use "the cross" as Protestants commonly did. That is, "the cross" (per Paul the Apostle) connotes God's redemptive plan.

Thus, in Hymn 65, "Great was the day, the joy was great," the first verse describes the coming of the Holy Spirit on the Day of Pentecost. The second and third verses lead to the impending mission of Jesus's twelve apostles—spreading "the myst'ry of his cross":

> What gifts, what miracles he gave!
> And power to kill, and pow'r to save!
> Furnish'd their tongues with wond'rous words,
> Instead of shields, and spears, and swords.
>
> Thus arm'd, he sent the champions forth,
> From east to west, from south to north;
> "Go, and assert your Savior's cause;
> Go, spread the myst'ry of his cross."

Then the fifth verse gives the devil's response and decidedly turns "the cross" into a "doctrine":

---

29. This and all other statements about Joseph's usage are based on a search of Truman G. Madsen, ed., *Concordance of Doctrinal Statements of Joseph Smith* (Salt Lake City: I.E.S. Publishing, 1985).

30. The quotations are from Andrew F. Ehat and Lyndon W. Cook, comps. and eds., *The Words of Joseph Smith: The Contemporary Accounts of the Nauvoo Discourses of the Prophet Joseph Smith* (Provo, Utah: Brigham Young University Religious Studies Center, 1980), 376 and 239, respectively.

31. In "The glorious day is rolling on," from Smith, *A Collection of Sacred Hymns* (1835), 93–94.

The Greeks and Jews, the learn'd and rude,
Are by these heav'nly arms subdu'd;
While Satan rages at his loss,
And hates the doctrine of the cross.

The sense of "the cross" as the Christian mission also appears in hymn 257, which begins with a self-interrogatory about the singer's valiance:

Am I a soldier of the cross,
A follower of the Lamb?
And shall I fear to own His cause,
Or blush to speak His Name?

If these new usages of "the cross" seem incidental, new references to "the blood of Jesus" are more potent.

THE BLOOD OF JESUS

Joseph Smith never referred to the "blood of Jesus" as such in his doctrinal writings and speeches. Although it was not uncommon for him to refer to *blood*, he did so almost always in the context of any of three themes: (1) the shedding of innocent blood as a grievous sin, (2) the blood of Abraham or related blood as a divine genetic marker, and (3) the spilling of the blood of the righteous in persecution (or, specifically, his enemies' "thirst" for his blood). The 1835 hymnbook mentions Jesus's blood most often in connection with the sacrament or in questions such as "Alas! And did my Savior bleed" (no. 80) or "And did my Savior die / and shed his blood for me?" (no. 84). The closest it comes to invoking the *power* of Jesus's blood is in the sixth verse of no. 89: "His blood can make the foulest clean."

The 1841 hymnbook vividly elevates the blood of Jesus in its imagery, matching the rhetoric of camp-meeting preachers. One example is referring to his flowing blood as the "crimson tide" in this stanza from no. 185:

Stretched on the cross, the Savior dies;
Hark!—his expiring groans arise!
See, from his hands—his feet—his side,
Descends the sacred—crimson tide!

In this Christian favorite (no. 176), we find his blood as an overflowing fountain in an extended metaphor connected to "redeeming love":

There is a fountain fill'd with blood,
Pour'd from Immanuel's veins;
And sinners plung'd beneath that flood
Lose all their guilty stains.

The dying thief rejoic'd to see
That fountain in his day;
And there have I, though vile as he,
Wash'd all my sins away.

O Lamb of God, Thy precious blood
Shall never lose its pow'r
Till all the ransom'd sons of God
Be saved, to sin no more.

E'er since, by faith, I saw the stream
Thy flowing wounds supply,
Redeeming love has been my theme,
And shall be till I die.

The idea of washing the soul in Jesus's blood occurs again in no. 66:

To him that lov'd the sons of men,
And wash'd us in his blood,
To royal honors rais'd our hands,
And made us priests to God.

Still another hymn (no. 52) contrasts the power of Jesus's blood with that of the sacrificial animals in earlier times:

Not all the blood of beasts,
On Jewish altars slain,
Could give the guilty conscience peace
Or wash away the stain.

But Christ, the Heavenly Lamb,
Bears all our sins away;
A sacrifice of nobler name,
And richer blood than they.

Hymn no. 110 ("O how happy are they") treats the blood of Jesus as a source of both comfort and joy as well as a link to God's "fulness":

This comfort is mine,
Since the favor divine
I have found in the blood of the Lamb;
Since the truth I believ'd,
What a joy I've receiv'd,
What a heaven in Jesus' bless'd name!

...

O the rapturous height
Of this holy delight,
Which I feel in the life-giving blood!
Of my Savior possess'd,
I am perfectly bless'd,
Being filled with the fulness of God!

Hymn no. 245 suggests that the blood of Jesus allows saints to conquer.

Rise, O my soul—pursue the path
By ancient worthies trod;
Aspiring, view those holy men
Who liv'd and walk'd with God.

Though dead, they speak in reason's ear,
And in example live;
Their faith, and hope, and mighty deeds,
Still fresh instruction give.

'Twas thro' the Lamb's most precious blood,
They conquered every foe;
To his almighty power and grace,
Their crowns of life they owe.

Lord, may I ever keep in view
The patterns thou hast given
And ne'er forsake the blesséd road
That led them safe to heav'n.

I have included the entire text here for its eloquence as well its appeal to the last of my three ideas, grace.

GRACE

The word "grace" appears many times in the 1835 hymnbook. Occasionally it has glowing adjectives attached—"heav'nly," "wondrous," "bounteous," "free," and "all-sufficient." The idea of grace rises high in three phrases: "the triumph of his grace," "the gospel of grace," and "my faith and hope relies / upon thy grace alone." In all his recorded doctrinal statements Joseph never accompanies "grace" with superlatives or exultant modifiers. Nor does he make salvation reliant "upon thy grace alone." Instead, he tends to use the term in a relatively generic sense, referring simply to "God's grace," "divine grace," or, on the negative side, "falling from grace."

But many hymns unique to Emma's 1841 hymnbook revel in the principle of grace. Fresh elocutions appear: "wonders of his grace," "riches of his grace," "God's redeeming grace," "boundless grace," "the power of sovereign grace," "the treasures of his grace"—all gifts of Jesus, who is called "the prince of grace" (see below). Some hymns emphasize grace in distinct, sometimes unprecedented ways. In this hymnbook, for example, the message of the church is not so much the restoration of the gospel (as in the apostles' hymnbook), but "proclaiming grace," as in hymn no. 175:

Proclaim, says Christ, my wond'rous grace
To all the sons of men;
He that believes and is immers'd,
Salvation shall obtain.
Let plenteous grace descend on those,
Who, hoping in the word,
This day have publicly declar'd,
That Jesus is their Lord.

With cheerful feet may they advance,
And run the Christian race:
And, through the troubles of the way,
Find all sufficient grace.

Another newly added hymn, "Come thou fount of every blessing" (no. 76), begins thus:

Come thou fount of every blessing,
Tune my heart to sing thy grace;
Streams of mercy never ceasing,
Call for songs of loudest praise.

The next verse emphasizes grace and the singer's propensity to stray:

Oh! to grace how great a debtor
Daily I'm constrain'd to be
Let they goodness like a fetter,
Bind my wand'ring heart to thee!
Prone to wander—Lord, I feel it—
Prone to leave the God I love.
Here's my heart—O take and seal it—
Seal it for thy courts above.

Hymn no. 60 is an extended meditation on grace, particularly as it arises from Jesus's empathy:

With joy we meditate the grace
Of our High Priest above;
His heart is made of tenderness,
His bowels melt with love.

Touch'd with a sympathy within,
He knows our feeble frame;
He knows what sore temptations mean,
For he has felt the same.

He, in the days of feeble flesh,
Pour'd out His cries and tears,
And in His measure feels afresh
What ev'ry member bears.

Then let our humble faith address
His mercy and his pow'r;
We shall obtain deliv'ring grace
In each distressing hour.

Still another hymn (no. 57) emphasizes the low state of sinners Jesus redeems through his grace:

Plunged in a gulf of dark despair
We wretched sinners lay,

Without one cheerful beam of hope,
Or spark of glimmering day!

With pitying eyes the prince of grace
Beheld our helpless grief;
He saw—and, O amazing love!—
He came to our relief.

References to "amazing love" and "wretched sinners," of course, draw the mind to that most beloved of grace songs, here included as hymn no. 118.

Amazing grace! (how sweet the sound),
That saved a wretch like me!
I once was lost but now am found,—
Was blind, but now I see.

'Twas grace that taught my heart to fear,
And grace, my fears reliev'd.
How precious did that grace appear
The hour I first believ'd.

Through many dangers, toils, and snares,
I have already come;
'Tis grace that brought me safe thus far
and grace will lead me home.

Such hymns, moving back to revivalist language and sentiment, seem almost at odds with the millennialist, restored-gospel language that characterizes the apostles' hymnbook.[32]

• • •

The October 1841 general conference of the church used Emma's 1841 hymnbook. In total, ten different hymns were sung (two of them twice). Of those ten, three had appeared in the 1835 hymnbook, six were in both the apostles' book and Emma's, and one was unique to Emma's. The new Relief Society (for women) began to meet in 1842 with Emma as president. The minutes show, not surprisingly, that they used her hymnbook. In 1843 the

32. For a fuller analysis of that hymnbook's contents, see James Nathan Arrington, "The Journey Home: A Root-Metaphor Analysis of the 1840 Mormon Manchester Hymnbook," MA Thesis, Brigham Young University, 2005.

Times and Seasons included a notice that read: "SACRED HYMNS. Persons having Hymns adapted to the worship of the Church of Jesus Christ of Latter Day Saints, are requested to hand them, or send them to Emma Smith, immediately." Clearly she planned another hymnbook. But it never came to be.[33] How far would this newer hymnbook have traveled in Emma's new direction? And would have it have put the apostles' book out of commission?

Competing hymnbooks may have aggravated the split between Emma and the Twelve. But the roots of the split went far deeper. By 1841 Joseph's relationship with the apostles had tightened, with Brigham Young and Heber Kimball being his favorites. Joseph clearly shared things with the Twelve that he concealed from her (or that she rejected). While Joseph had purveyed plural marriage, Emma, as president of the Relief Society, led a public crusade against it. She had privately said that she "did not believe a word" of the revelation drafted to convince her of the doctrinal premise for her husband remarrying dozens of women. That rejection was doubtless one factor—maybe the only one—that moved Joseph to shut down the society after slightly less than two years of operation. Some evidence suggests that Emma may have been on the verge of divorcing Joseph. In turn, the marriage revelation threatened her with being "destroyed" if she continued to resist her husband's divine dalliances. The 1841 hymnbook seems a concession to Emma, a counterweight to the apostles' book, if not a new incentive to remain faithful despite the spreading mutations in her and her friends' households.

The apostles who surrounded Joseph tried to keep women tamped down on old-fashioned biblical grounds. Young's right-hand man, Heber Kimball, explained, "I do not want a woman to tell me that she loves me, when she does not keep my commandments, for her statement would be vague and foolish."[34] Marital love only counted when it conveyed woman's submission. "It is the duty of a woman to be obedient to her husband, and unless she is, I would not give a damn for all her queenly right and authority;

33. *Times and Seasons* 4 (Feb. 1, 1843): 95.

34. JD 4:65 (Nov. 2, 1856).

nor for her either, if she will quarrel, and lie about the work of God and the principle of plurality [of wives]."[35]

Solidarity with priesthood colleagues and leaders trumped any competing loyalties, especially to women. "I would not give a dime for a man that does not love [his brethren] better than they love women. A man is a miserable being, if he lets a woman stand between him and his file leader; he is a fool, and I have no regard for him; he is not fit for the Priesthood."[36]

After Joseph was shot to death, Emma could find no common ground with the Twelve. She spurned their successorship and fought with them over who owned what properties in Nauvoo. Late in 1845 Benjamin Johnson and Newell Whitney were assigned to visit Emma and "persuade her to remain with the Church." She said she would, Johnson recalls, "on condition she would be the leading spirit."[37] But Young had already rejected her. He would twice publicly claim that Emma had tried to poison Joseph at Nauvoo. In turn, he said, Joseph had called a meeting of the Twelve to denounce her in front of them.[38] Young also said that Emma had destroyed Joseph's marked Bible and "connived" with the mob that killed him, even persuading Joseph to remove his allegedly protective temple garment before going to Carthage Jail.[39] Young called her a "devil" and "one of the damnedest liars I know on earth"; anyone who followed her, he said, would be "damned."[40] Still, he played the saint, saying "There is no good thing I would refuse to do for her, if she would only be a righteous woman." He held the keys to eternity and would save her if she bowed to him. Heber Kimball explained that "Joseph stood for the truth and maintained it; [Emma] struck against it. … She declared that she would leave [Joseph], if he would not sustain her instead of sustaining brother Brigham, and Heber, and the rest of

35. Ibid., 82 (Nov. 9, 1856).

36. Ibid., 138 (Dec. 4, 1846).

37. Benjamin F. Johnson, *My Life's Review* (Independence, Missouri: Zion's Printing & Publishing Co., 1947), 107.

38. *The Complete Discourses of Brigham Young*, ed. Richard S. Van Wagoner, 5 vols. (Salt Lake City: Smith–Petit Foundation, 2009), 3:1531 and 4:2157–59.

39. For the three assertions in this sentence, see ibid., 2:1009 and 914, and 5:2658.

40. For the three quotations in this sentence, see ibid., 4:2378.

the Twelve Apostles of God. … She had her choice, but Joseph would not follow her." The principle that overrode all else in such disputes was this: "Women are to be led."[41] By the time of that statement, Emma had married a Methodist, leading some to claim that she had joined his church. That proved untrue, but in time she joined the so-called "Reorganization," with her son Joseph Smith III at the head. The Reorganization's first hymnbook was essentially a revised version of her 1841 hymnbook.

By then the main body of the church, now gone west, completely discarded her hymnody. Once Joseph died, her book became an albatross around the spiritual neck of his successors. Whatever its content, what it symbolized as a dare to their authority rendered it unusable. And that blocked the new direction toward which Emma was coaxing Mormon hymnody.

The split between Emma and the apostles may help explain why she tilted her hymnbook's character in the direction she did. Increasingly isolated, she resonated more to hymns of personal solace and the intimate, graceful Savior than to the bold, millennialistic, group-oriented hymns of, say, Parley Pratt, which celebrated the newness of a fresh dispensation rather than the comforts of an ancient one being restored. In 1853 the *Millennial Star* noted that, in the last dispensation, "God will send forth, by His servants, things *new* as well as *old*, until man is perfected in the truth."[42] Over time it became clear that in her hymnody Emma pursued the old, at least when it came to familiar revivalist themes and rhetoric. Yet it was new, if only for how it transgressed the men's hymn choices. Emma Smith's 1841 hymnbook went backward to go forward.

Hymns flavor worship. They also color our perception of orthodoxy. Again and again, the character of the hymns we sing asks us: what themes shape us? What texts distill into memorable phrases and, by repetition, saturate our minds?

Whether or not Emma Smith had stayed with the apostles, the apostles could have stayed with her. They could have kept what she brought, by divine authority, to the canon of Mormon hymnody. But leaving her choices behind grew out of this priesthood

41. JD 5:29 (July 12, 1857).

42. "Our Father Adam," MS 15 (Nov. 26, 1853): 780, italics in the original.

principle: men overruled women. For a woman, even one so well-connected, to hold sway over a branch of the canon was intolerable. And the Kingdom of God had no room for community property. So the men's hymnody, plump with masculine airs, militaristic undertones, and monarchial visions, overrode the woman's intimate divine impulses. That's how the church left Emma Smith and why you should care.

APPENDIX

Hymnbooks through 1845 (not including multiple printings)

Smith, Emma. *A Collection of Sacred Hymns for the Church of the Latter Day Saints*. Kirtland, Ohio: F. G. Williams, 1835. 90 hymns.

Rogers, David W. *A Collection of Sacred Hymns for the Church of the Latter Day Saints*. New York: C. Vinten, 1838. 90 hymns (including one duplicate).

Elsworth, Benjamin. *A Collection of Sacred Hymns for the Church of the Latter Day Saints*. N.p.: Elsworth, 1839. 112 hymns.

Young, Brigham, Parley P. Pratt, and John Taylor. *A Collection of Sacred Hymns for the Church of Jesus Christ of Latter-day Saints in Europe*. Manchester, England: W. R. Thomas, Spring Gardens, 1840. 271 hymns (one printed twice).

Smith, Emma. *A Collection of Sacred Hymns for the Church of Jesus Christ of Latter Day Saints* Nauvoo, Illinois: E[benezer]. Robinson, 1841. 304 hymns (one printed twice).

Page, John S., and John Cairns. *A Collection of Sacred Hymns for the Use of the Latter Day Saints*. N.p.: Page and Cairns, 1841[?]. 47 hymns.

Merkley, Christopher. *A Small Selection of Choice Hymns for the Church of Jesus Christ of Latter Day Saints*. N.p.: Merkley, 1841. 19 hymns.

Hardy, John. *A Collection of Sacred Hymns, Adapted to the Faith and Views of the Church of Jesus Christ of Latter Day Saints*. Boston: Dow and Jackson's Press, 1843. 155 hymns.

Little, Jesse C., and George Bryant Gardner. *A Collection of Sacred Hymns, for the Use of the Latter Day Saints*. Bellows Falls,

Vermont: Blake and Bailey, 1844. 48 hymns (some with musical notation).

Adams, Charles A. *A Collection of Sacred Hymns for the Church of Jesus Christ of Latter Day Saints*. Bellows Falls, Vermont: S. M. Blake, 1845. 104 hymns.

Rigdon, S[idney]. *A Collection of Sacred Hymns for the Church of Jesus Christ of Latter Day Saints*. Pittsburgh: E[benezer] Robinson, 1845. 182 hymns.

3 TRACKING "THE SPIRIT OF GOD"

It feels like cheating to start with a big block quote. But I do not think anything conveys the weight of "The Spirit of God" better than this statement by Brigham Young's most famous ex-wife:

> This hymn always stirred the Saints to the very depths of their natures. It was as appealing and sonorous as a battle-cry, as exultant as a trumpet-note of victory. Without understanding it, I was powerfully affected by it; my cheeks would glow, my eyes flush with tears, and my little heart grow so large that I would almost suffocate. The sublime exaltation of the Saints, as they sung this, was felt by me, child as I was, though I could not comprehend it. I shut my eyes now, and see a large company gathered together, in the fast-falling twilight, on a wide plain, that seems as endless as the ocean; the blue of the star-studded sky is the only covering for the heads of this company. In the dusk the white-covered wagons look weird and ghostly. Campfires are burning; men, women, and children are clustered together, and the talk goes back to the old days and the trials and persecutions which these people have borne, and forward to an independent and happy future, blessed of God and unmolested by man. In the glow of anticipation, some one strikes up this fervid hymn,—the rallying-song of the Mormons,—and the wide plains echo back the stirring strains. I nestle by my mother's side, awed and subdued, but content to feel the clasp of her hand and meet the loving light of her eyes. The song is over, and "hosannas" and "amens" resound on every side, and out of the blue sky the stars smile down on the wanderers with a calm, hopeful light.
>
> Never, to the very last, up to the time of my abandoning Mormonism and leaving Utah, could I hear this hymn unmoved; and even now the very thought of it thrills me strangely.[1]

1. Ann Eliza Young, *Wife No. 19, or The Story of a Life in Bondage* … (Hartford: Dustin, Gilman & Co., 1876), 119–20.

If you are now or ever have been a Latter-day Saint, that rapture at the "rallying-song of the Mormons" still echoes, faintly or noisily, in your life. The song premiered in 1836 at the dedication of the first Mormon temple and has been sung prominently at the dedication of every temple since. It was the last song in the first Mormon hymnbook with words, the first song in the first Mormon hymnbook with music, and appears in every Mormon hymnbook since. Congregations sing it lustily in every ward, branch, and stake in the church to this day. Its sturdy, fist-waving character makes it feel like the Mormon national anthem. So, let me tell you some things about the song that you may not know.

• • •

First, the text of "The Spirit of God" seems born of what we might call the "tongues culture" of early Mormon Pentecostalism. Here are the roots of that culture: At the Day of Pentecost after Jesus' resurrection, speaking miraculously in other languages was a sign of God's bestowal of the Holy Spirit on the young church. By the time of Paul's first letter to the Corinthians, ecstatic tongues ("real" languages or not) and their interpretation had become an information delivery system, a two-step gift of prophecy by which messages were given to the church. According to the fourteenth chapter of that epistle, one might not only speak in tongues but also sing in tongues, as long as an interpretation was given in either case. Some revivalist churches, from post-colonial America onward, claiming to perpetuate ancient Christian practices, resumed this tongues+interpretation method. The Church of the Latter Day Saints (as it was called when "The Spirit of God" was written) was one of those churches.

In 1834 E. D. Howe explained that tongues among Mormons were "practiced almost daily." In meetings, they often came by assignment, with the assignee having the choice of speaking or singing. Even when "spoken," Howe said, tongues were always "a medium between speaking and singing" (not unlike modern glossolalia). Still, they "would frequently sing in this gibberish, forming a tune as they proceeded. The same songs, they said, would be sung when the lost tribes appeared in Zion."[2]

In that context, realize that to Mormons such a new song was something more. The opening line to the preface of the first Mormon hymnbook—probably written by its publisher, William Wines (a.k.a. "W. W.") Phelps, who also wrote "The Spirit of God"—invokes 1 Corinthians 14's discussion of "singing with the spirit"—that is, in *tongues*—and "singing with the understanding" (i.e., in one's own language). The last line of the preface divides the sources of the new church's hymnody into two branches. "It is sincerely hoped," the preface concludes, "that the following collection, selected with an eye single to [God's] glory, may answer every purpose till more are composed, *or till we are blessed with a copious variety of the songs of Zion*" (emphasis mine).[3] Those are the two sacred-song genres of early Mormonism: hymns and songs of Zion.

A July 1830 revelation had told Emma Smith it would be "given" to her "to make a selection of sacred hymns … to be had in my church" (D&C 25: 11). Two years later, in the first issue of the church's first newspaper, *The Evening and the Morning Star*, Phelps began publishing on its last page "Hymns, Selected and prepared for the Church of Christ, in these last days." ("The Church of Christ" was still the church's name before it was switched to "Church of the Latter Day Saints" in 1834.) Seven hymns appeared on that page, presumably "selected" by Emma, although the first one was written by Phelps himself. In the next seven issues, more appeared, though the heading shortened or disappeared, and the number of "selected" hymns dwindled—respectively, to two, three, two, two, one, one, then none. Only in the ninth issue did Phelps offer something labeled "New Hymn" (no tune, no credits). And in the tenth issue he printed his own hymn "Now Let

2. E. D. Howe, *Mormonism Unvailed* […] (Painesville, Ohio: Published by the author, 1834), 134–36.

3. Emma Smith, *A Collection of Sacred Hymns for the Church of the Latter Day Saints* (Kirtland, Ohio: F. G. Williams, 1835), iii–iv. For more on this hymnbook and its dating, see Peter Crawley, *A Descriptive Bibliography of the Mormon Church*, 3 vols. (Provo: Brigham Young University Religious Studies Center, 1997–2012), 1:57–59; and Shane Chism, comp., *A Selection of Early Mormon Hymnbooks 1832–1872: Hymnbooks and Broadsides from the First 40 years of The Church of Jesus Christ of Latter-day Saints* (Tucson, Arizona: Published by the author, 2011), 20–24.

Us Rejoice," a hymn which would be sung at the Kirtland temple dedication where "The Spirit of God" premiered.

In the thirteenth issue, May 1833, Phelps introduced a new heading: "Songs of Zion." We know by comparing these two new texts with the Kirtland Revelation Book, February 27, 1833, that they are versified paraphrases of a text on that date labeled "sang by the gift of Tongues and Translated." (One of these hymns was part of a larger *23-stanza* versification of that tongues-revelation and were indeed published as a broadside with the heading "Mysteries of God.") Two more "songs of Zion" appear in the next issue of the newspaper, and one more in the issue following. Then, in the January 1834 issue "Moroni's Lamentation" appears without the "Song of Zion" (or any other) heading. Yet we know from a manuscript copy that it was a versified paraphrase of a song originally sung in tongues by Joseph Smith's mother.[4]

Elizabeth Ann Whitney later explained how she came to this gift of tongues-singing in a meeting during which "I received the gift of singing inspirationally, and the first Song of Zion ever given in the pure language was sung by me then, and interpreted by Parley P. Pratt, and written down." The tune to which she sang was that of "Adam-ondi-Ahman" and the text detailed some of Adam's exploits.[5] Whitney gained a reputation for such singing, according to an 1880 account: "Sister Whitney then sang one of her sweet songs of Zion in the language which was spoken and sung (the Prophet Joseph said) by our first parents in the Garden of Eden. Sister Snow explained that Joseph Smith told Mother Whitney 'If she would use the gift with wisdom it should remain with her as long as she lived.' Sister Zina then gave the

---

4. To understand this in context, see Lavina Fielding Anderson, ed., *Lucy's Book: A Critical Edition of Lucy Mack Smith's Family Memoir* (Salt Lake City: Signature Books, 2001), 35–36. The broadside is in CHL, and is reprinted in Chism, *Selection of Early Mormon Hymnbooks*, 101. For more on tongues culture, see Dan Vogel and Scott C. Dunn, "The Tongue of Angels: Glossolalia among Mormonism's Founders," *Journal of Mormon History* 19, 2 (1993): 1–34; Matthew R. Davies, "The Tongues of the Saints: The Azusa Street Revival and the Changing Definition of Tongues," in *Joseph F. Smith: Reflections on the Man and His Times*, ed. Craig K. Manscill et al. (Provo, Utah: Religious Studies Center/Salt Lake City: Deseret Book Co., 2013), 470–85.

5. Elizabeth Ann Whitney, "A Leaf from an Autobiography," *Woman's Exponent* 7 (1878): 83.

interpretation. The theme of which was rejoicing and praise to the Great Author and Giver of good."[6]

Thomas Bullock has in his papers a few such songs in manuscript. One—marked on the outside "Song of Zion"—is headed "Lines sung in tongues by Ann Elizabeth Whitney [sic]. Interpreted an[d] written by Prescendia L. Kimball." The song's opening lines aptly describe the genre: "I'll sing a song of Zion, / 'Tis with an angels tongue." Fully sixteen stanzas ensue, many addressed to various people, presumably in the congregation at the time. Another Bullock manuscript, unattributed but marked "Song of Zion," has four verses and a chorus all urging repentance and preparedness for the second coming.[7]

From these sources and others the genre of "song of Zion" and its difference from mere "hymn" seems clear. In that light consider the earliest description we have of the composition of "The Spirit of God," which comes from an 1838 Church of England article on Mormons. Before reprinting the entire text, the author notes that "a correspondent informs us" that "the Mormonites say, [this hymn] was most beautifully sung in an unknown tongue, and afterwards translated as it now appears." The temporal proximity of this description to the song's premiere—a mere two years—gives it some credence. But, more to the point, the temporal context of the song's premiere makes the description even more plausible. Indeed, I would like to propose the month, if not the specific meeting, at which the singing in tongues that gave birth to this song of Zion took place.

Phelps first published "Hosanna to God and the Lamb" in the January 1836 issue of his newspaper *Messenger and Advocate* (sequel to *The Evening and the Morning Star*). On the 17th of that month a unique meeting had been held. It was the first meeting in which Joseph Smith's diary reports that tongues had "come upon us … like the rushing of a mighty wind." This was by far the most explicit citation of the New Testament Day of Pentecost that Smith had yet made. But Phelps's own account of the meeting is more explicit. While he almost never mentions specific meetings

6. "R[elief], S[ociety]. Reports," *Woman's Exponent* 9 (Sept. 1, 1880): 54.
7. Thomas Bullock Papers, CHL.

in his terse diary of these years, of this meeting Phelps writes: "There was speaking and singing in tongues, and prophesying, as on the day of Pentecost."[8] The timing, rhetoric, and spirit of this diary entry seem an apt context for the tongues-singing that would mutate into "Hosanna to God and the Lamb."

On January 21 we read that "we shouted Hosanah to God and the Lamb" and, later in the day, "loud hosanahs and glory to God in the highest, saluted the heavens." The next day "the congregation shouted a loud hosanah [and] the gift of toungs, fell upon us." On January 28, Sidney Rigdon "cried hossannah that all [the] congregation should join him & shout hosannah to God & the Lamb & glory to God in the highest." On February 6 Smith said that "all the quorums are to shout with one accord a solemn hosannah to God & the Lamb with an Amen amen & amen" (the latter echoing the twofold "amen" that closes Phelps's new song of Zion). Later in the meeting the quorum of the Seventy "could not hold their peace but were constrained to cry hosannah to God &the Lamb & glory in the highest."

On March 30, the Kirtland temple dedication finally arrived. Near the close of the dedicatory service, the choir premiered "Hosanna to God and the Lamb," a.k.a. "The Spirit of God," then the congregation unanimously shouted multiple hosannas to God and the Lamb, and "President Brigham Young gave a short address in tongues, and David W. Patten interpreted, and gave a short exhortation in tongues himself."[9] A new Pentecost indeed.

• • •

The six successive verses of Phelps's "Hosanna to God and the Lamb" spool out in an orderly way, like a tract or a sermon, padding the lines as needed to fill up the meter and form rhymes. Verse 1 offers the clearest hint of the text's origin: the spirit burning

8. On Joseph Smith's journal entries here and in the next paragraph, see www.josephsmithpapers.org/paper-summary/journal-1835–1836 (accessed June 7, 2019). For Phelps's diary entry, see Bruce van Orden, *We'll Sing and We'll Shout: The Life and Times of W. W. Phelps* (Salt Lake City: Deseret Book Co., 2018), 227.

9. The Kirtland temple dedication minutes, from which many of the facts here and later in this essay are derived, have been reproduced in many places, including www.scottwoodward.org/churchhistory_kirtlandtemple_accounts_firstdedicatory-service.html (accessed June 7, 2019).

We then returned to Savanna, where we baptized five more, stayed about two weeks, and went to greenwood, Stuben co. N. Y. where we found a little branch of about 30 members, we preached twice and baptized one: and from this place we returned to Kirtland, arrived the 15 day of Oct.

H. STANLEY,
J. GRANT.

To J. WHITMER.

J. WHITMER, Esq. SIR:—

I must ask pardon of the portion of your readers whom it may concern for a neglect to present to you the following circumstance for publication before this time.

At our Conference in Bradford Mass. it was proved that the character and conduct of Elder James Paten, of North Providence R. I. rendered him unworthy of a place in the church of the 'Latter Day Saints.' His licence had been called for before this by some official member of the church in that quarter, but he refused to deliver it up The conference therefore voted that he should be published.

I am, Sir, Yours
in the Bonds of
the New Covenant.
ORSON HYDE,
Clerk of Conference.

Kirtland Jan. 12, 1835.

Extract of G. Burket's letter, dated, Wood river, Ill.

Dear brother:

After laboring for a season in the branch of the church of Latter Day Saints, through the providence of our God, I have baptized four, in Madison co. Ill.

Yours &c.
G. BURKET.

To J. WHITMER.

HOSANNA TO GOD AND THE LAMB.

TUNE—*American Star.*

The Spirit of God like a fire is burning;
The latter day glory begins to come forth;
The visions and blessings of old are returning;
The angels are coming to visit the earth.
We'll sing & we'll shout with the armies of heaven:
Hosanna, hosanna to God an the Lamb!
Let glory to them in the highest be given,
Henceforth and forever: amen and amen!

The Lord is extending the saints' understanding—
Restoring their judges and all as at first;
The knowledge and power of God are expanding:
The vail o'er the earth is beginning to burst.
We'll sing and we'll shout &c.

We call in our solemn assemblies, in spirit,
To spread forth the kingdom of heaven abroad,
That we through our faith may begin to inherit
The visions, and blessings, and glories of God.
We'll sing and we'll shout &c.

We'll wesh, and be wash'd, and with oil be anointed
Withal not omitting the washing of feet:
For he that receiveth his PENNY appointed,
Must surely be clean at the harvest of wheat.
We'll sing and we'll shout &c.

Old Israel that fled from the world for his freedom,
Must come with the cloud and the pillar, amain:,
A Moses, and Aaron, and Joshua lead him,
And feed him on manna from heaven again.
We'll sing and we'll shout &c.

How blessed the day when the lamb and the lion
Shall lie down together without any ire;
And Ephraim be crown'd with his blessing in Zion,
As Jesus descends with his chariots of fire!
We'll sing & we'll shout with *His* armies of heaven:
Hosanna, hosanna to God and the Lamb!
Let glory to them in the highest be given,
Henceforth and forever: amen and amen.

The glorious day is rolling on—
All glory to the Lord!
When fair as at creation's dawn
The earth will be restor'd.

A perfect harvest then will crown
The renovated soil;
And rich abundance drop around,
Without corroding toil:

For in its own primeval bloom,
Will nature smile again;
And blossoms streaming with perfume,
Adorn the verdant plain.

The saints will then, with pure delight,
Possess the holy land;
And walk with Jesus Christ in white,
And in his presence stand.

What glorious prospects! can we claim
These hopes, and call them our's?
Yes, if through faith in Jesus' name,
We conquer satan's pow'rs.

If we, like Jesus bear the cross—
Like him despise the shame;
And count all earthly things but dross,
For his most holy name.

Then while the pow'rs of darkness rage,
With glory in our view,
In Jesus' strength let us engage,
To press to Zion too.

For Zion will like Eden bloom;
And Jesus come to reign—
The Saints immortal from the tomb
With angels meet again.

THE LATTER DAY SAINTS'
Messenger and Advocate,
IS EDITED BY
JOHN WHITMER,
And published every month at Kirtland, Geruga Co Ohio, by
F. G. WILLIAMS & Co.

*At $1, per an. in advance. Every person procuring ten new subscribers, and forwarding $10, current money, shall be entitled to a paper one year, gratis. All letters to the Editor or Pubn*tiz*must be*
POST PAID.
No subscription will be received for a less term than on year, and no paper discontinued till all arrearages are paid, except at the option of the publishers.

The first appearance of the text to "Hosanna to God and the Lamb" (a.k.a. "The Spirit of God").

like a fire references the original Day of Pentecost, with its visible tongues of fire signaling the aural sign of speaking in tongues. The verse continues to claim, more generally, that ancient miraculous blessings are now resurging on earth. Verse 2 introduces the idea of restored judges. That is, beyond mere signs and wonders, actual personalities have arrived to govern the budding kingdom. Verse 3 refers to the "solemn assemblies" of which the temple dedication was the summit. Verse 4 refers to actual rituals the temple will house. Verse 5 refers to a three-person panel, no doubt the First Presidency of the church, likened to Moses, Aaron, and Joshua, who will preside and "feed" the people of the new Israel. Verse 6 projects into the Millennium, with images of subdued beasts, kingly crowns, and fiery chariots.

Tucked between these verses, though, is a far less dramatic, almost punctuational refrain. It has no place in the unfolding narrative of the verses, but is almost boilerplate praise constructed from a few common elements. It takes up the hosanna shout itself: "Hosanna, hosanna to God and the Lamb." The third line echoes the angels' declaration at Jesus' birth: "Let glory to them in the highest be given." The chorus concludes with a quasi-legalistic formula that seals the chorus as a kind of proclamation: "Henceforth and forever, amen and amen."

Which brings us to an argument against the "Song of Zion" genesis of Phelps's text: all the language of the hymn, both verse and chorus, is prefigured in other hymns of the era, most notably "My Heart's Experience," first published in 1803. Its fifth verse begins, "We'll sing and we'll shout and we'll shout and we'll sing." (This dual verbal formulation appears in no other extant hymns of the era.) In verse 2, "the news of his mercy is spreading abroad" foreshadows Phelps's line "to spread forth the kingdom of heaven abroad." And in verse 6, Jesus' chariots make their appearance. Moreover, the seventh verse of "My Heart's Experience" supplies the "armies of heaven" idea in the words "angels do sing / And with that bright army [we] make heaven to ring."

To what extent such language might have bled into a tongues-interpretation—or vice versa—who can say? I believe that both sources, a tongues interpretation and glimmers of an

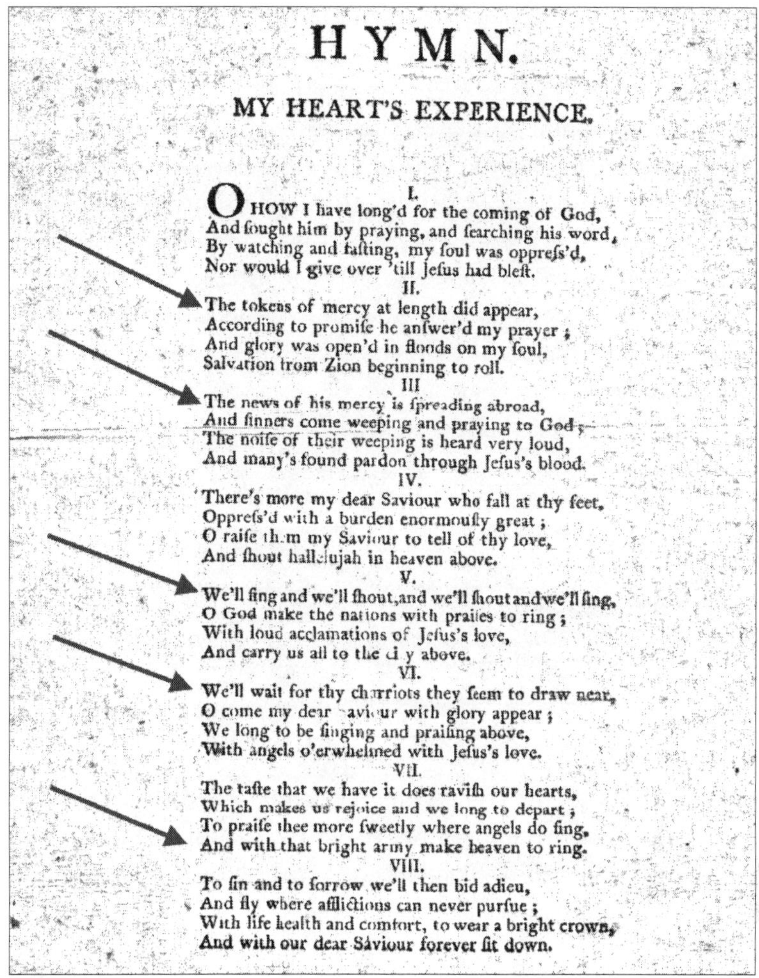

HYMN.

MY HEART'S EXPERIENCE.

I.
O HOW I have long'd for the coming of God,
And ſought him by praying, and ſearching his word,
By watching and faſting, my ſoul was oppreſs'd,
Nor would I give over 'till Jeſus had bleſt.

II.
The tokens of mercy at length did appear,
According to promiſe he anſwer'd my prayer;
And glory was open'd in floods on my ſoul,
Salvation from Zion beginning to roll.

III
The news of his mercy is ſpreading abroad,
And ſinners come weeping and praying to God;
The noiſe of their weeping is heard very loud,
And many's found pardon through Jeſus's blood.

IV.
There's more my dear Saviour who fall at thy feet,
Oppreſs'd with a burden enormouſly great;
O raiſe them my Saviour to tell of thy love,
And ſhout hallelujah in heaven above.

V.
We'll ſing and we'll ſhout, and we'll ſhout and we'll ſing,
O God make the nations with praiſes to ring;
With loud acclamations of Jeſus's love,
And carry us all to the ci y above.

VI.
We'll wait for thy ch rriots they ſeem to draw near,
O come my dear aviour with glory appear;
We long to be ſinging and praiſing above,
With angels o'erwhelmed with Jeſus's love.

VII.
The taſte that we have it does raviſh our hearts,
Which makes us rejoice and we long to depart;
To praiſe thee more ſweetly where angels do ſing,
And with that bright army make heaven to ring.

VIII.
To ſin and to ſorrow we'll then bid adieu,
And fly where afflictions can never purſue;
With life health and comfort, to wear a bright crown,
And with our dear Saviour forever ſit down.

"My Heart's Experience" (1803), a common hymn text that prefigured phrases in "The Spirit of God" (as marked).

existing hymn, fused in Phelps's imagination to bring about his text "Hosanna to God and the Lamb."

• • •

Tracking texts is one thing, tracking tunes is another. The biggest obstacle: we have no recordings. And printed versions of tunes, when they exist at all, mutate from one printed source to another. The "authenticity" of any tune relies on dubious criteria. Consider two examples, both well known to Latter-day Saints.

The first is William Clayton's hymn text "Come, Come, Ye Saints." It's refrain "all is well" was well-known from a song by that name. So, tracing the tune of our hymn back to its borrowed source seems easy. For years, the most-cited source for the tune was the well-known *Sacred Harp* of 1844. But an earlier version of the tune, this one in 6/8—a so-called *compound* meter, in which each beat divides equally into three parts—yields a rolling, lilting tune, notably different in character from the marchlike version in the *Sacred Harp*.[10] Here are all three:

Incidentally, if the compound meter tune was the one Clayton had in mind for "Come, Come, Ye Saints," we can see a different intention for the words "come, come": with the accent on the first "come," as in the *Sacred Harp* version, the repeated words sound like an urgent exhortation. But with the accent on the second "come," as in the earlier version, the idiom "come, come" emerges—that is, a "tsk tsk" of disapproval, which makes far more sense with the words that follow it in Clayton's song. Still, one can never know which version of this tune he had in mind, if either. He might have only vaguely recalled something like either of these published versions, one he most likely picked up through oral tradition, not the printed page.

The second example is "A Poor Wayfaring Man of Grief." The same tune ("Duane Street") appears with the text in many

10. David W. Music, "A New Source for the Tune 'All Is Well,'" *The Hymn* 29, 2 (Apr. 1978): 76–82.

Protestant hymnbooks. It is in a simple meter, not the compound one Mormons use. Although obviously derived from "Duane Street," the Ebenezer Beesley tune that Mormons use for James Montgomery's text appears in no other hymnbook. Meanwhile, a transcription of Apostle John Taylor singing the song as he did at Carthage Jail in 1844 reveals something *between* those other two.[11] Here are all three:

All this begs the question: how accurate was the transcription of Taylor's version? And how differently might Taylor have sung it from one occasion to the next, during the three decades he kept the song alive as a commemoration of Joseph Smith's martyrdom?

In tracking the proper music for "The Spirit of God," note that when Phelps published the text in his newspaper *Messenger and Advocate*, he identified the intended tune as "American Star." The problem is that "American Star" was not a "tune" per se. Penned by John McCreery, "American Star" became equally popular with "The Star-Spangled Banner" and had a hallowed presence in that era's culture, spawning imitations galore, from a Fourth of July song by McCreery himself to prize-winning texts in song competitions. In 1817, McCreery even published *The American Star Songster*, the first book to denote the tune we still use for "Star-Spangled Banner" (tune: "To Anachreon in Heaven").

"American Star" had four eight-line stanzas, each alternating

11. See Frederick Beesley, "A Sketch of the Musical Compositions of Ebenezer Beesley and Conditions Which Inspired Him to Compose," as cited in Sterling E. Beesley, *Kind Words: The Beginning of Mormon Melody: A Historical Biography and Anthology of the Life and Works of Ebenezer Beesley: Utah Pioneer Musician* (Privately published, 1980), 398.

12- and 11-syllable lines respectively, dutifully. It had no refrain or "chorus" as Phelps's "Hosanna" did, but ended each stanza with the words "American Star," a reference to the national flag. The opening suggests the snarling, combative tone of most of the lyric:

Come, strike the bold anthem, the war dogs are howling,
Already they eagerly snuff up their prey.

The stanza goes on to paint a scene of inevitable war, in which "youths grasp their swords," "beauty weeps," and ensuing generations "rush to display the American Star."

The second stanza urges brave defiance against "ruffians" who would drag women down with insults, etc., and envisions a "proud eagle [who] comes swooping, / And waves to the brave the American Star." The third stanza opens with a promise of patriot angels:

The spirits of Washington, Warren, Montgomery,
Look down from the clouds, with bright aspect serene;

The fourth stanza calls for a uniting of hands "round liberty's altar" as "united, we swear by the souls of the brave." The "American Star," we learn in the final lines, will fly over the imminent death of "oppression and tyranny."

One finds other song texts before 1836 that give "American Star" as the tune. But all of the extant pre-1836 printings of the "American Star" text that name *its* tune only name one: "Humors of Glen"—a sturdy, war-drummy tune, that rolls and thumps its way through sixteen bars in a minor key, diverging to major, then returning to minor at the end. Here is "The Spirit of God" set to that tune:

Its musical punch suits a national anthem for the Mormon Zion. But its serviceability for a choir, particularly a newly formed group of assorted volunteers with varying levels of training, falls short. Not only would one have to create parts for the tune, but, more important, the melody itself requires a level of flexibility and preciseness that a group of treble singers—women and perhaps boys—would be hard-pressed to negotiate synchronously. I will just say it: I do not think "The Spirit of God" was ever sung to "Humors of Glen" except perhaps in Phelps's mind.

So, was the tune we sing today the tune sung at the Kirtland temple dedication? The current LDS hymnbook seems to say no. The annotation for "The Spirit of God" there says that the tune is "ca. 1844.," which would disallow it from being the one sung in 1836. But it is a trick annotation. All we know is that the tune's earliest known *publication* was in 1844.

I believe the current tune is the same one sung at the Kirtland temple, as at all temples since. Consider three points.

First, why would we discard that original tune for another one and never use the first one again? Mormons love to commemorate. The first Mormon temple is the ripest picking ground for commemoration. No reason to junk its music and every reason to cherish it.

Second, if the one we sing today is not the tune sung in 1836, then the latter would have to be another that would *work for the text*. One boon of the Internet is the ability to search hundreds of thousands of tunes from tens of thousands of hymnbooks and instrumental tunebooks. Such a search reveals an important fact: while there are at least thirteen hymns with 12–11 alternating lines overall—the best-known being the Thanksgiving favorite "We Gather Together"—there are none *from that era* that are of the right length or that have a verse-chorus structure. At the same time, none of the over 244,000 indexed instrumental tunes online match the "Spirit of God" tune we use today.

Third, the tune we use today is so memorable that, if it existed previously, it would certainly have appeared in print outside of Mormondom to some other text either before 1844 or since. After at least a century of searching in books and now online for any other use of the tune, no one has found a match. Despite any lingering mystery about whether Phelps's text was first sung to any other tune or whether any other words were first sung to this tune, one thing seems sure: once this tune and text were printed together in 1844 neither this text nor this tune has been printed with any other partner since.

Knowing the demands of preparing choral music, especially among amateur and probably unauditioned singers, and knowing that the singing school for the temple dedication was organized at the beginning of January 1836, I suspect that the tune used for both songs began to be rehearsed first for "Now Let Us Rejoice," an existing text, and then served double duty for the new text, "Hosanna to God and the Lamb." Phelps's new hymn *text* was a perfect finale but came along too late for the choir to learn new music for it, especially when it had music that already fit. Meanwhile, as I said above, a choral arrangement of "American Star" was implausible. In any case, the tune they used for both hymns appears to be new for the Kirtland services, since, even though the other tune names for hymns at the dedication were known, this one only had a tune name that matched the name of the *new song's* text. That is, both "Now Let Us Rejoice" and "The Spirit of God" carry the tune name "Hosanna."

Given the uniqueness of the tune as it was published in 1844, it makes sense to posit three options.

1. The tune was composed by a Mormon and then written down.
2. The tune was remembered by a Mormon and then written down.
3. The tune as printed in 1844 was a combination of remembered and composed.

Of the three, the last seems truest to music circulated in a mostly oral culture. That explains why we have the variant tunes discussed above and why so many tunes that are "the same" are only similar: one person remembered a tune one way, then wrote it down as best as he or she could. In the process, notes were added or subtracted and a new variation emerged.

But let me put it this way: *I believe this tune is, in fact, the first indigenous Mormon music to be written down and published.* Let me show you how I think it came together.

One can break down the "Spirit of God" tune into idiomatic fragments of popular pre-1836 hymn tunes, building blocks from which a new tune easily could have been constructed in 1836. (In what follows, I have transposed all tunes into the key of C and followed the "Spirit of God" tune *as it was published* in 1844.)

I have three tunes in mind. The second phrase of "The Trumpet," for example, overtly prefigures the opening of "The Spirit of God." The next two measures of "The Spirit of God" overtly echo the opening of "Northfield." The final measures of the first phrase echo the end of "Muhlenberg." And there we have the tune to "The Spirit of God."

In "The Spirit of God" that whole first phrase is repeated exactly and thus accommodates a full stanza of text.

The "Spirit of God" *chorus* begins with a brief, nondescript chant, after which the entire chorus unfolds as a series of variations on the verse.

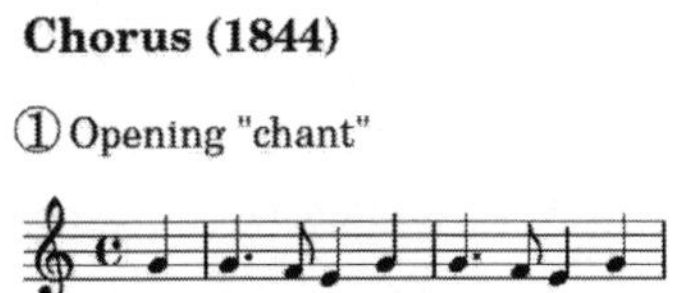

② Derivations from verse

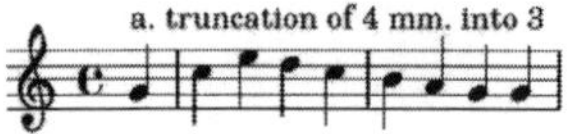

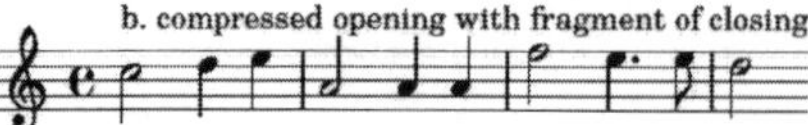

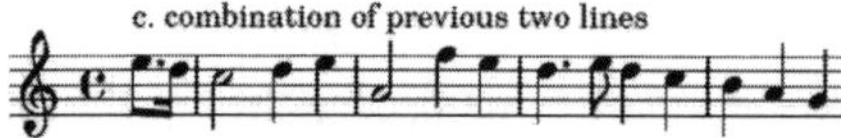

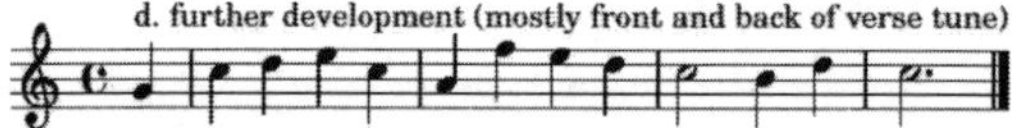

Overall, the melodic segments of "The Spirit of God" develop simply and naturally from idioms of the time. But assembled into a setting of an elaborate text, this fresh national anthem for Zion proved both brilliant and sturdy.

• • •

So much for the tune. What about its accompaniment? The first printing in 1844 adds to it a bass line that is mostly pro forma and slightly less than ingenious.

In the music's second printing, 1877, full harmonies were added. That took the next step, a huge one, in the song's journey toward what we sing today.

It was not until the coming of the railroad to Utah that musical type was readily available in Mormondom's capital. That meant that printed music happened piecemeal, most commonly in magazines printed either by the church or the leading musicians of the day. The *Utah Musical Bouquet*, published by Mormon Tabernacle organist Joseph Daynes, issued at least ten issues during 1877–78. Each brief issue contained untexted solo keyboard scores and a page of "Catechism of Harmony and Thorough Bass." The fifth issue contained "The Spirit of God."

Unlike the 1844 printing, this one had four parts, representing soprano, alto, tenor, and bass, the standard layout of music intended

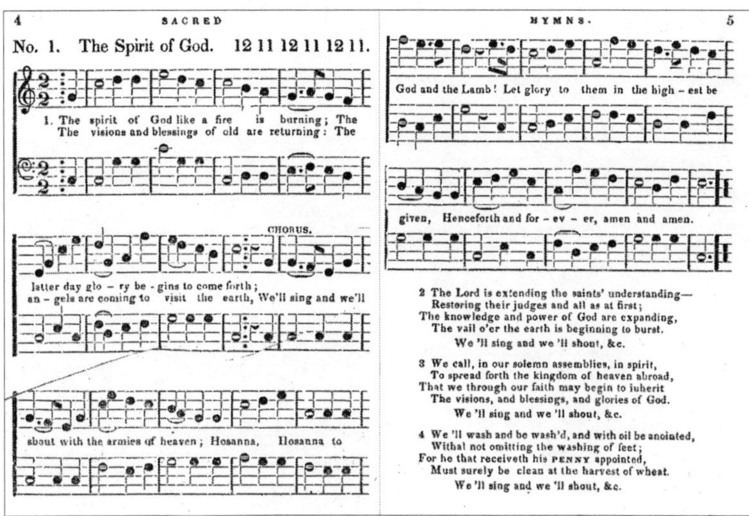

The first appearance of "The Spirit of God" with musical notation (1844).

for four-voice part singing. The key was down a step from the 1844 version C to Bb), and the harmony veered slightly from the original, most notably in the third measure of the verse, which in 1844 had the first scale-degree in the bass of the third measure of the verse, but now had the fourth scale-degree (and in 1844 had the fourth scale-degree in the bass of the chorus's third measure but now had the first scale degree). It also added some chromatic harmony not contemplated in the original (see mm. 9–10 of the chorus, for example).

Two aspects of the 1877 melody differed in memorable ways. First, this version removed the lilting dotted-quarter + eighth-note combinations that opened the chorus of the 1844 original. Second, it introduced more ornamented figures here and there, as in the fourth and twelfth measures of the chorus, where simple repeated quarter-notes become a rising and falling figure that echoes several tunes of the day (most notably the repeated motif that fills the second half of the popular fuging tune called "Lonsdale").

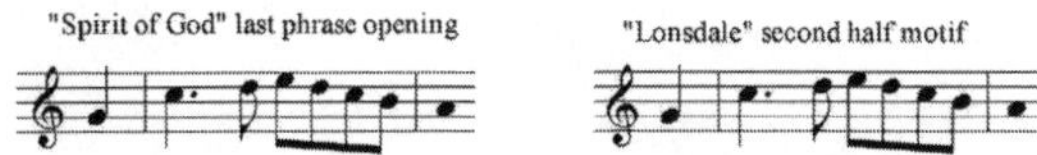

The first appearance of "The Spirit of God" music in four parts (1877).

The hymn's next appearance, in the *Primary Tune Book* three years later, offers a slightly different take.

The harmony is simpler and the melody returns in several details to the 1844 version, most obviously in the opening of the

The first appearance of "The Spirit of God" in four parts, reharmonized, with words (1880).

chorus. Perhaps Eliza Snow, the tune book's compiler, felt that children would prefer the uneven rhythms at the chorus' opening to the march-like, beat-driven notes that Daynes had given them.

The four-part setting in the 1889 *Latter-day Saints' Psalmody* became the standard, now given the tune name of "Assembly." It is the setting that has appeared in all Mormon hymnbooks since. It holds closer in its tune to the *Musical Bouquet* version but closer in its harmony to the *Primary Tune Book* version.

• • •

So, at the end of this fussy archaeology, what should we carry away from the "The Spirit of God"?

First, the song is a conduit back into the creative, spiritually improvisatory fountainhead of Mormonism. It was an era when Latter-day Saints could open themselves up to public inspiration that went from unintelligible (tongues) to intelligible (interpretation) to formal (versification). Early Mormons had faith in instantaneous, unplanned, unique flows of utterance that they knew might yield new canon.

Second, the song carries us back into a wider cultural stream of idioms that surrounded the generation after the War of 1812. Tunes were everywhere, texts were everywhere, and one could mix, match, adapt, revise, and rewrite at will, knowing there was, at some deep level, a common coinage of speech and music that the whole nation shared.

Third, the song leads us to reconsider the questions of literacy itself. What do we really know of what was not written down? How did Mormons sing—but also, how did they preach, or talk, or pray in public? We project backwards from the present, thinking perhaps, in an age reliant on recordings, that written documents mimic the sounds on which they were predicated. But the mysteries locked up in "The Spirit of God" should lead us to wonder: how do we negotiate between the acoustic and the written? If "the *voice* of the Lord" is what we seek, maybe the *written* word—or tune—cannot suffice. And *that* is one of the founding principles of Mormonism itself.

4 MINISTERING MINSTRELS

Dozens of men who stormed Carthage Jail and shot Joseph Smith on June 27, 1844, had put their wet hands into gunpowder and smeared it on their faces.

It was an old trick, this cheap disguise: darkened faces were harder to identify. Or, as at the Boston Tea Party, this ruse might not have been to obscure identity but to misdirect. Dark skin matched dark deeds, and so blacks and Indians made handy surrogates: mimic one of those groups, confirm the stereotype, and walk away from crimes a free man. Mormon scripture and lore, of course, reinforced that premise: God darkened bad people's skin as a sign. The mark God put on Cain to identify him to others was blackened skin. That shade among his descendants blocked them from holding the priesthood. God smote Nephi's evil brothers and generations thereafter with darker skin. In the Book of Mormon, granted, people sometimes work against type—the dark-skinned suddenly and confoundingly act more worthily than the light-skinned. But the exception relied on the rule. Skin color aspired to match the content of one's character. God had designed it that way, cursing bad men and women with an overflow of melanin.[1] Dark-faced mobs played on that divine rule.

Yet, as Northrop Frye puts it, one should always expect a

1. The literature on Mormons and race has mushroomed in the twenty-first century. Consider just the following five volumes in chronological order: Armand Mauss, *All Abraham's Children: Changing Mormon Conceptions of Race and Lineage* (Urbana: University of Illinois Press, 2003); Newell G. Bringhurst and Darron T. Smith, eds., *Black and Mormon* (Urbana: University of Illinois Press, 2004); W. Paul Reeve, *Religion of a Different Color: Race and the Mormon Struggle for Whiteness* (New York: Oxford University Press, 2015); Max Perry Mueller, *Race and the Making of the Mormon People* (Chapel Hill: University of North Carolina Press, 2017); and the entire issue of *Dialogue: A Journal of Mormon Thought* 51, 3 (Fall 2018).

Detail of 1851 engraving of darkened-face assassin threatening to decapitate Joseph Smith.

"demonic parody."[2] And in the divine skin trade, the darkening of mob faces had just such a parody—the entertainments known as "minstrelsy," which infused and infested British and American stagecraft throughout the nineteenth century. Smear the ashes of burnt cork on one's light-skinned face and *pretend* to be dark-skinned, with all the warping and twisting of character that implied, but now in the direction of comedy, not tragedy. On the one hand, minstrel shows were populated by "darkies" who were

2. Frye uses this idea, for example, in *The Great Code: The Bible and Literature* (New York: Harcourt Brace Jovanovich, 1982).

ugly, unclean, lazy, and cunning. On the other hand, these same black characters were often portrayed as tender, devout, familial, and more sensible than whites when it came to politics and religion. Minstrels strove to depict blacks as both uncivilized and endearing, fit objects of the paternalism of whites, that strange mix of pity and domination.[3]

While Mormons echoed centuries-old myths about blackness and whiteness (i.e., darkness and lightness), actual responses to dark skin and its owners in early Mormonism range from distrust to indifference to pity to fascination, with none of those responses unmixed. When black Mormon Hark Lay was convicted of seducing women, that might have seemed a validation of prejudice. When Elijah Abel served the Mormon cause like a champion, his dark skin may have seemed unremarkable. On the Zion's Camp march, George A. Smith wrote that they ate near a plantation and "the half-naked negro waiters excited considerable curiosity."[4] These varied takes on black skin had hints of both Old and New Testament curiosity and even titillation: think of the Queen of Sheba and Solomon, the Ethiopian eunuch and the Apostle Philip, or even Simon of Cyrene, who carried Jesus' cross.

During Joseph Smith's lifetime, minstrelsy seemed more of a seduction than a reality. One tell-tale hint of longing comes from then-secret wife of Smith, Helen Mar Whitney, who recalled that she and her friends would sometimes awaken at night to the sound of minstrel entertainments from the showboats on the Mississippi.

> For a time after we settled on the flat there were but few houses built between ours and the river, and "oft in the stilly night" waking from our slumbers we would hear delicious strains of music wafted by the breeze over our quiet city from some steamer passing up or down the river, as they were frequently accompanied by minstrels, sometimes colored people and their music was perfectly enchanting—"Behold how brightly breaks the morning," "The Cracovion Maid" and

3. Two fine overviews of minstrelsy are Robert C. Toll, *Blacking Up: The Minstrel Show in Nineteenth-Century America* (New York: Oxford University Press, 1974), and the "Blackface Minstrelsy" section of Dale Cockrell, "Nineteenth-Century Popular Music," in David Nicholls, ed., *The Cambridge History of American Music* (Cambridge, England: Cambridge University Press, 1998), 165–75.

4. See George A. Smith, "The Return to Kirtland," *Instructor* 81, 6 (June 1946): 288.

"Home, Sweet Home," and in many Ethiopian airs they excelled. The following verse will, no doubt, remind many beside myself of their most charming serenades—

> "My skiff is by the shore
> She's light and free,
> To ply the feathered oar
> Is joy to me,
> And as she glides along,
> My song shall be,
> Dearest maid, I love but thee!"

> Negro melodies are always sweet, and there is something most exquisite in the sound of music from the water. [5]

Whitney's recollection of that verse may be off: "My Skiff Is by the Shore" was a wildly popular blackface minstrel song different from the non-minstrel song she quotes. However that may be, Whitney aptly reminds us how the Mississippi River was as much an entertainment stage as a shipping route or conduit for emigrants. Jeannette Cooperman writes as colorfully about that as one can:

> The river was not, in those years, a sullen and muddy conveyor belt for barges. There were circus boats stuffed with clowns and poodles; theater boats wailing over villainy; opera boats that sent heralds ashore to trumpet their performances. Minstrels did the Cakewalk and the Buzzard Lope and the Buck and Wing, told tall tales, sang spirituals, shook tambourines, mocked current events. All the persuaders were on the river: preachers and card-readers, lecturers on mesmerism and the significance of bumps on the skull.[6]

Beyond the waterfront sound of minstrelsy, consider also this flirtation with the comedic side of blackface entertainment: what Mormons came to call their "creed" was earlier known as "the negro's eleventh commandment." Joseph Smith's grandfather Asael Smith cited it as such in a letter to Jacob Towne in 1796: "Give my

5. Helen Mar Whitney, "Scenes in Nauvoo," *Woman's Exponent* 10 (Sept. 15, 1881): 58.

6. Jeannette Cooperman, "In Their Golden Age, Riverboats Were Our Nightclubs, Our Theater District, Our Parade Ground: A Look Back at the History of the Mississippi River," www.stlmag.com/history/Mississippi-River-History/ (accessed June 2, 2019).

best regards to your parents, and tell them that I have taken up with the eleventh commandment, that the Negro taught to the minister, which was thus:—The minister asked the Negro how many commandments there were, and his answer was, 'Eleben, Sir.' 'Aye,' replied the other, 'What is the eleventh? That is one I have never heard of!' 'Why, sir, the Elebenth Commandment, sir, is MIND YO' OWN BUSINESS.' And so I choose to do, and give myself but little concern about what passes in the political world."[7] Without mentioning either the "negro" derivation or its comic quasi-biblical Ten-Commandments trope, in 1844 Joseph's brother William formulated the "Mormon Creed" this way: "To mind their own business, and let everybody else, *do likewise.*" The creedal stature of that phrase remained for decades in Mormonism thereafter. Yet few could miss its vernacular pre-existence as a comic negro bit.[8]

With these glimmers of faux-black culture as background, let me tour you through three phases of minstrel entertainment in early Mormondom: (1) Local Blackface, (2) Imported Blackface, and (3) Black.

LOCAL BLACKFACE

While I find no evidence of Mormon blackface in Nauvoo or earlier, traces of the practice show up in early Utah. In 1847 Brigham Young complained about elders who, despite their glorious calling to preach and minister, were dancing "as niggers … they will hoe down all, turn summersets, dance on their knees, and haw, haw, out loud," unmistakably describing energetic minstrel-style dancing. (Young added, "I don't mean this as debasing the negroes by any means.")[9]

7. Asael Smith, Letter to Jacob Towne, Jan. 14, 1796, www.geni.com/people/Asael-Smith-I/6000000005953053862 (accessed July 11, 2019). For more on the creed and its uses as the "eleventh commandment" (though not necessarily "the negro's"), see www.barrypopik.com/index.php/new_york_city/entry/eleventh_commandment_mind_your_business (accessed July 11, 2019). On the Mormon Creed generally, see Michael Hicks, "Minding Business: A Note on 'The Mormon Creed,'" BYUS 26, 4 (Fall 1986):125–32.

8. Meanwhile, Frederick Douglass adopted the phrase interestingly, without the comedic intent. See his "The Key to Uncle Tom's Cabin," Apr. 29, 1853, www.utc.iath.virginia.edu/africam/afar03nt.html (accessed July 18, 2019).

9. *William Clayton's Journal: A Daily Record of the Original Company of "Mormon" Pioneers from Nauvoo, Illinois, to the Valley of the Great Salt Lake* (Salt Lake City: Deseret News Press, 1921), 196.

The 1850s yield a few references to local "in-house" blackface. In January 1853 a local group calling itself "The African Band" performed minstrel songs at the Salt Lake Social Hall.[10] In 1854 the *Deseret News* described a 13th Ward party at which "a solo dance was also performed by a 'genuine Ethiopian' [the standard term for a blackface performer], in a style somewhat original, and 'werry pecoolia'"—a nod to faux black dialect. But the paper added a note typical of Mormon legitimizations of public fun: "Indeed the whole entertainment was not unbecoming true intelligence." In other words, this schtick, however lowbrow, had a tinge of "the glory of God" to it and therefore could not be indicted by normal critical judgment.[11] The Utah Reformation of 1856–57 likely tamped down the spread of minstrelsy in Deseret. But in the late spring of 1857 the *Deseret News* described a festival at the Social Hall at which "Ethiopian minstrel performances added much to the amusement of the audience." The list of players who took part consists mostly of well-known names from the Salt Lake music scene.[12] In 1858, as Colonel Albert Sidney Johnston's troops approached Salt Lake City, minstrelsy appeared even among the armies of Deseret.[13] Minstrel *music* so captivated the Saints that Apostle Wilford Woodruff warned in 1855 that scripture reading was being neglected in Mormondom in preference for "negro songs," which he placed in the same category as French novels.[14] Let us take a quick inventory of such songs.

First and most popular were the sentimental minstrel songs, of which Stephen Foster composed the best known—songs that celebrated lost love and innocence or the beauties of Southern plantation life. Several of Foster's songs were widely played in Utah during the 1850s and 1860s, and Brigham Young reportedly liked to hear Eliza Snow's "O My Father" sung to the tune of

10. DN, Jan. 22, 1853.

11. "Ward Party," DN, Mar. 2, 1854. My reference to the glory of God qua intelligence comes from Mormonism's well-known dictum: "the glory of God is intelligence" (D&C 93:36).

12. "Flora's Festival," DN, June 17, 1857.

13. See Clarence Merrill, Autobiography, 326, typescript, HBLL.

14. Scott G. Kenney, ed., *Wilford Woodruff's Journal: 1833–1898,* 9 vols. (Midvale, Utah: Signature Books, 1983), 4:353.

Foster's "Gentle Annie.'"[15] (Indeed, after the Civil War, Young's daughter recalled, he became quite fond of such "Negro melodies.")[16] A song of this type written by John Hugh McNaughton became quite popular among nineteenth-century American religious groups, including the Mormons. Popularized by Christy's Minstrels in the late 1850s, the song depicted the tender feelings of plantation servants bound together by family ties. It began: "There is beauty all around when there's love at home. There is joy in every sound, when there's love at home. Peace and plenty here abide, smiling sweet on every side: Time doth softly, sweetly glide when there's love at home."[17]

Anti-slavery songs, though relatively few, also appeared in minstrel shows. One of these, Henry Clay Work's "Babylon Is Fallen," beguiled the Saints with its militant religious dialect:

Don't you see de black clouds risin' ober yonder
Whar de Massa's old plantation am?
Neber you be frightened, dem is only darkies
Come to jine an' fight for Uncle Sam.
Look out dar, now! We's a gwine to shoot!
Look out dar, don't you understand?
Babylon is fallen! Babylon is fallen!
An' we's agwine to occupy de land.[18]

A third type of minstrel song was the jubilant "walk-around" type used for minstrel finales, of which Dan Emmett's "Dixie" was the most popular. "Dixie" was so popular in Mormondom that it was sung in the general conference priesthood meeting at Salt Lake City in April 1863.[19] W. W. Phelps also wrote new lyrics to "Dixie" as a tribute to Brigham Young. In order that Young and

15. See Augusta Joyce Crocheron, *Representative Women of Deseret* (Salt Lake City: J.C. Graham, 1884), 1–2.

16. Susa Young Gates and Leah D. Widtsoe, *The Life Story of Brigham Young* (New York: Macmillan, 1930), 249.

17. The earliest known imprint of "When There's Love at Home" is dated 1859. A photocopy of an undated imprint bearing the printed subscript "Christy Minstrels Song" is in the Church Music Department Subject and Correspondence Files, CHL.

18. The chorus to "Babylon Is Fallen" appears in the George Careless cornet part book (labeled "Dramatic Music"), CHL.

19. George Goddard Journal, Apr. 7, 1863, holograph, CHL. The minutes of the conference (as published in DN) do not mention the song.

his children might sing the song, Phelps effusively wrote, "in that spirit that sounds like heaven, and swells the soul to thoughts that breathe, by words that burn, with sense and sound."[20] One verse is suggestive of the whole:

> We love the words of the prophet Joseph,
> While the gentile only knows of
> war and wo, war and wo, war and wo,
> Israel reigns.
>
> Up. Up! Ye royal priesthood holders,
> Joseph's robe's on Brigham's shoulders,
> clear the way, clear the way, clear the way,
> Israel reigns.

The fourth type was the comic song, the bread and butter of blackface minstrelsy. Thus, we find "The Nigger's Lament" sung at a July 24, 1856, "Literary and Musical Festival" in Salt Lake City, the minstrel favorite "Lucy Long" being one of the "favorite songs" of the Mormon Battalion, and "Blue Blood Colored Coons" appearing in the Beesley Band part book of the era.[21]

At the dedication of the Salt Lake Theatre in 1862, Brigham Young asked that only entertainment of the highest literary and moral value should appear on its stage.[22] Some suited the times, such as the productions of *Uncle Tom's Cabin* in 1864 and 1865, a play the *Deseret News* praised for its "allegorical vision."[23] But productions at the theatre throughout the Civil War years featured blackface skits and entr'actes, with local singers and comedians—particularly the convert William C. Dunbar—presenting more "negro songs" and, in one case, a production of *The Octoroon: A*

---

20. "Israel Reigns," hymn and postscript of Phelps, Letter to Young, Jan. 2, 1862, holograph in CHL.

21. "Nigger's Lament" is mentioned in "Literary and Musical Festival–Anniversary July 24," DN, Aug. 20, 1856. "Blue Blood Colored Coons" appears in the Beesley Band part book ("Music") in the Sterling Beesley Papers, HBLL. On "Lucy Long," see Norma B. Ricketts, *Mormon Battalion: The Western Odyssey of Melissa Burton Coray: 1846–1848* (Salt Lake City: Daughters of the Utah Pioneers, 1994), 39.

22. "Propriety of Theatrical Amusements," JD 9:242–45.

23. The production dates of these plays appear in Therald Francis Todd, "The Operation of the Salt Lake Theatre, 1862–1875," PhD Diss., University of Oregon, 1973, 286–87.

Life in Louisiana, which featured a "Grand Ethiopian Chorus," with "Ethiopian," again, connoting blackface.[24] All these appeared against the backdrop of the *Deseret News* using occasional "Sambo" quotes as column fillers.[25]

The final burst of local minstrelsy came at the end of 1868. With the completion of the railroad months away, the first minstrel group as such booked itself in the theatre. The newspapers took notice: "This attraction is something new for our theatre-goers and we have no doubt they will enjoy the novel and highly amusing performances of the songsters hugely. These are the first professional 'Negro Minstrels' that have appeared in this city." And such a group, the paper added "is certainly a great attraction for Salt Lake City." *The Curtain*, a local theatrical paper, called it a "grand novelty ... a kind of performance very popular in the States and will no doubt create a sensation among our people. Many of them have not seen 'Negro Minstrels' before."

The group appeared for the three final nights of the year with six members, a typical roster of comic, percussion ("bones"), lithe dancing and boisterous singing:

Add Weaver – Prince of Comedians
Ben Hoyt – The Inimitable Bones
Samuel Rickey – Champion Cloggist
Professor King – Violinist, Director of Music
Henry Kendall – The Great Basso
Joseph Russell – Interlocutor

After the first performance, it seemed clear that Weaver was the star, with the *News* noting his "really good jokes." *The Curtain* called the show a "rare treat" for "lovers of [the] strongly sensational."

But on January 2 the *News* reported that group was now "defunct."[26] With so much success and attention, the odds are that something other than theatrical failure caused them to pull up

24. See "Theatrical," DN, May 18 and Oct. 19, 1864. Also, Alfred S. Morris, Jr, "Music History of the Salt Lake Theatre, The Formative Years: 1862–1870," MA Thesis, Brigham Young University, 1957.

25. See DN, Oct. 5, 1864, and Mar. 1, 1865.

26. For this and all quotations in the preceding two paragraphs, see the theatrical notices in DN, Dec. 28, 1868, through Jan. 2, 1869; also *The Curtain*, Dec. 19 and 31, 1868.

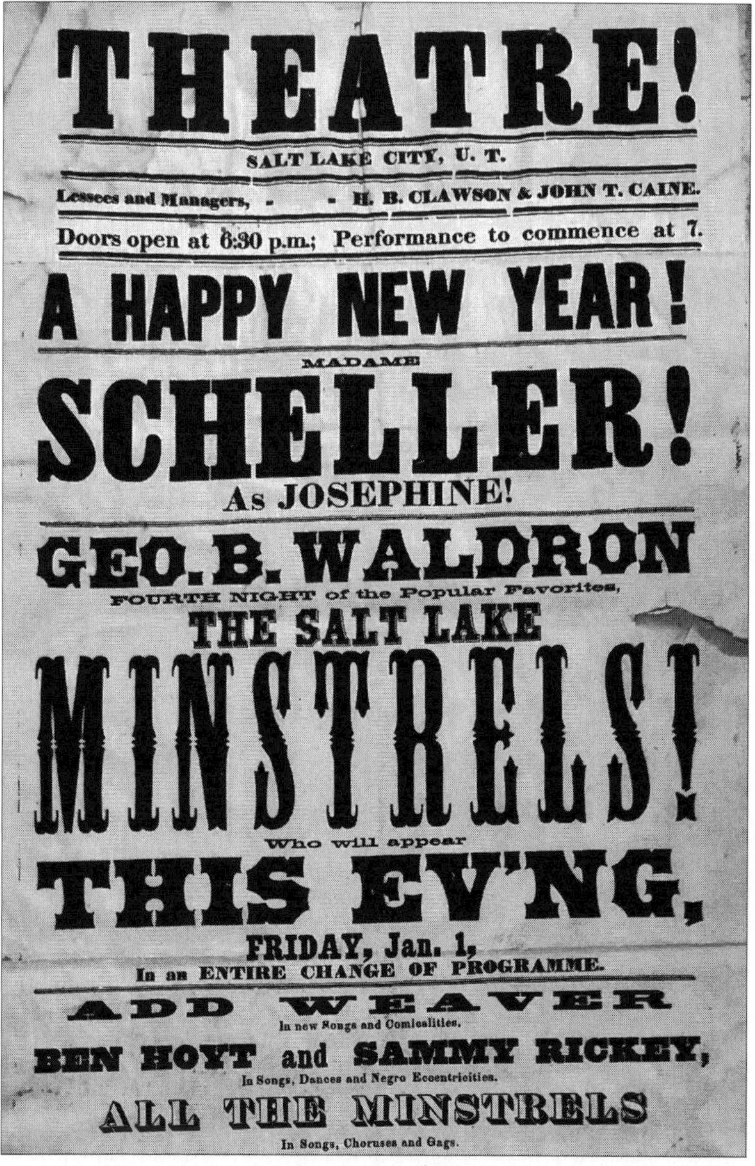

Detail of Salt Lake Theatre poster for Utah's first homegrown minstrel troupe (1869).

stakes. Brigham Young himself possibly put an end to it. Minstrelsy often used grimacing and facial contortions for comic effect, a practice which he generally denounced in the theater unless it produced "pleasurable emotion."[27] Young appears to have been most troubled by the blacking of the face to perform pseudo-Negro skits and music. He did not object to burnt cork makeup when it was called for in legitimate plays, because he insisted upon authenticity of theatrical detail.[28] But after he attended the Salt Lake Minstrels, he insisted that the elders who performed in it stop darkening their faces, adding that if any of them should die suddenly with their faces in burnt cork they would be disgraced.[29] Undoubtedly gratuitous blacking suggested to Young a mockery of God since dark skin was God's curse on blacks, an affliction that would bar them from the priesthood and, consequently, the highest degree of celestial glory.

Still, a Salt Lake Theater prop inventory in 1877—the year Young died—listed three calico "nigger coats," two "nigger undershirts," eight "nigger wigs," and a banjo, all the property of the venue.[30] And if we needed more evidence of the persistence of local minstrelsy in Mormondom, consider notices in the *Utah Musical Times* from 1876–77. The Salt Lake 20th Ward Institute had a party at which "W. T. Harris gave stump speeches in the irrepressible 'Nigger style,' and caused much merriment." The Salt Lake 6th Ward presented an "Ethiopian Sketch." The 3rd Ward offered a comedic "Negro Music Lesson."[31] Blackface entertainment was by now woven into Mormon life.

IMPORTED BLACKFACE

The driving of the Golden Spike in 1869 began the next phase of blackface in Mormondom. The Salt Lake Theatre managers had recently closed the venue because, as they wrote to British theater

27. As Young put it, "The distortion of the muscles of the face and body … should … be studiously avoided." See "Theatres," DN, Jan. 11, 1865.

28. See the account of George Pyper, *Romance of an Old Playhouse*, rev. ed. (Salt Lake City: Deseret News Press, 1937), 261.

29. See the excerpt from the Laura McBride Smith Papers in Robert Sayers, "Sing Anything: The Narrative Repertoire of a Mormon Pioneer," *Journal of the Southwest* 29 (Spring 1987): 76–77. A photograph in this article (43) shows the minstrel group after they abandoned blackface makeup.

30. Inventory of the theatre, Oct. 10, 1877, in Deseret Dramatic Association Papers, CHL.

31. *Utah Musical Times* 1 (Apr. 15, 1876): 29; and 2 (Apr. 1, 1877): 11.

entrepreneur Sheridan Corbyn on July 31, 1869, "we wanted to give the audience a respite from so much *Drama*. We think they have become satiated with it. Minstrelsy would no doubt be a very agreeable change." They explained to Corbyn that "We believe and have always believed that a first class minstrel troupe would do well in this city, for we have never had anything of the kind here." Yes, they had had the local group, but "first class" implied performers from further east. They proposed that Corbyn book such a group in Salt Lake for at least two weeks, with the theatre furnishing house, lights, posters, ads, props, doorkeepers, ushers, and ticket-takers and the minstrel troupe furnishing the "entire entertainment"—no locals to assist them. They'd then split the after-tax gross receipts, 50/50. But, the inevitable catch:

> It is perhaps unnecessary to tell you that a performance to be acceptable here must be chaste and first class in every particular, and a company to be well thought of and respected by the community, must respect themselves and avoid drunkenness, swearing and all such vices while performing here. Doing this and attending strictly to their *own business* [a reference to the "Mormon Creed"] and leaving everybody else alone is all that is necessary to get along in this community. We are thus particular, so that you may know what is expected and if you have any such in your company better leave them behind as they will be sure to injure you here.

Corbyn booked Murphy and Mack's twenty-eight-member minstrel troupe to come to Utah from San Francisco for a ten-day engagement on Salt Lake's terms.[32] News of the engagement caused a commotion in the city and prompted the *Deseret News* to observe that if its readers did not pack the house to overflowing, "they will manifest a most unparalleled lack of taste and appreciation."[33] The troupe, like most minstrel companies, played a fresh program every night and did very good business for late summer in Salt Lake City when the hot, poorly ventilated theatre was quite uninhabitable. The newspapers claimed that the only fault that

32. See Clawson and Caine, Letter to Sheridan Corbyn, July 31, 1869, Deseret Dramatic Association Letterpress Copybooks, CHL.

33. "The Minstrels," DN, Aug. 27, 1869; compare the various notices in DN, Aug. 18–26, 1869.

could be found in this gentile minstrelsy was that "we could not have more of it."[34] The minstrels' success troubled some of the city's intellectuals, however, who argued that not only did it speak ill of the public's taste, but that it also may have constituted a breach of President Young's admonitions to cultivate "home talent.'" Could not the Saints appreciate their own George Careless and Ebenezer Beesley playing classical music, one critic asked, as much as they did gentiles in blackface?[35]

In 1870 and 1872, respectively, two more professional minstrel troupes came to Utah. The first of these, Duprez and Bendedict's, was also the first East Coast company to visit the territory. On their arrival in Salt Lake City, they drew huge crowds and tumultuous applause, especially for their clog dancing, stump preaching, and female impersonations.[36] Their return visit that September was regarded as nothing short of miraculous, since it had been reported in the Utah press that the minstrels had been massacred by highwaymen on their way to San Francisco. Duprez and Benedict's minstrel parade through the streets of Salt Lake City in September 1870 delighted the citizens with the news that the troupe had not been, as the *Deseret News* put it, "dispatched to the spirit world."[37] When the Purdy, Scott, and Fostelle Minstrels arrived in 1872, the press and public lavished them with praise. The *Salt Lake Tribune* observed that "there's a good deal in the darkey when properly brought out, and the present minstrels appear to have got all of his interesting points. They present a greater variety by far than we have ever before witnessed in a performance of this kind."[38] But music critic John Tullidge slammed their performances. He called them unprofessional "pretenders" whose agents had "deceived" the "public of Salt Lake City [who] were egregiously gulled" by these minstrels. *Footlights* magazine assailed the troupe for misrepresenting themselves as first class, when they

34. "The Minstrels," DN, Aug. 25, 1869.

35. John Tullidge, "Murphy and Mack's Minstrel Troupe," *Utah Magazine* 3 (Sept. 11, 1869): 298–99, and "Our Orchestra," *Utah Magazine* 3 (Sept. 18, 1869): 314–15.

36. See "Duprez Minstrels," DN, Aug. 4, 1870.

37. "The Minstrels Ho!" DN, Sept. 16, 1870.

38. "The Minstrels," SLT, Feb. 16, 1872. Tullidge's critique is in "The Americus Combination," *Footlights*, Apr. 11, 1872.

were "very ordinary" performers. "They hadn't a note of music; the musical director of the Theatre wrote their music for them, giving much of his time for their benefit, for which Mr. Scott refused to remunerate him, and by his profanity and obscenity made himself disgustingly obnoxious." Purdy used "old, vile gags which were older than himself. When the audience refused to laugh, he'd leave the stage for up to twenty minutes." And on and on.

More scandal erupted when the minstrels' manager breached agreements with theatre employees who painted the scenery, the performers left huge unpaid debts in town—especially for cigars—and, to add insult to injury, the troupe complained in the eastern press about Utah's backwardness. Some Salt Lakers reversed their earlier positive assessments of the minstrels and took the episode as further confirmation that home talent was the only safe sort. The scandal appears to have fostered the brief reemergence of the Salt Lake Minstrels, who toured the Wasatch Front in March 1872, right after Purdy, Scott, and Fostelle's left the region.[39]

The theatre, though, faced other troubles. The winter of 1872–73 was particularly harsh, so patrons could not walk to the theater and horse sickness kept them from riding. There were rumors of a smallpox outbreak. People had begun complaining about the dirty seat cushions in the theatre. And two competing venues were siphoning theatre goers away. In March 1873, George Reynolds complained to Brigham Young that the opening of the Theater Comique and Bowery in town was "drawing away patrons." Worse than that was a new venue: "a Melodeon or Music Hall has been opened on Main St., where I am told brazen women dance lewd dances. This hall is well attended, some going out of curiosity, others because they have a liking to such exhibitions."[40]

As business slowed and rivals increased, no more blackface minstrel troupes were booked into the theatre until 1878. When Milt G. Barlow, one of the nation's most famous blackface artists, brought his troupe to Salt Lake City in 1879, it briefly reunited

39. On Purdy, Scott, and Fostelle's visit, see also the notices in DN, Feb. 17 and 21, 1872; SLT, Feb. 20, 1872; and *The Footlights*, Feb. 19 and Mar. 11–14, 1872. On the Salt Lake Minstrels tour, see notices in *The Footlights*, Mar. 11, 13, and 18, 1872.

40. George Reynolds, Letter to Brigham Young, Feb. 5 and Mar. 7, 1873, Deseret Dramatic Association Letterpress Copybooks.

a Mormon family: Barlow was the son of a dentist in the 15th Ward and the two men had not seen each other since the father left his wife and family in Lexington, Kentucky, thirty-two years earlier.[41] Meanwhile, a new "sensation" was rising in the ranks of American entertainment.

BLACK

Utahns, like the rest of the nation, began to clamor for real blacks to perform for them on the stage. To employ black entertainers was seen as something of a philanthropic enterprise during Reconstruction years, but it was also a chance to see the novelty, some people felt, of *blacks imitating whites imitating blacks*. Real black entertainers were referred to as "colored" to distinguish them from the more common "negro" or "Ethiopian" entertainers (i.e., white men in burnt cork). All-black minstrel troupes had begun to appear with greater frequency throughout the nation after the Civil War. Not wanting to disappoint their audiences, black minstrels retained the style and content of blackface minstrelsy. And because they were "authentic" Negroes, these players lent an air of genuineness to the portrayals of blacks to which people had grown accustomed in previous decades.

But a new vision of how and what blacks could perform also emerged. The teenage Hyers Sisters were at the vanguard. As Jocelyn Buckner would later write of them, these two black, classically trained vocalists "pushed boundaries of acceptable and expected roles for black and female performers by developing works that moved beyond stereotypical caricatures of African American life."[42] The sisters came to the Salt Lake Theatre in 1871, billed as "musical wonders" with the qualifier "colored" beneath their names. It was only their second performance, following their debut in San Francisco.

In interpreting classical music, the sisters proved more than equal to their white peers. That might be what led the theatre to change its billing from the novelty-oriented "musical wonders" to the more respectful "wonderful musical artistes." They

41. "An Interesting Fact," DN, June 4, 1879.

42. Jocelyn L. Buckner, "'Spectacular Opacities': The Hyers Sisters' Performances of Respectability and Resistance," *African American Review* 45, 3 (Fall 2012): 309.

performed works that included scenes from Donizetti's 1842 opera *Linda di Chamounix*. Mormon music critic John Tullidge declined even to mention that the sisters were black in his glowing review of their concerts, and near the end of their run the theatre dropped the word "colored" from its advertisements. In a final turn of events, a coalition of Mormon and gentile musicians and businessmen arranged a benefit concert to raise money for the sisters to continue their vocal training in Italy. But, returning the proceedings to stereotype, the theatre scheduled to play on the same bill with the sisters Dick Brown, "The World's Champion Banjoist," who would appear in "Five or Six Ethiopian Sketches."[43]

In 1873 a black solo artist made his first appearance in Salt Lake City. The former slave Thomas Bethune toured the nation after the Civil War under the name "Blind Tom," displaying his strange musical abilities, which ranged from playing by ear works of Liszt, Chopin, and other luminaries, to imitating various instruments with his voice, to singing minstrel-style plantation songs of his own composing, to duplicating at first hearing any piece played by an audience member. In April 1873, three years after Blind Tom's exploits had been publicized on the front page of the *Deseret News*, the Salt Lake Theatre managers wrote to Bethune's agent that there was "considerable anxiety" in the city to hear this phenomenon.[44] They set an engagement for May, billing Tom as the "Most Wonderful Living Curiosity of the Nineteenth Century."

His performance was showy: he played Lizst, Thalberg, and many other moderns at the piano, told stories and jokes, did vocal imitations of guitar, banjo, bagpipes, music boxes, and more. But Blind Tom failed to meet the public's expectations. The audiences' greatest disappointment came when Joseph Daynes, one of Utah's most prominent "home composers," played one of his own pieces

---

43. On the Hyers (sometimes billed as "Hyer") Sisters' visits, see John Tullidge's review in DN, Aug. 16, 1871; the notices in *Footlights*, Aug. 12, 16, and 17, 1871; and the theatre posters on file in CHL. See also the racism-tinged review of a subsequent concert in *Salt Lake Times*, Feb. 4, 1879.

44. See George Reynolds, Letter to Thomas Warwick, Apr. 30, 1873, Deseret Dramatic Association Letterpress Copybooks. Bethune was publicized in DN, Apr. 13, 1870.

for Bethune to imitate. Bethune balanced on one foot, rubbed his head, and twitched his fingers "as though under the influence of great nerves and mental excitement." He then played his imitation, which, though it was similar to Daynes's original, "no musical ear could consider it anything like an exact reproduction of the original."[45] Although Blind Tom did return to Salt Lake City twice more in the next twenty-one years, he drew only small crowds of fans willing to pay high prices.[46]

When the Original Georgia Minstrels came to Utah in 1876, local observers concluded that their performances were cruder and less polished than those of burnt cork minstrels but that "they are superior for the reason that they are genuine negroes, and nothing unnatural to them is assumed,"[47] and "the whole is probably perfectly characteristic of negro amusements away down south in Dixie."[48] The *Utah Musical Times* went into greater detail, taking the concert very seriously:

> This band of twenty real negro performers drew large houses, and sent their audiences home somewhat fatigued with the vocal exercises they were compelled to make on account of the comicalities of the four end men of the troupe. The company possess little excellence as vocalists. In solo singing they are very deficient. The instrumentalists are very good, and but for their fine accompaniments the singing would be a failure. The dancing was superior, and much of it better than has yet been seen here. The acting scenes (farces) were miserable, and detracted much from what might be said to be very fair entertainments of the class.[49]

But what Utahns seemed to prize most about the Georgia Minstrels was the oral contortionism of Billy Wilson who, the *Salt Lake Times* indelicately noted, "has the most expansive [food trap] of any nigger we ever saw," a mouth which the *Deseret News*

---

45. See DN, May 13–14, 1873, and SLT, May 13, 1873.

46. Blind Tom returned to the Salt Lake Theatre on June 20–21, 1876, and August 13, 1894. See especially SLT, June 21, 1876, and *Utah Musical Times* 1 (July 15, 1876): 77.

47. "The Minstrels," SLT, Apr. 28, 1876. See also the following day's notice, which credits the group with "extreme naturalness."

48. DN, Apr. 28, 1876.

49. *Utah Musical Times* 1 (May 15, 1876): 45.

likened to that of a hippopotamus.[50] The *Ogden Junction* ended their review with just these four words: "But, oh! That mouth."[51]

From 1873 to 1877 local Mormon minstrelsy continued to thrive in parties and entertainments, as we have seen. But during those years—the last five years of Brigham Young's life—gentile minstrel troupes appeared only twice at the Salt Lake Theatre. The Purdy, Scott, and Fostelle affair had left lingering ill will in Utah toward gentile minstrels. Moreover, the Panic of 1873 curtailed touring for many minstrel groups, and few were willing to venture as far as Salt Lake City from either coast."[52]

The novelty of such acts quickly wore off in Utah, and subsequent black minstrel groups attracted less attention than their white counterparts, perhaps because of what one Salt Lake newspaper called the "Ethiopian uncouthness" that blacks inherently conveyed.[53] But during this same period Utahns faced a new and troublesome form of blackface minstrelsy. Scantily costumed female minstrels began to replace the traditional blackface female impersonators in the 1870s. Less concerned with imitating blacks than with exciting exotic male fantasies, the most famous national female minstrel troupe began to appear in Salt Lake City early in 1878. The Rentz-Santley Female Minstrels drew crowds of elders, but Mormon leaders balked at the obvious eroticism of the shows. The *Deseret News* loquaciously walked the tightrope on this guilty pleasure:

> The singing was mostly good, and some of it first-class. So with the dancing. The costumes were elegant, but in some instances not too profuse, and in others very conspicuous by their absence. There was

50. See "The Georgia Minstrels," *Salt Lake Times*, Apr. 28, 1876, and DN, Apr. 28, 1876. The *Ogden Junction* review of that troupe, April 27, 1876, does not refer to Wilson by name but simply closes with the words, "oh! that mouth."

51. "Those Minstrels," *Ogden Junction*, Apr. 27, 1876.

52. For the quote and a discussion of the theatre's problems, see George Reynolds, Letter to Brigham Young, Feb. 5, 1873, CHL.

53. See "The Minstrels," SLT, May 10, 1876. For notices on other black troupes, see especially those surrounding engagements at the Salt Lake Theatre during September 18–20, 1878, March 14–15, 1879, and April 18–19, 1882. The last of these engagements was by Callendar's Georgia Minstrels whose elaborate stage show impressed Salt Lake City audiences. The SLT noted that the whole show was so varied that it was "like a minstrel show, circus, camp meeting and picnic combined" (Apr. 19, 1882). The most stunning aspect of this show was its opening panorama of Africa in which the minstrels were shown in their "natural" state (DN, Apr. 18, 1882).

> lots of fun and the audience applauded vociferously. There was plenty of the entertainment, and though it was not of a very intellectual character, it will no doubt draw again immensely, for it is full of life, and the multitude run after such performances. It is a variety show No. 1 of its kind, but we cannot say it is a very good kind for the people of this territory.[54]

When the troupe returned to the Salt Lake Theatre on the Monday night following the April 1878 general conference, the *Deseret News* refused to review the show and church leaders forbade the minstrels from using the theatre for any further engagements. The following January the group played at Salt Lake's Liberal Institute where many scrutinized the troupe to see how bad they really were. Some protested that nothing the female minstrels did was any more vulgar than the burlesque opera troupes who were among the Salt Lake Theatre's most popular attractions. The theatre managers, however, insisted that the Rentz-Santley troupe was "a perfect stink" and that it was "suicidal" to foist them on the predominantly Mormon public.[55]

Nevertheless, the female minstrels returned to the Salt Lake Theatre in 1885 with a show called *An Adamless Eden,* a show vulgar enough that the *Salt Lake Tribune* now accused the Mormon theatre of corrupting the city, even though the performance garnered the lowest receipts of any show held in the theatre up to that time. Astonishingly, the Rentz-Santley minstrels returned once again to the Salt Lake Theatre in 1888 with a show entitled *Adam and Eve.* Mormon president Wilford Woodruff was seduced by the title into attending the performance—much to his outrage—and the *Deseret News* expressed horror that "sacrilege" had now been added to these already immodest shows. With the

54. "The Minstrels," DN, Jan. 23, 1878.

55. This treatment of the Rentz-Santley Minstrels is based on DN notices for Jan. 23 and Apr. 9 , 1878, and the editorial "Debasing Performances," June 29, 1888; SLT, Jan. 1–12, 1879, and Mar. 11, 1885;Kenney, *Wilford Woodruff's Journal,* 8:506 (June 28, 1888); and especially the following letters from the Deseret Dramatic Association Letterpress Copybooks: to J. T. Maguire, Mar. 12 (?), 1881; Messrs. Spies and Smart, July 3, 1882; M. B. Leavitt, Mar. 6, June 10, 1884, and Mar. 13, 1885; and W. D. Mann, Feb. 20, 1885. See also the editorial "The Nude Drama," published in direct response to the performance of Rentz-Santley, *Ogden Junction,* Jan. 11, 1879.

performance of *Adam and Eve,* church leaders at last decisively banished the Rentz-Santley minstrels from the Salt Lake Theatre.

By the 1880s Utah audiences, who only a few years earlier had not known professional minstrelsy, were well versed in the genre. Groups that did not meet their high standards were flouted at the box office and scorned in the press.[56] By the middle of the decade, many Utahns regarded minstrel entertainments as generally stale and predictable; only exceptional virtuosity and spectacle could get their attention.[57] Like many Americans, the Mormons had developed a taste for grandiosity, one that was reflected not only in their holding of massive music festivals but also in their passion for "mastodon" minstrel shows of the sort popularized by Jack Haverley, the late nineteenth century's most prominent minstrel entrepreneur. Haverley transformed the raucous caricaturing of early minstrelsy into the slick, pseudo-aristocratic extravaganzas that dominated the minstrelsy of the 1880s. His minstrel troupes had been featured performers at the Salt Lake Theatre during both general conferences of 1878, and his brand of entertainment was known to be "of the most chaste character."[58] In 1879 he brought his first forty-man mastodon minstrel show to Utah. This new troupe became so popular that it soon found itself at the center of Mormon-gentile competition in Salt Lake City.

In June 1882 the Walker brothers, the city's most affluent ex-Mormons, opened the Walker Opera House. To attract a predominantly Mormon clientele, the owners announced that not only would its house orchestra be led by "home talent" George Careless, the former Salt Lake Theatre music director who had refused to unionize, but also that Jack Haverley and his minstrels would book exclusively through the Opera House for the next two years. Determined not to be upstaged by the Walkers, the Salt Lake Theatre managers leased their hall to Haverley for three years on the condition that he alternate his attractions between the two houses.[59] The

56. See, for example, the reviews in DN, Nov. 15–17, 1880, and Feb. 11, 1881.

57. See "Barlow and Wilson's Minstrels," DN, July 8, 1885.

58. This characterization is from SLT, June 5, 1879. See also the reviews in DN, Apr. 4–5 and Oct. 5, 1878.

59. On the Haverley dealings, see David McKenzie's letters to Charles Frohman (Dec. 7, 1881), J. H. Haverley (Feb. 2, 1882), Charles McConnell (June 12, 1882),

Salt Lake Theatre managers took this unusual step because they were worried that they would lose general conference business to apostates, especially since, as the managers wrote, "the best attraction for Conference is a first class Minstrel Company."[60]

But the move was unpropitious. Anti-polygamy prosecution began to drive many potential ticket buyers into hiding or into prison.[61] Because of the intensity of the prosecution, the church held no general conferences in Salt Lake City from 1884 to 1887. The succeeding years saw the rise of vaudeville or "specialty" shows in theatres throughout the nation, generally at the expense of minstrelsy. By the early 1890s, Utah was preparing for statehood and Salt Lake City aspired to be a metropolis with its own big-city-style minstrel companies: the Salt Lake Mastodon Minstrels and the Deseret Minstrels. Of the former, the *Salt Lake Tribune* wrote: "As the curtain slowly rose, disclosing thirty negro faces, a number of ladies in the audience fainted. It was afterwards learned that, fancying they espied resemblances to the faces of their husbands, these ladies swooned at the thought of the scandal." Of the Deseret Minstrels, "One lady expressed the doubtful compliment that the minstrels 'looked better as "niggers" than white men." In 1895 the women of Salt Lake City high society began producing their own female minstrel shows, allegedly more chaste and benevolent than earlier such shows had been.[62] At the same time, the gentile "Minstrel King," Jack Haverley, retired from show business and

---

Frederick W. Bert (Nov. 2, 1882, and Feb. 13, 1883), and M. B. Leavitt (Nov. 7, 1882), all in the Deseret Dramatic Association Letterpress Copybooks. See also the account in Pyper, *Romance of an Old Playhouse*, 295–97. The Walker Opera House tried to secure the exclusive rights to minstrel performances by Leavitt's minstrels, Haverley's chief rivals. But Leavitt declined, partly out of loyalty to the Salt Lake Theatre managers and partly because he doubted that any non-Mormon house could survive in Salt Lake City. See M. B. Leavitt, *Fifty Years in Theatrical Management* (New York: Broadway Publishing, 1912), 411–12.

60. David McKenzie, Letter to Frederick W. Bert, Feb. 13, 1883, Deseret Dramatic Association Letterpress Copybooks.

61. Minstrel scenes were also staged by Mormon polygamists in prison. See Abraham H. Cannon, Journal, July 5, 1886, photocopy of holograph, HBLL.

62. On the Salt Lake Mastodon Minstrels, see the notices in DN, Dec. 18, 1891, SLT, Dec. 19, 1891 (the "swooning" quote is from here), and *Salt Lake Times*, Dec. 19, 1891. On the Deseret Minstrels, see especially DN, Feb. 18, 1893, and SLT, Feb. 22 (the "looked better" quote is from here), Mar. 23, and Apr. 12, 1893.

Cover of minstrel book that includes the stump speech "Mormons and Mormonism" (1888).

settled in Deer Creek, Utah. His death in Salt Lake City in 1901 signaled the end of an era.[63] Or not.

Mormon polygamy continued to give comedic grist for the minstrel mill. The popular minstrel "Governor" Add Ryman gave

63. See "Minstrel King Dead," SLT, Sept. 29, 1901.

a faux stump speech on Mormonism and its multi-wife addiction that made its way into a standard book of blackface patter in 1888.[64]

And in 1905 a popular blackface song called "The Mormon Coon" by Raymond Browne and Henry Clay Smith acquired some traction both in print and on record. It seems to say that blacks and Mormons both belong to the same lust-bound clan—though blacks, quite awkwardly, remain at once interlopers and fellow-travelers. Thus, the spoof, while two-fisted, is also ham-fisted:

A coon named Ephraim skipped the town one day.
Nobody knew just why he went away,
Until one night a friend he got a note,
It was from Eph and this is what he wrote:
"I'm out in Utah, in the Mormon land,
And going to stay, because I'm living grand,
I used to rave about a single life.
Now ev'ry day I get a brand new wife."

Chorus:

"I've got a big brunette,
And a blonde to pet.
I've got 'em short, fat, thin and tall …
I've got a Cuban gal,
And a Zulu pal.
They come in bunches when I call;
And that's not all—
I've got 'em pretty, too.
Got a homely few,
I've got 'em black to octoroon …
I can spare six or eight.
Shall I ship 'em by freight?
For I am the Mormon coon."

There's one gal I ain't married yet, but say,
I'm saving her up for a rainy day.
If you ain't never heard a cyclone roar,
Come up and hear just how my wives can snore.
If you stay out late you can "con" your wife.

64. *Standard Stump Speeches and Ethiopian Lectures : A Choice Collection of Stump Speeches and Negro Burlesque Recitations* … (New York: M. J. Ivers & Co., 1888).

If I got gay that mob would have my life,
It keeps me hustling in loving line.
They all yell out, "I saw him first, he's mine."

(Chorus)

Next Fall they'll make me Gov'nor of the State;
The Parsons give me commutation rate;
I wish for ev'ry wife I had a cent,
Why, just for photographs, a house I rent.
I've got so many, I forget a lot.
I keep the marriage license door bell hot,
If on the street into a wife I run,
I have to ask her, "What's your number, Hon?"

(Chorus)[65]

• • •

If my three phases are a way into the subject, there is no way out of it. American minstrelsy metamorphosed well into and even beyond the twentieth century. Vaudeville used blackface and the same old "coon" dance steps and jokes. Al Jolson took his blackface into the first "talkie," *The Jazz Singer*. The first variety show ever broadcast was a 1924 performance by Dailey Paskman's Radio Minstrels. Sheet music featured comic imagery with characters straight out of minstrel show posters. In 1936 a major music publisher produced Paskman's *Blackface and Music* a full-scale minstrel show "ready for performance." It stayed in print for decades. The hugely popular Amos and Andy on the radio were essentially invisible minstrels—although when the white actors who played them appeared in public or photographs, they did so in blackface. Restaurant chains kept minstrel stereotypes alive: Coon Chicken Inn, a four-location chain that lasted from 1925–57, and Sambo's, founded in 1957 and multiplying to more than 1,100 locations half of whom endured into the early 1980s. Even into the twenty-first century, comic blackface in one's past bedeviled a Supreme Court justice's confirmation hearings and a Canadian prime minister's reelection campaign.

65. One can hear the recording at www.youtube.com/watch?v=_oyK1qLIinY (accessed July 16, 2019).

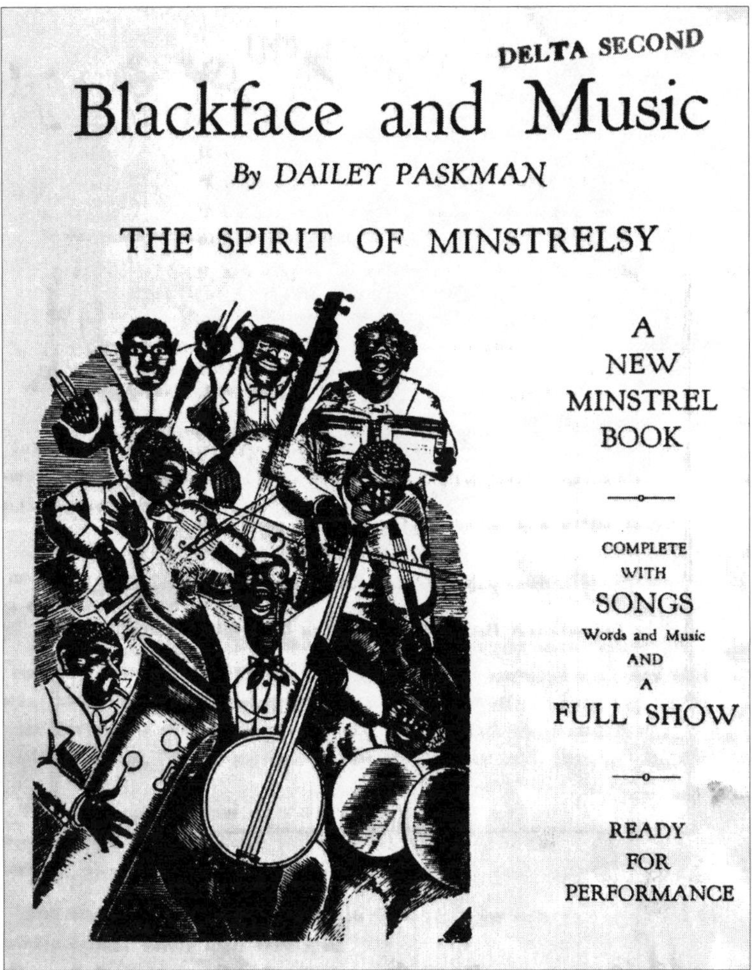

Title page of 1936 minstrel show book formerly in the Delta Second Ward (Utah) library.

Professional minstrelsy gradually subsided in Utah, as elsewhere, but ad hoc local minstrelsy persisted. Paskman's minstrel show folio landed in at least some Mormon ward libraries. In the early 1920s, before being named Tabernacle Choir director, Spencer Cornwall directed the Swanee Singers Minstrel Show.

Images of blackface entertainments in 1940s Utah appear in the photograph archives of the *Salt Lake Tribune*. Pseudo-minstrel

Spencer Cornwall (standing, back center) as director of a minstrel group years before his tenure as conductor of the Mormon Tabernacle Choir.

road shows cropped up in the 1950s and even the 1960s. The racism behind it all still tangles Mormonism up: the church's longstanding priesthood ban of anyone with African lineage (a ban finally ended in 1978); the *Book of Mormon* musical's neo-minstrel caricatures of Africans; even the "Africanizing" of pop songs by the black Latter-day Saint Alex Boyé, on which other scholars have begun to dote.[66]

In their affection for blackface entertainment, nineteenth-century Mormons showed themselves to be more or less in step with the nation at large. Yet one wonders if certain features of minstrel entertainment did not have a special appeal for the Saints.

First, Mormons were fond of spoofing sectarian beliefs and practices. This they did not only in songs, recitations, and holiday toasts but also in tracts and, most potently, in their temple ritual, where sectarian ministers were portrayed as loquacious buffoons. Minstrelsy also satirized sectarian religions as in this blackface

66. See, for example, Jeremy Grimshaw and Ali Colleen Neff, "The Sounds of Sal Tlay Ka Siti: Alex Boyé's 'Africanized' Covers and Mormon Racial Dynamics," Society for Ethnomusicology Annual Meeting, College of William and Mary, Pittsburgh, Nov. 16, 2014.

character's definition of faith: "Faith am a compounded conglomeration ob phantasmagorical whichness, absolved from someness by a liberal infusion ob de impossibly mixed up when."[67] Thus, minstrelsy helped augment a well-established Mormon repertoire of religious parody.

Second, Mormons needed the attention of outsiders to help reinforce their sense of self-importance and maintain their identity as a distinctive people. Minstrels, like cartoonists and comic writers, regarded Mormonism and its people as apt subjects for topical humor.[68] References to themselves in minstrel shows allowed the Saints who attended them to see their own reflection in the mirror of gentile culture. And it was undoubtedly of some comfort to see outsiders thinking of them in a non-threatening way.

Third, while they espoused the virtues of high culture in building up Zion, Mormons also depended on simple, popular entertainment to help bind them together as a community. Cooperation and social equality being among Mormonism's highest values, blackface entertainment united most Mormons around images that were common to even the least of Saints.

Admittedly, these images were caricatures. In the white American tradition, Mormons built a sense of community partly on the foundation of bad faith toward blacks. This is ironic when one considers the underlying affinities of Mormons and blacks in nineteenth-century America. In Mormon Nauvoo, Heber C. Kimball had expressly connected the Saints' plight to that of non-whites: "We are not accounted as white people, and we don't want to live among them."[69] But pioneer Utahns seem not to have exploited that implied empathy nor to have discerned the theme that tied together black American culture and white Mormon culture: their common use of imagery from ancient Israel. Blackface music and theatre regularly used images of captive Israel to articulate the sense of oppression and loneliness that blacks in nineteenth-century America felt. In their songs and sermons Mormons used

67. From the routine "A Question of Faith" in Charles Townsend, *Negro Minstrels with End Men's Jokes, Gags, Speeches, Etc.* (Chicago: T. S. Denison, 1891), 26–27.

68. See, for example, the joke mentioned in Wittke, *Tambo and Bones*, 162.

69. *Times and Seasons* 6 (Nov. 1, 1845): 1012.

similar images to express their frustration at persecution and their estrangement from American Babylon. In the domain of metaphor, then, Mormondom and the world of minstrelsy converged.

As for "demonic parody," consider minstrelsy's own update of Cain's curse. Jack Haverley, the "Minstrel King" who died in Utah, published this bit of minstrel show humor, updating the curse of Cain so cherished and exploited by Christians of all stripes: Cain was really the first *white* man. Why? Because when the Lord spoke to him after he killed Abel, he was so terrified, his skin paled.[70]

70. See "The First White Man," in Jack Haverley, *Negro Minstrelsy* (Chicago: Frederick J. Drake & Co., 1902), 67.

II

5 THE *MORMON PIONEERS'* TREK EAST

Whenever I go to New York City, I scope out which musicians will be playing in what clubs and take their albums with me on the chance of getting them signed. In summer 2001 I saw that the legendary Ramblin' Jack Elliott would be playing the Bitter End one of the nights I would be there. My wife, Pam, and I went to the club, saw the show, and afterwards I followed him backstage with the only record of his I had: the 1965 Columbia Legacy album called *The Mormon Pioneers*, on which he'd recorded three songs.

He looked at it and said, "I've never seen this."

"Well, you're on it."

He studied its track listings and said, "I think I remember the recording sessions but I've never seen the record before."

"I'm pretty sure most of the copies of it ended up in Utah."

"If I gave you my address, could you get me a copy and send it to me?"

"I can, and I'd be honored to."

He wrote his address on an envelope, signed my album, and within two weeks I'd bought him a still-sealed copy for five bucks at Starbound Records in Salt Lake City, boxed it carefully, mailed it to him, and never heard a word back.

If one of its makers had lost track of this album, Mormon record hounds hadn't.

It showed up all the time in the racks of Utah thrift stores and antique shops, attics and basements, and sale bins of public libraries. It was one of the media trophies of Mormonism: a gleaming 12 x 12-inch silver-gatefolded LP made by the world's biggest record company, with a 48-page book of photos, artwork, essays, and lyrics bound into it. It was a pillar in Columbia's showcase of Americana, the "Legacy" series. But the trail that led to this

The cover of Columbia Legacy LP *The Mormon Pioneers*, signed by singer Ramblin' Jack Elliott.

elegant improbability has never been tracked. It winds through the backroads of the recording industry, the folk music revival, and an American faith's quest for respectability. Thank Ramblin' Jack for getting me to walk that trail with you now.

• • •

The year 1959 had given the Mormon Tabernacle Choir three reasons to rejoice. First, it was the thirtieth anniversary of their national radio show. They had spent almost all of that time under contract with CBS, the Columbia Broadcasting System, whose sister company, Columbia Records, gave them the second reason to celebrate. On November 29, their conductor, Richard Condie, received a Grammy for "Best Performance by a Vocal Group or Choir." The object of the award was the choir's Columbia release of "The Battle Hymn of the Republic." At the same time, their Christmas season release of Handel's *Messiah* shot up the charts on its way to outselling the Leonard Bernstein Columbia release of the work that Easter by ten to one.

Early in February 1960 Columbia gave the LDS Church a check for the sale of 1,202,134 units of "Battle Hymn" and *Messiah*—almost unimaginable for a church choir.[1] Choir president Lester Hewlett wrote that "I handed the record royalty check personally to President [David O.] McKay" and was told that the money would be "used entirely by our organization. … the Church officials want the Choir to use the money … to expand and improve our Choir program."[2]

A few days before the church got that check, Columbia's president, Goddard Lieberson, sent Hewlett copies of two lavish Civil War-inspired albums in what Columbia called its "Legacy" series. The first, *The Confederacy,* had come out in 1954, and its sequel, *The Union*, was brand new. Each of these featured songs and narrations of the era on long-playing vinyl records bundled together with large booklets of song texts, photos, and essays.[3] Destined for home hi-fi stereo systems, the albums looked and felt like coffee-table books. In an accompanying letter, Lieberson wrote, "In addition to the other work being done by the Mormon Tabernacle Choir, would it not be interesting to enter upon a project of this sort devoted to the history of the westward movement as it affected the Mormon Church. In fact, I suppose, it could be a history of the Mormon Church, but I should think with an emphasis on the pioneer aspect of the move to the west." It would not mimic the Tabernacle Choir's usual records but would be like

1. On this and events described in the previous paragraph, see Michael Hicks, *The Mormon Tabernacle Choir: A Biography* (Urbana: University of Illinois Press, 2015), 115–17.

2. Lester Hewlett, Letter to Goddard Lieberson, Mar. 8, 1960, Mormon Tabernacle Choir Correspondence Files, 1942–68, CHL. This collection is hereafter referred to as "MTCCF."

3. For more on these, see "Columbia Sets 'Legacy' LP Series Line," *Billboard,* Sept. 5, 1960.

the Civil War albums, including a booklet "prepared by an historian of the Church."[4]

Hewlett wrote back, excited about this new project, for which "the Choir would produce enough music to make a record or two to go along with the book-record album" that would "contain the early history of the Mormon Church, especially emphasizing the move of the Church to the West." David Evans, the choir's publicity agent, made plans for meetings with church leaders, noting that he had two "competent professional writers" he wanted to invite to write the booklet. They would give it "real quality … and perhaps name prestige," he said. Within two weeks, the church's president, David McKay, gave his blessing to the project. And who wouldn't? It promised a publicity coup for a church still mistrusted and shadowy to most Americans.[5]

It is hard to say whether it was Columbia or the church that was barking up the wrong tree. Lieberson had written to the president of the Tabernacle Choir, the record label's gateway into the church and also its classical cash cow. Thus, Hewlett had no reason to think this was anything but a choir record that could promote its sponsoring faith like a giant billboard. The word "Legacy," though, might have misled—whose legacy? The church would have seen it as *its* legacy. But for Lieberson, it was Columbia's legacy first and America's second. The album was a showcase for the label, not the church. It would extend Columbia's reach into the burgeoning folk song market—now headlined for them by Bob Dylan—and create a tie-in product for its ultra-popular choir. Whatever map there was for this new genre, Columbia wanted to be on it, from the company president's idea to the accountants seeing black ink.

The next two letters that passed between Lieberson and Hewlett signaled the disconnect. Hewlett searched his library to find "the best Mormon history to send" to Lieberson and came up with the notably lightweight but serviceable oversize gift book by Salt Lake City attorney Rulon Howells, *The Mormon Story* (1957). He sent it to Lieberson, who thanked him but tried to clarify that this

---

4. Goddard Lieberson, Letter to Lester Hewlett, Feb. 5, 1960, MTCCF.

5. Lester Hewlett, Letter to Goddard Lieberson, Feb. 19, 1960, and David W. Evans, Letter to Lester Hewlett, Feb. 12, 1960, both in MTCCF.

would be an album about history, not religion. "I do not know if I mentioned this to you earlier," he wrote to Hewlett on March 17, 1960, "so perhaps I should say now that it is my feeling that we should stay very clear of the religious aspects in telling the story of the westward movement. I certainly do not mean to avoid them, but for both of our sakes, I do not think it would be advantageous were this album to look like a publication of the Church of Jesus Christ of the Latter-Day Saints. I think, as a matter of fact, it would be a disservice to the Church if this were the case." It was imperative "that we must present the Mormon story as a part of American history, and the articles that accompany it should not be by Mormons, but by historians who are interested in that history."[6]

Lieberson handed the project off to Columbia's "literary utility man" Charles Burr, who wrote to Hewlett in hopes the latter could send him three books and one article that the company wanted to consult for this "Legacy" album. Those sources made it clear what Columbia wanted for the music.[7]

• • •

In 1932 the Daughters of the Utah Pioneers published a green hardback called *Pioneer Songs*, a motley collation of anything connected with old Utah, with "pioneer" apparently meaning any Utahn active before the twentieth century.[8] Though the title sounds comprehensive, *Pioneer Songs* cobbled together ditties that nineteenth- and early-twentieth-century Mormons would have known and sung, but with no definitively "Mormon" flavor to them. Hymns, love songs, political songs, and other genres bump up against one another, forming an album, a scrapbook, a handbook of recreational songs, oldies to warm the heart. Still, some latter-day saintly songs pop up, such as Apostle John Taylor's rewrite of "The Rose that All Are Praising" into "The Upper California," which cheerleads for the people's imagined westward pursuit.

6. Lester Hewlett, Letter to Godard Lieberson, Mar. 8, 1960, and Goddard Lieberson, Letter to Lester Hewlett, Mar. 17, 1960, both in MTCCF.

7. Charles Burr, Letter to Lester Hewlett, July 27, 1960, MTCCF. Burr requested the first three books and the Lester Hubbard article mentioned in the paragraphs that follow this.

8. *Pioneer Songs*, comp. Daughters of Utah Pioneers, arr. Alfred M. Durham (Salt Lake City: Daughter of Utah Pioneers, 1932).

A year after *Pioneer Songs* appeared, George Briegel, a trombonist and publisher with an eye for niche markets, published *44 Old Time Mormon and Far West Songs*.[9] The "Mormon" in Briegel's title promised more than it delivered. Indeed, the book's subtitle reads: "Including—Railroad, Cowboy, Hobo, Rocky Mountain, Love & Comedy Numbers." Of the forty-four songs, fewer than ten could arguably count as "Mormon." The rest were just as the subtitle outlined, including chestnuts like "Oh Susanna," "I've Been Working on the Railroad," and "Home on the Range." A rewrite of Stephen Foster's "Camptown Races," a spoof on the so-called "Mormon War" of 1857, is one of the few bona fide "Mormon" songs, even though the tune was well-known from anywhere but the Great Basin. At the same time, Foster's popular "Hard Times Come Again No More" includes the annotation "This was Brigham Young's favorite song," which, one supposes, converts it to a "Mormon" song.

In 1946 the Utah State Centennial Commission published its *Source Book* for commemorations of the 100th anniversary of the Mormon pioneers entering the Salt Lake Valley in 1847.[10] Given its purpose, the mimeographed *Source Book* was all-Mormon and all-Utah, the difference between the two mostly indistinguishable. The thirty-six songs in the book's music section ranged from hymns to trail songs, all celebrations of the switchback between Mormon history and desert life. Reverence held sway, the lyrics safe and noble.

In line with the pioneer centennial, scholarly journals published Mormon folksong research in 1946–47: an article by Levette J. Davidson in the *Journal of American Folklore*, another by Austin and Alta Fife in *Western Folklore*, and a third by Lester Hubbard in the *Utah Humanities Review*.[11] These all offered the songs as

9. George F. Briegel, comp. and arr., *44 Old Time Mormon and Far West Songs* (New York: George F. Briegel, 1933).

10. *Arts Division Source Book: Basic Materials on Music, Drama, Art, Pageantry, Parades for the Utah Centennial, 1847–1947* (Salt Lake City: Utah Centennial Commission [1946]).

11. Levette J. Davidson, "Mormon Songs," *Journal of American Folklore* 58 (1946): 273–300; Austin E. Fife and Alta Fife, "Folksongs of Mormon Inspiration," Western Folklore 6 (1947): 42–52; Lester Hubbard, "Songs and Ballads of the Utah Pioneers," *Utah Humanities Review* 1 (1947): 74–96.

specimens of Utah Mormon *folklore*, pieces of a collective regional consciousness, rather than exemplars of broader American folk song tradition.

In 1952 two recordings of Mormon folk songs hit the shelves. The Library of Congress had amassed a deep well of field recordings called the "Archive of Folk Song," whose Mormon exemplars had mostly come from Austin and Alta Fife. The Fifes had made many folk song collecting excursions, recording what they heard onto discs, and tabulating the singer and the location. Still early in the history of the "LP" (the "long-playing" record), the Library of Congress now issued *Songs of the Mormons and Songs of the West*, edited by Duncan Emerich.[12] It contained thirteen tracks, only six of which (the A-side of the LP) were "Songs of the Mormons," all of them field recordings by the Fifes. A little skittish about seeming to hoist up a religion, especially one with a dicey history in the states, the preface in the album's twelve-page insert started with this line: "The traditional Mormon songs on the A side of this record are secular and historical, and should be seen in that light." They were "items of general Americana," but also pertained to "a single group of people and to the final establishment of a single State." The "References for Study" that preceded the texts and extensive notes for each song directed the listener to the scholarly articles on Mormon music by Davidson, the Fifes, and Hubbard. It then cited the three basic published collections (*Pioneer Songs*, Briegel's book, and the *Source Book*).

That same year, the Smithsonian Institution's allied label, Folkways Records, put out its own take. Lavovi McMurrin ("L. M.") Hilton had been a police chief for years in the mildly rowdy whistle stop of Ogden, Utah. As a sideline, he sang old Utah songs in church and civic gatherings, using his authoritative, yet plaintive unaccompanied baritone voice. Folkways recorded him singing "The Handcart Song," "Whoa! Ha! Buck & Jerry Boy," "Sego Lily," "Seagulls and Crickets," "Echo Canyon Song," "Zack, the Mormon Engineer," "Oh Babylon, Oh Babylon!," "Come, Come

12. *Songs of the Mormons and Songs of the West: From the Archive of Folk Song*, Library of Congress Recording Laboratory AFS L30 [with twelve-page booklet], ed. Duncan Emerich.

Ye Saints," "Hard Times Come Again No More," "Gather Round the Camp Fire, Brethren," "Have Courage, My Boy, to Say No," and "What's the Use of Repining?"–the richest collection of Mormon-specific folk performances yet.

Four years later Indiana University Press published Austin and Alta Fife's definitive *Saints of Sage and Saddle: Folklore among the Mormons*. Its twenty-two-page epilogue, "Lyre of the Lord's Anointed," updated the authors' earlier *Western Folklore* article. The opening paragraphs drove down some stakes, not only about the authors' own credibility but the subject's larger import:

> So abundant are the songs that the Mormon folk have composed and sung at all of the critical moments in their history that, were every other document destroyed, it would still be possible, from folk songs alone, to reconstruct in some detail the story of their theology, their migrations, their conflict with the Gentiles, and the founding and development of most of their settlements from New York to San Bernadino. On one occasion we made a systematic attempt to record all of the songs about St. George—one Mormon town. In a week, more than forty items had been recorded and we had gained positive knowledge that our repertoire was incomplete.

The songs that followed "form at best a random sampling from the hundreds of Mormon songs in our collection, which in turn is but a fraction of the inexhaustible supply."[13]

• • •

In the summer of 1960, Charles Burr asked Jay Wright of Utah's LDS Church-owned KSL Radio for some ideas about authors for the Mormon LP booklet. Wright gave him two names, both professors at University of Utah: J. H. Adamson and Lester Hubbard. When Burr approached them, both begged off. Adamson said he lacked the expertise. Hubbard had the expertise, having field-recorded many singers performing Utah folk songs, not to mention knowing the Fifes' trove well. But he refused to compete with his soon-to-be-released book about Utah folk songs

13. Austin and Alta Fife, *Saints of Sage and Saddle: Folklore among the Mormons* (Bloomington: Indiana University Press, 1956), 316.

by collaborating with Columbia. Burr fretted to Hewlett that he should have offered them more money.

It took nearly a year for Hewlett to recommend another prospect: Wallace Stegner. In some ways Stegner fit superbly, smack in the sweet spot where Columbia's ambitions and the church's vainglory met. His respectful and eloquent *Mormon Country* had come out almost twenty years earlier. He knew pioneer history and admired it. He was not Mormon yet loved Mormons and wrote solidly. "He will do a superb job," Hewlett wrote.[14]

Initially, Hewlett had assured Lieberson that, "after this [booklet] has been written, our choir director, Richard P. Condie will suggest the numbers that should be included with the record-book album and these numbers can be submitted to your [bosses, John] McClure and [Schuyler] Chapin." But by September 1960, Hewlett changed his tune and recommended a BYU English professor to take charge of the album's repertoire: Thomas Cheney, then preparing a book manuscript with the working title "Songs of the Wasatch and Tetons."[15]

Cheney had piggybacked on the work of the Fifes but went farther. He had made recordings of 800+ Mormon-related songs and bound the lyrics into two thick volumes. Hewlett got Cheney to send his entire collection of lyrics to Burr at Columbia in October with the promise they would have no exclusive rights to the songs Cheney had unearthed. Burr loved them and asked Cheney to pick 40–50 songs he thought were "important to the Mormon cause."

Hewlett visited Burr in New York when there on Tabernacle Choir business. "I am sorry I kept you so late that night and trust your wife did not scold you too severely," he wrote Burr when he got back to Salt Lake City, "but I did want to try to give you the spirit of this religion we call Mormonism, to tell you about its beginnings, about the trek across the uninviting prairies, how the Mormons put five stars into the American flag, the Mormon

14. Charles Burr, Letter to Lester Hewlett, Sept. 9, 1960, and Lester Hewlett, Letter to Charles Burr, Aug. 7, 1961, both letters in MTCCF.

15. Lester Hewlett, Letter to Goddard Lieberson, Mar. 30, 1960, Charles Burr, Letter to Lester Hewlett, Sept. 30, 1960, and Charles Burr, Letter to Lester Hewlett (responding to Hewlett's telephone call that day), Sept. 30, 1960, all in MTCCF.

REEL 14

Side 1

The Postman	Don Brady	
The Two Sisters	Bob Christmas	55
The Farmer and the Crow	Renee Christmas	165
The Gallows Tree	Renee Christams	190
The Wreck of Number 9	Mary Pratt	310
Birdie I Am Tired Now	Mary Pratt	375
Froggie Went A Courtin	Bob Christmas	415
Blue Mountain	Bob Christmas	475
St. George and the Drag-on	Bob Christmas	600
The Iron Horse	Bob Christmas	700
Passing Through	Bob Christmas	760

Side 2

Mottos on the Wall	Jesse Jepsen	
Sweet Evelina	Jesse Jepsen	100
Spanish Jaunita	Jesse Jepsen	185
Down By the River	Jesse Jepsen	325
Fallen Leaf	Jesse Jepsen	450
Just Thirty Five	Jesse Jepsen	610
I Can't Change It	Jesse Jepsen	710
Sweet Nola Shanna	Jesse Jepsen	820

Inside cover of one of the 7" reel-to-reel tape boxes of Thomas Cheney's 800+ field recordings of Mormon folksong.

Battalion." He assured Burr that "we here are really very excited about our 'Story of the Church' album that you are working on."[16]

In February 1961 Cheney sent Burr forty-one songs, with words, lead sheets, taped samples of the songs, annotations on them, and a price list for making tapes of song excerpts. He had

16. Charles Burr, Letter to Lester Hewlett, Oct. 31, 1960, and Lester Hewlett, Letter to Charles Burr, Nov. 1, 1960, both in MTCCF.

spent fifty-two hours of his time, he said, but billed Columbia officially only for secretarial costs, which amounted to $53.75. The songs he had picked, he told Burr, would "have not only appeal to Mormon people, but also to a good segment of the American people."[17]

It took six more months for Columbia to officially "green light" the project and make its selection from Cheney's set. Burr wrote to Hewlett that he wanted to keep working with Cheney, record all the selected songs in Salt Lake City, and—bone duly thrown—involve the Tabernacle Choir in some way. But much of the repertoire "seems to call for either individual soloists or smaller combinations of voices than the entire Choir. We want to retain as much as possible the folk flavor of the materials. Just how we will solve this is not yet apparent." But they would have to proceed "without preconceptions."[18]

Hewlett wrote back that the choir was ready to move on this, had the soloists to do it, a double mixed choir, and a small choir of about fifty voices. Then Lieberson stepped back in to take the reins. He and his staff had whittled down Cheney's list of songs and the Tabernacle Choir would not suit most of them. "The songs are too intimate and personal, for the most part, to be presented well, or, in some cases, even understood, by so many voices." Some could be arranged, others needed just a singer and a guitar. Cheney recommended folk singers—which included Hilton and the young Bob Christmas—who would need to be hired and recorded quickly. For group numbers, east coast arrangers should be used, because Mormon arrangers perhaps "are a bit too familiar with the material to be able to take a fresh viewpoint towards it."[19]

Columbia's Cheney-derived song list was this:

> Six solo songs: "Whoa, Haw, Buck and Jerry Boy," "St. George and the Dragon" ([i.e., "drag-on," a word play), "Once I Lived in Cottonwood," "Waste Not, Want Not," "Tittery-irie-ay," and "Don't Marry the Mormon Boys."

17. Thomas Cheney, Letter to Charles Burr, Feb. 15, 1961, MTCCF.

18. Charles Burr, Letter to Lester Hewlett, July 24, 1961, MTCCF.

19. Lester Hewlett, Letter to Charles Burr, Aug. 1, 1961, and Goddard Lieberson, Letter to Lester Hewlett, Aug. 4, 1961, both in MTCCF.

Four small group songs: "Hand Cart Song," "This Is the Place," "Wait for the Wagon," and "Hard Times Come Again No More."

Four Tabernacle Choir songs: "The Ox Team Trail," "Echo Canyon," "Come, Come, Ye Saints," and "Our Mountain Home So Dear."

Six vocal-instrumental medleys: "Mormon Battalion Song," "On the Road to California," "The Upper California," "The Seagulls and the Crickets," "Mormon [Johnston's] Army Song," and a "Mormon Love Serenade."

It was a tepid list, a set of compromises and mostly zingless choices. "Hard Times" was a Stephen Foster song, although this version a Mormon-slanted rewrite. The "Mormon Love Serenade" was a made-up medley that puzzled Cheney, who had not submitted any such thing. "Come, Come" and "Our Mountain Home" were straight out of the hymnbook. Cheney did not like "Waste Not, Want Not" and "Tittery-irie-ay." Church leaders, understandably, would veto "Don't Marry the Mormon Boys."

Cheney wrote back a possible song order, including a few substitutions, then added what would become another sticking point: "Zack, the Mormon Engineer." Ostensibly a train song, it spoofed the romantic whimsy of a railroading Mormon bishop who had a wife at every whistle stop. Cheney thought this should be in the "Love Serenade" medley. "The total song has some references which might not be wise to present to Columbia's big audience," Cheney wrote, "yet I want to use [it] because of its fine audience appeal."

Strangely, Hewlett seemed to keep missing the cue from Columbia. He wrote to Lieberson on August 28, 1961, that Richard Condie was working with Cheney on arrangements. Lieberson shot back: "I'm sure you will understand that this is not directed towards the Choir when I say that we do not want this to be exclusively a Mormon Tabernacle Choir album." The choir had its own brand and series of albums and Lieberson did not want this to "run into" those. More important, "we will want to have in some instances, for some of the songs, voices which sound—shall I say—not only unprofessional, but of a folk quality, perhaps even a rough quality. We would also like to have, if possible, some vocal exercises by 'old-timers' which would have the ring of authenticity."[20]

At the same time, two new contestants—or allies—emerged. First, in 1961 the University of Utah Press published Lester Hubbard's magnum opus, *Ballads and Songs from Utah*. Its 475 pages contained 250 songs, some with just text, others with tunes, but all with scholarly apparatus—whom he heard the song from, when, and where. Its scattershot breadth of repertoire vaguely resembled that of *Pioneer Songs*: although it was barely Utah-specific, it was far from Mormon-specific. Nevertheless, it contained all the songs on Cheney's list.

Second, the obscure Festival label issued a new LP: *Rosalie Sorrels Sings Songs of the Mormon Pioneers*. It contained many of the songs used in earlier recordings but included two specific songs connected with Joseph Smith: "The Unknown Grave" and "A Poor Wayfaring Man of Grief." This LP seemed almost a gauntlet thrown down: no record thus far had covered the terrain so fully. Yet the piecemeal distribution of what was a far lower grade production than Columbia had in mind assured that Sorrels's anthology of Mormon song would stay mostly in-house, destined for collectors of esoterica with a folky bent. That in itself, during this folk music revival era, counted for more than one might think. But Columbia had far bigger game in its sights, both in slickness and sheer heft.

On September 8, 1961, Hewlett wrote to Burr that Cheney and he had brought three singers with guitars into his office and listened to some of the album's proposed songs with Richard Condie. Most of the songs worked, he said. But couldn't a Mormon arrange them? He had mentioned Leroy Robertson before and now tried to justify that choice above "arrangers in the East." As evidence, Hewlett brought up two things. First, Robertson's arrangements for the choir on the recent Tabernacle Choir album *Songs of the North and South*: could Burr listen to those? Second, Robertson had the "rough" disposition Columbia wanted because "his father was a sheep man in Southern Utah and Leroy … was raised in the forest and had to herd his father's sheep during the summer time.

20. Lester Hewlett, Letter to Goddard Lieberson, Aug. 28, 1961, and Goddard Lieberson, Letter to Lester Hewlett, Sept. 1, 1961, both in MTCCF.

While he was herding sheep, he made [violins] from the raw wood of the forest."[21]

Burr took almost a month to mull this over and reply. Robertson's *North and South* arrangements were "beautifully sung and arranged [but] it seems clear to me that they are nevertheless in strict contrast in the *kind* of sound" Columbia wanted. Instead, he praised the solo folk versions Cheney had sent. What Columbia wanted on this album was the "rugged intensity and vigor" that the folk singers offered. "The sound of the massed choir, however lovely, tends to be relatively impersonal, panoramic, and somewhat remote." This "massed sound" could be "an element in the record, and most appropriately toward the end, where the achievement of the Mormon Church in successfully establishing itself and prospering might well be represented by this sound of many voices." But, overall, "small groups and individuals would still give us the best results."

As for the album's repertoire, Burr had two requests. First, songs that used well-known tunes with Mormon words added "might strike some listeners as too definite a mockery of the non-Mormon population." His main example: the two Johnston's Army songs, one of which parodied Stephen Foster's "Camptown Races," the other, "Yankee Doodle." Then there was "Zack, the Mormon Engineer." After talking with Hewlett, Cheney had rewritten it for palatability. Burr wrote back that Cheney's rewrite "seems to us to be innocuous and indefinite. If the verses that more specifically describe the romantic habits of Zack are offensive to you, then it would seem better to me not to use the tune at all. In fact, it may occur to some people who know the verses to this tune that the omission of the more specific and ribald stanzas would necessarily give the song an apologetic or hypocritical aspect."[22]

In December Burr scheduled three recording sessions for the following month. If Cheney could come and oversee them for authenticity, that would help, though he knew Cheney's teaching schedule might hinder such a visit.[23] He did not mention who would be performing the songs. He also did not mention the side

21. Lester Hewlett, Letter to Charles Burr, Sept. 8, 1961, MTCCF.
22. Charles Burr, Letter to Lester Hewlett, Oct. 2, 1961, MTCCF.
23. Charles Burr, Letter to Thomas Cheney, Dec. 20, 1961, MTCCF.

deal he had going on another "Legacy" album, one spawned by leading collectors of Mormon folksongs, who had been snubbed in the *Mormon Pioneers* project.

• • •

In October 1959, Austin Fife had met Goddard Lieberson in Washington, DC. Lieberson gave Fife and his wife and collaborator, Alta, three albums: the *Confederacy* and *Union* "Legacy" albums and *Songs of Our Soil* by Johnny Cash, a country-folk singer whom Columbia had recently lured away from Sun Records in Memphis, Tennessee. Lieberson hoped the Fifes might be able to mount some Americana project for the "Legacy" series. Austin proposed three possibilities: *Bad Men Ballads*, *Women of the West*, and *Songs of American Railroading*. He and Alta would select song texts and tunes, supply illustrations, and pick narratives for recitation. By December, they all settled on the *Bad Men* (or *Badmen*) project, and Austin turned negotiations over to his agent, T. W. Raines, who wrote Lieberson that Austin would be "acting as his own 'publisher,' and ... make a few changes in this public-domain material in order to copyright it and obtain performance royalties."[24]

Burr replied for Lieberson. Fife's new copyrights were off the table. Columbia was not paying for retreads of material long in the public domain, although *the company itself* might copyright its own arrangements of old songs. Burr also asked Fife to write an article for the album's booklet, but for a flat author's fee. Raines wrote to Fife that, in conversation, Burr "seemed less sure of your role as a consultant in the presentation of the material." His research, yes, but no further oversight.[25]

After more debate with Columbia, Raines wrote to Austin on March 9, 1960, that the label refused to pay the Fifes anything close to what they wanted or even involve them much in the project they

24. The information and quote in this paragraph come from Austin Fife, Letter to Goddard Lieberson, Nov. 3, 1959; T. W. Raines, Letter to Goddard Lieberson, Dec. 21, 1959; and Austin Fife, Letter to Goddard Lieberson, Jan. 16, 1960. All of these are in the Austin E. and Alta S. Fife Papers, Special Collections, Merrill–Cazier Library, Utah State University, Logan.

25. Charles Burr, Letter to Austin Fife, Feb. 5, 1960, and T. W. Raines, Letter to Austin Fife, Feb. 9, 1960, both in Fife Papers.

had devised. Raines and Burr settled on $1,000 for the Fifes' work so far and maybe $100 per song used. But the Fifes could not control or direct how the performers played the songs.[26] After hearing no acceptance or counter-offer from Columbia by the end of May, Austin asked Raines to back out and retrieve their tapes and manuscripts from Burr unless the label quickly settled the money and control issues with them.[27] On June 7, Burr wrote Raines that Columbia would give Austin $200 for his work thus far and $300 more for all further help and advice. Columbia would hold all of the Fifes' materials for the time being.[28] Austin fired back that their offer was "wholly unacceptable." He calculated his and Alta's time spent thus far as worth at least $650. Have Columbia return the tape and manuscript, he said. "If at a later date they decide that they really want to go ahead with the project they may reopen negotiations with us."[29]

Complicating the process, upstart Elektra Records had already done "badmen" albums—twice, once in 1955 and again in 1957. In the first case, they issued a ten-inch record entitled *Badmen and Heroes*. Each category got one side of the record, with five songs apiece. That album then became part of a double-LP reissue set in 1957, bundled with the LP *Pirate Songs*.[30] Although only three of the five "badmen" songs would make it onto the upcoming Columbia record, Elektra's performers suited Columbia's needs well—not only for their own *Badmen* album but, as it turned out, for the *Mormon Pioneers* set.

Meanwhile, in 1961 Cheney published a tough critique of Fife's methodology and scholarly acumen. The Fife archive, Cheney wrote, was "absurdly disorganized," a "mulligan stew" with "many faults," which he seemed happy to enumerate. Fife wrote a testy letter to Cheney in reply—just after Cheney made the Columbia deal.[31] And that was that.

• • •

26. Austin Fife, Letter to Charles Burr, Feb. 14, 1960; T. W. Raines, Letters to Austin Fife, Feb. 16 and Mar. 9, 1960; all in Fife Papers.

27. Austin Fife, Letter to T. W. Raines, May 31, 1960, Fife Papers.

28. Charles Burr, Letter to T. W. Raines, June 7, 1960, Fife Papers.

29. Austin Fife, Letter to T. W. Raines, June 12, 1960, Fife Papers.

30. The two LPs are Elektra EKL 16 and EKL 129.

31. Thomas E. Cheney, "Mormon Folk Song and the Fife Collection," BYUS 3, 1: 57–63; Austin Fife, Letter to Thomas Cheney, Apr. 25, 1961, Fife Papers.

By March 1962—two years into the project that even Burr still called the "History of the Mormons" album—Columbia recorded basic tracks not with L. M. Hilton, Bob Christmas, or any of the Tabernacle Choir singers, but with the three Elektra *Badmen* singers—Ramblin' Jack Elliott, Oscar Brand, and Ed McCurdy (along with Clayton Krehbiel). Burr sent acetates of the sessions to the church for response. There was still room for ten to twelve more minutes of music, he added, even before cutting any of these. Hewlett countered with the idea of adding five classic hymns: "The Spirit of God Like a Fire Is Burning," "Praise to the Man," "Joseph Smith's First Prayer," "O My Father," and "A Poor Wayfaring Man of Grief."[32]

That September, though, at the age of sixty-six, Hewlett suddenly died. On the one hand, the project lost its original Mormon champion and liaison. He had overseen and shaped every decision from the church's side for two and a half years. On the other hand, the project would now slip out of the purview of the president of the Tabernacle Choir. Columbia lost an institutional ally, but also was freed from the singleminded focus of the man who had been in his church-corporate position for twenty-four years.

A week before Christmas 1962, Elder Richard Evans gave his apostolic take on the album's contents. "From our particular point of view I feel the one of Johnston's Army and the reference to 19 wives, and the one about Betsy, who blubbered and bawled would better be cut; also the one of advice to the girls not to marry a Mormon boy. It's the kind of thing that might 'catch on.' Also," he added, "technically and musically, [the songs] are exceedingly well done, but the series has a bit of the 'hill billy' flavor and isn't quite in keeping with the dignity of the Church or the Choir, and doesn't convey the image we should have. However, if we are committed to it, and if we can get some concessions and modifications, and some solid assurance that the script that goes with it will be made acceptable to us, I should think we should proceed and clear it with the First Presidency, if that has not already been done—especially

32. Charles Burr, Letter to Lester Hewlett, Apr. 18, 1962, and, regarding the hymns that could be added, a document appended to one headed "The Mormons as recorded in New York in March," both in MTCCF.

if we can get Joseph Smith's First Prayer and Our Mountain Home included by the choir."[33] No letter could have made it clearer: the church saw this as a record about the *Mormon* pioneers, while Columbia saw it more as about the Mormon *pioneers*.

As 1963 arrived, Lieberson finally began confirming prospective authors for the Mormon project in earnest. Cheney, understandably, would write notes about the songs. But Lieberson approached noted poet, songwriter, historian, and folklorist Carl Sandburg, requesting "a kind of poetic preface" to the album. He also invited historian of Americana Carl Carmer for "a piece on the origins of the Mormon faith with respect to the times, the New York State background of Joseph Smith and the broader emotional and religious aspects of the founding of the Church in the last century." Carmer accepted the invitation. The 85-year-old Sandburg, although well-versed in Illinois Mormon history, declined.

For a history of the Mormon trek west Lieberson turned to another Mormon, BYU history professor LeRoy Hafen. Lieberson loved LeRoy and Ann Hafen's 1960 book *Handcarts to Zion*, a documentary history based on diaries and other personal accounts. This "Legacy" album, Lieberson told Hafen, would be "a project about pioneers, rather than a religious album. Our emphasis, then, is on the kind of individuals who participated in the building of the Church during the time of hardship, and less on the developments during the colonization period and the present achievements of the established faith." Would Hafen write such an essay of about 3,000 words? If Hafen was "in doubt about the proportions or the seriousness of our approach to the subject," Lieberson said, he should consult the now *four* previous "Legacy" albums: the Civil War sets, one on the American Revolution, and even one on the birth of the Lincoln Center for the Performing Arts.[34]

Hafen accepted on behalf of himself and his wife. Lieberson handed the matter over to Burr, who offered Hafen $750 for an essay by July. Burr sweetened the deal with this bit of praise: "There is something about the documented story of even one man's life, if

33. Richard L. Evans, Letter to Isaac Stewart et al., Dec. 17, 1962, MTCCF.

34. The information and quotes in the previous two paragraphs come from Goddard Lieberson, Letter to LeRoy Hafen, Mar. 29, 1963, in Leroy Hafen Collection, HBLL.

that man is appealing and real, that can tell the reader more than page after page of digested opinion, we feel, and you and your wife have demonstrated a sympathy with this approach." Hafen agreed, submitting his essay on June 19. Ann, though, wanted an addendum. "Inasmuch as the woman's part in the Mormon difficulties and trek is not adequately included," LeRoy wrote, "I am enclosing my wife's poetic tribute to the pioneer woman. You are welcome to use it if you care to; indeed, it would be gratifying to me if you can."[35] They passed.

The production team still had far to go. Readings and readers had to be chosen, illustrations, design, and typography—all remained to be done. And other "Legacy" projects were ahead of this one in the pipeline—not only *The Badmen*, but another album ahead of it, *Mexico*. At the end of 1963, though, one event derailed everything: the killing of President Kennedy.

As the shock wore off, tributes to Kennedy blossomed in all sorts of media, from garish newspaper inserts to scholarly tomes. A few LPs even appeared, often anthologies of Kennedy speeches and quips. Lieberson wanted to produce the most elaborate of these yet as part of his "Legacy" series. It would be an oral history, a two-disc spoken-word portrait of JFK, with a 240-page hardbound coffee-table book as part of the box set. Lieberson spent the front half of 1964 inviting Kennedy friends and colleagues to be interviewed for the recording.[36]

• • •

By then, yet another album foreshadowed Columbia's. The 3-Ds, a Utah-based folk group about to be signed to Capitol Records, recorded an album entitled *Mormon Folk Ballads*, pressed by Century Records for the Education Media Services at BYU. Its thirteen songs included the two Joseph Smith songs that Sorrels had recorded, along with, by now, some Mormon folk standards, such as "Woah! Hah! Buck," "St. George and the Dragon," "The Iron Horse," and the Mormon rewrite of Foster's "Hard Times."

35. The information and quotes in this paragraph are from Charles Burr, Letter to LeRoy Hafen, Apr. 16, 1963, and Leroy Hafen, Letter to Charles Burr, June 19, 1963, both in Hafen Collection.

36. Responses to both the invitations and the final album are in the Lieberson Papers.

The market for the LP was unclear. As early as June 1963, the trio had played some of the songs on the New York radio show *Folk Music Worldwide* hosted by newsman Alan Wasser, to whom they explained Mormon history and said they had just taped the tracks for this album. "Now these aren't the hymns that you'd usually find in a hymnal," group member Dick Davis said, "but rather the songs that they would sing going along in their wagons or around their campfires in the evening, and many of these songs actually tell the history of the trek of the Mormon pioneers as they crossed the continent to Utah."[37]

When Columbia's *Mormon Pioneers* album finally came out late in 1965, here was how it looked: an arresting silver-foil coating to the gatefold cover with "The Mormon Pioneers" in a stylized font based on one from the 1870s Hamilton Wood Type Foundry in Wisconsin—a lettering that now reflected the Victorian past, yet in its earliest days, was itself pioneering. (After the *Mormon Pioneers* LP, it would tellingly appear on psychedelic posters from San Francisco, the cover of Jimi Hendrix's *Axis: Bold as Love* album, and a host of other youth-targeted pop artifacts.) The letters floated above a spectral crowd of bearded men standing behind their reflections in a lake. On the interior pastedowns on both sides of the gatefold was a detail from *The Mormon*, a newspaper edited by the man who would become the third Mormon president—and who popularized "A Poor Wayfaring Man of Grief" in Mormondom—John Taylor. The paper's date is March 3, 1855, a date of no particular import in Mormon history. Yet, starkly visible on this page, appeared a fitting headline: "Mind and Money."

The booklet begins with a title page whose reverse carries an introduction and dedication by Lieberson. Then the contents unfurl:

— Carl Carmer on "The Birth of the Mormon Church"
— LeRoy R. Hafen on "The Mormons on the Frontier"
— Thomas Cheney's "Notes on the Music"
— Biographies, book credits, and the record's track listing

37. A recording and transcript of the show can be found at www.folkmusicworldwide.com/three-ds-mormon-folk.html (accessed May 27, 2019).

Samples of how the historic typeface used for *The Mormon Pioneers* became associated with psychedelia in the later 1960s.

Strewn throughout the prose pieces are dozens of photos (full page, montage, and so forth), engravings, maps, and facsimiles of holographs (prose and drawings), with that Hamilton Foundry wood typeface in the headings.

Inside the sleeve, the album:

Side 1: Come Come Ye Saints (Chorus)
Tittery-Irie-Aye (Jack Elliott)
The Ox-Team Trail (Chorus)
Whoa, Haw, Buck, and Jerry Boy (Ed McCurdy)
Mormon Battalion Song (Jack Elliott)
On the Road to California (Ed McCurdy, Clayton Krehbiel, Chorus)
This is the Place (Ed McCurdy, Chorus)
The Sea Gulls and the Crickets (Oscar Brand)
Brighter Days in Store (Ed McCurdy, Chorus)

Side 2: The Campfire Meeting (Chorus)
Waste Not, Want Not (Clayton Krehbiel)
The Handcart Song (Chorus)
Johnston's Army Song (Clayton Krehbiel, Chorus)
Root Hog or Die (Jack Elliott)
Once I Lived in Cottonwood (Clayton Krehbiel)
Echo Canyon (Clayton Krehbiel, Chorus)
Come, Come Ye Saints (Mormon Tabernacle Choir)

Strewn among these sixteen songs, one hears readings from the period, most of them close-miked and introspective.

All told, the church had both won and lost: "Sweet Betsy from Pike" was gone. "Zack the Engineer," gone. The last verse of the Brigham Young song, gone. "Don't Marry the Mormon Boys," gone. But Columbia had kept "Johnston's Army" and rejected all Mormon hymns except for the one Tabernacle Choir performance at the end of the LP—"Come, Come Ye Saints." Still, church leaders could not have foreseen one final trophy: Goddard Lieberson's Introduction, in which he not only dedicated the LP to LDS then-president David McKay but torqued the project's meaning in a new direction.

> Many will be curious to know why this literary-musical essay on the Mormon pioneers should come from a source outside of the Church of the Latter-day Saints. To begin with, we are not concerned here with Mormon theology, and this is not a religious album. … [This is] the dramatic story of the Mormon pilgrimage, a flight from bigotry and intolerance into a western wilderness. … [T]he most poignant factor

> in this history was that they were truly—in this "land of religious freedom"—the victims of prejudice. It is always difficult for Americans to think of themselves as capable of the brutality of bigotry, particularly in the light of the enunciations of the Bill of Rights and the Constitution.

In other words, to be Mormon was to be a token victim of civil rights violations, whose African-American victims had filled recent headlines and provoked some of President Lyndon Johnson's best rhetoric. The irony, of course, was that the church had a cultural bullseye on its back for banning blacks from its priesthood, its temples, and even its Tabernacle Choir.

When David McKay got his copy, he called it an "excellent production," one made with "thoughtful and meticulous care." And he thanked Lieberson for the personal touch: "I note that you have honored me by dedicating this album to me as the present President of the Church, and want you to know that I am grateful for this tribute. I shall treasure this album not only for the honor you pay our intrepid Pioneers, but for your own manifest friendship and spirit of good will."[38]

A vivid oblong "Legacy" series advertisement appeared in *Billboard.* It depicted and described the latest four albums in this order: *John Fitzgerald Kennedy . . . As We Remember Him*, *The Mormon Pioneers*, *The Badmen*, and *Mexico.* The ad copy for the Mormon set recapitulated the themes with which the project began: "One hundred years ago, it was dangerous to be a Mormon. Driven from their homes by the bigotry of their neighbors, the Mormons set out on a pilgrimage across our Western wilderness to establish a church and a commonwealth. . . . This is not a religious album. It is a tribute to the spirit, imagination, courage and heritage of these zealous, hearty people."[39]

The church's official bookstore chain, Deseret Book, quickly advertised the record in a full-page ad for the official church magazine *Improvement Era.* It proclaimed "NEW FOR CHRISTMAS—BRING THE SONGS AND STORIES OF THE PIONEERS RIGHT INTO YOUR HOME through The Mormon Pioneers[,] a recorded tribute in song and prose to our noble forebears by COLUMBIA RECORDS." The

38. David O. McKay, Letter to Goddard Lieberson, Oct. 15, 1965, in Lieberson Papers.

39. From the full-color advertisement in *Billboard,* Nov. 27, 1965.

November 1965 Billboard ad for the Columbia Legacy Series, with *The Mormon Pioneers* flanked by other recent discs in the series.

record had become a mirror in which Mormons could see their identity shining back with the legitimacy only the world's largest record label could offer.

• • •

The Mormon Pioneers signaled a mid-1960s breakthrough in Mormon studies. The same year it came out the Mormon History Association began convening. A year later, the first issue of *Dialogue: A Journal of Mormon Thought* came off the press, containing a review of *Mormon Pioneers*. Its author, Laurence Lyon, praised the album's good public relations value: "a refreshing package of Mormon history in capsule form" that "prove[d] that not all good things about Mormons must originate in the West." Its version of Mormon history was "executed with good taste and dosed out in amounts appropriate for the millions of people … the record will reach." What might follow this foretaste tantalized Lyon. The album signaled that "the time is ripe for a more ambitious offering from within the Mormon culture itself." This album took "a small but important first step." But more must follow "if Mormon culture is to be preserved and passed on to a more urbane, but forgetful, generation."[40]

40. A. Laurence Lyon, "Saints of Song and Speech," *Dialogue: A Journal of Mormon Thought* 1, 1 (Spring 1966): 149–51.

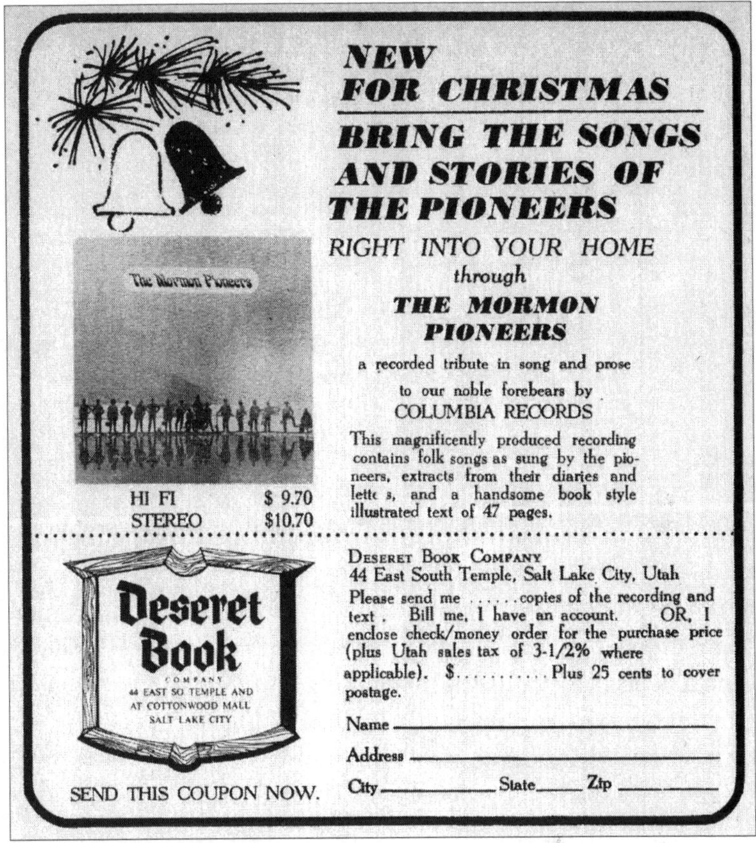

Ad for *The Mormon Pioneers* in *The Improvement Era* (Dec. 1965).

Two years later, Tom Cheney's book came out, now called *Mormon Songs from the Rocky Mountains*. In 1969, the church's seminaries and Institutes published a guitar book and record entitled *Songs of the Mormons*, containing eighteen folk favorites—including "Zack, the Mormon Engineer," which, its introduction said, "depicts in comic form, life in one type of plural marriage. It is not intended to be sarcastic." Then, in 1970, a coda to the Columbia project: Doubleday published Carl Carmer's short but eloquent book *The Farm Boy and the Angel: The Mormon Vision and the Winning of the West*, replete with prose drawn from his essay for *The Mormon Pioneers*.[41]

41. Thomas E. Cheney, *Mormon Songs from the Rocky Mountains: A Compilation of Mormon Folksong* (Austin: American Folklore Society/University of Texas Press,

But by then, the "Legacy" series was dead. As of 1968, Columbia had twelve albums in the series and at least two more in the talking stages, all ranging widely in design and production values. That spring corporate accountants asked for sales figures for all "Legacy" albums. The oldest sets had the highest sales: the *Union* package, with just under 48,000 units sold, and the far more popular *Confederacy* package, which had just over 90,000. Well below those numbers but still high on the list were the Kennedy package (16,545) and the much newer *Irish Uprising* (16,012). At the bottom of the pack was *The Mormon Pioneers*, with 3,683 total units sold. The label, with rock groups now heading their roster, cancelled the whole series.[42]

In 1969, Lieberson spoke to the International Music Industry Conference at Paradise Island in the Bahamas. The title of his speech? "Music as an International Social Force." Music is essential to a society's identity, he said, "just as its language is, and just as the kind of clothes the people wear is, and just as their attitude toward their families and their friends and their work is." Music can unite societies or divide them. It "can tell you who you are and what you can do." And that is "powerful … in an age when loss of identity is a serious problem."[43]

The masthead of *The Mormon* reprinted in *The Mormon Pioneers* carried this epigraph: "It is better to represent ourselves than to be represented by others." But the album refuted that claim. The vision of Lieberson, the narrative by Carl Carmer, the gritty performances by non-Mormon folk singers, the slick production values, and the sure-footed marketing campaign made this a Mormon tract of unmatched potency. Why? Because it asked for no converts, just empathy.

1968), and Carl Carmer, *The Farm Boy and the Angel: The Mormon Vision and the Winning of the West* (Garden City, New York: Doubleday & Co., 1970). In 1980 Cheney gave his recordings and their index to HBLL.

42. The details, sales figures, and related memos are all in the Lieberson Papers.

43. The text of the speech is in the Lieberson Papers.

6 PEOPLE OF THE (OTHER) BOOK

As 1967 closed, a strange LP rolled off the conveyor belts at Artisan Sound Recorders in Los Angeles. The jacket's front cover showed a full-headdressed Indian chief painted by Wallace Parker. On the left side the words "People of the Book"—a term of art for Semitic nations—descended in faux-Mayan white letters on a black stripe. When one played the record's A-side, one heard an odd mélange of exotica, from spooky sound-effects to playful dances in simple harmonies, with instrumentation that included ocarinas, pan flutes, bone rasps, slit drums, and other ancient Mesoamerican sound-makers. On Side 2, a choir sang excerpts from Handel, Sunday school songs, and the "Battle Hymn of the Republic."

The record was a souvenir of an ambitious BYU-bankrolled pageant. Held at the Starlite Bowl in Burbank that October, the pageant featured this musical stew beneath a script cribbed from the Book of Mormon, a cast of Native Americans from a federal boarding school, television actors in leading roles, costuming borrowed from the wardrobes of B-movie westerns and *Camelot*, quasi-Israeli folk dancing, slide projections of Nephite war scenes, and a manifesto at its outset that included this mini-sermon: "Science, which must find an answer for everything, soon advanced a theory (which still prevails) that is based on human deduction, drawn from insufficient evidence. Against the fallible theories of human logic, however, there is a divine explanation for America's mystery that is rapidly gaining ascendancy. ... That instead of nameless strugglers who crossed the Bering Straits from Asia into Alaska, [American Indians'] forefathers could have been Hebrew people who came out of Jerusalem at the time of the Babylonian

Cover of the 1967 program for *People of the Book* (illustration by Wallace Parker).

captivity!"[1] In some ways the LP was a mere drop in the river of psychedelic-surrealist albums that flooded the record market in 1967. In other ways it documented a unique Mormon encounter with race, legend, and pop culture.

• • •

The Mormon church has largely dropped any claims that North American Native Americans are Israelites per se—maybe some

1. From the script to "People of the Book," Institute of American Indian Studies and Research Papers, HBLL (hereafter IAISR Papers).

intermingling of bloodlines, mostly South or Central American, but not so much North American. Yet the religion's founder, Joseph Smith, was blunt, almost cheerily so: "The Book of Mormon is a record of the forefathers of our western Tribes of Indians. … By it we learn that our western tribes of Indians are des[c]endants from that Joseph that was sold into Egypt, and that the Land of America is a promised land unto them."[2] Throughout the prophet's career, Smith identified Native Americans as the progeny of the Hebrew migrants described in the Book of Mormon, which was buried in a hill in upstate New York. Given American Indians' Israelitish bloodline, Smith taught, gentiles like him and his followers owed a debt to them. Mormons must raise them from their fallen state into a civilization worthy of their noble line.

Smith's successor, Brigham Young, mounted a crude, but more pragmatic "lifting" of Laman's savage descendants: servitude. Buying up Indians was the way, he explained, to make sure they were not slaughtered or carted off by others for slavery in Mexico, California, and elsewhere. It also ensured they were surrounded by civilized white saints. On June 28, 1851, the *Deseret News* reported that Young had "advised [the people] to buy up the Lamanite children, as fast as they could, and educate them and teach them the Gospel, so that not many generations would pass ere they would become a white and delightsome people." Five years later the church's First Presidency noted with pleasure that "so many of the children of the Lamanites [are] in the families of the Saints, where they have the same opportunities and privileges as the white children."[3] The Lamanite indenture plan had succeeded. And it thrived, sporadically, for another two decades. It was a strange mixture of veneration and domination—or indeed was veneration by domination.[4]

2. Joseph Smith, Letter to Noah C. Saxton, Jan. 4, 1833, www.josephsmithpapers.org/paper-summary/letter-to-noah-c-saxton-4-january-1833/4 (accessed July 1, 2019).

3. MS 18 (Jan. 26, 1856): 50.

4. This history has been treated many times over the years, but I refer the reader to the most recent, which not only gives an authoritative overview but introduces all previous treatments of note: Brian Q. Cannon, "'To Buy Up the Lamanite Children as Fast as They Could': Indentured Servitude and Its Legacy in Mormon Society," *Journal of Mormon History* 44, 2 (Apr. 2018): 1–35.

From Young's death in 1877 until 1946, the church did little overtly to "lift" the Lamanites. But in that latter year, church president George Albert Smith assigned Arizonan Spencer Kimball, now in his fourth year in the Quorum of the Twelve Apostles, to "look after the Indian program in all the Church and in all the world." Kimball spent the rest of his life as a putative apostle to the Indians. In the fall of 1947, the church took its first tentative steps in a less galling sequel to the indenture program of the previous century. The Indian Placement Program, as it became known, recruited Indian *foster children* into white homes. In 1954 the First Presidency and Quorum of the Twelve approved this as a general program of the church. The church persuaded parents on reservations to send their children to what amounted to mini-boarding schools in the homes of approved Mormons.

For decades the federal government had built non-LDS boarding schools for Indian children. These schools included "outing" programs, by which the boys went to work on ranches, farms, and orchards, while the girls became "home helpers." The Bureau of Indian Affairs reported as early as 1924 that the "immediate results to the students of the outing system are better English, more self-confidence, less of the characteristic Indian diffidence, better manners, [and] more attention to personal appearance." While the federal government was attempting a kind of penance for its slaughter and decimation of Native American tribes, Mormons saw their mission as one given by God to "civilize" and convert Native Americans because they were Israelites and thus God's chosen people. Along the way, they would not only facilitate these tribes' peace with "the white man," but literally transform them into white men and women.

In 1950 the church's flagship school, Brigham Young University, installed a new president, attorney Ernest Wilkinson. Prior to his appointment, Wilkinson's legal career had focused on Indian land rights versus federal and state governments. As BYU president, Wilkinson in 1951 began to make the case for avidly ushering Indian applicants through BYU's gates. In 1953 he explained his foundational views in a speech to a group of teachers in Brigham City, Utah. His terse notes to the talk give the standard view of the spiritual schematic: "As a member of Mormon Church [I] have always believed in divine destiny of American Indian. … Because of iniquity into which they fell they were stricken with a dark skin. Through obedience to commandments—righteous living—they will again become a white and delightsome people." He added, "Don't infer some are not delightsome people now."[5]

During this period Wilkinson repeatedly explained that there were four "pillars" for advancing Lamanites. "It is my humble opinion," he said in 1955, "that the future of [the] American Indian is irretrievably tied to his advancement in the field of education, in the arts and sciences, in true Christian morality, in industry—in short, in civilization itself."[6] So Wilkinson endorsed the scholarshipping of American Indian students to BYU that year, giving them special tutoring, assigning them hand-picked faculty, and laying a foundation for what became a long-term structure of Lamanite higher education.

In 1960, Wilkinson established the Institute of American Indian Studies and Research at BYU, which would fuse Book of Mormon teachings and Latter-day Saint ambitions with archival, archeological, and sociological study of Native American tribes.[7] That same year, BYU announced plans for a new library whose outer walls would be covered with Mesoamerican glyphs. This was partly to honor Lamanites generally and partly to showcase the library's chief purpose beyond ordinary book stacks and carrels. The *Church News*'s front page displayed the artist's rendering with the headline "Indian Treasures: New BYU library to house outstanding collection."[8] The premise of the library was simply this: the "Red Men's history and sociology is the testimony of the Book of Mormon as to the exalted past and promise of this race." BYU director of libraries Lyman Tyler invited church members to donate

5. "Notes for Address to Teachers and Administrators of Indian Services at Brigham City—June 22, 1953," Ernest L. Wilkinson Papers, HBLL.

6. "Speech Given at Missoula, Montana on April 23, 1955 to An Indian Institute Held at University of Montana," Wilkinson Papers.

7. See Paul E. Felt and S. Lyman Tyler, "The Institute of American Indian Studies and Brigham Young University," BYUS 6, 1 (Jan. 1965): 52–54.

8. *Church News*, Nov. 5, 1960. The quotes and information that follow in this paragraph are from this issue, Edwin J. Butterworth, "Treasure-house of Indian Lore," 8, 15.

money and materials for the proposed archive, which would include "paintings, books, manuscripts, early grammars of the Indian languages, bibliographies of early Spanish and North American scholars and similar materials which will be of inestimable value to researchers the world over."

Meanwhile, in San Diego a talented housewife named Mildred Handy was writing lessons for an "Understanding Israel" course that would spiral out from Mormon study groups into actual experience with Jewish culture via a folk dance group she called "The Yovail Dancers." Over the next four years the group's rolls grew to about sixty members as she developed its repertoire to include not only ancient and modern urban and rural choreography, but also a narrative she bundled with the dancing into a presentation called "Fire of Israel." During those years, which included a move to Pasadena, the group's venues grew larger and more diverse. In 1964 they toured Europe and the Holy Land, where the group received the Pilgrim's Medal from the Israeli government.[9]

Handy hoped to link Mormons and Jews not only with mutual understanding but some under-the-table proselytizing. Her shows sometimes quoted Book of Mormon prophets as scripture, leading Jewish audiences to inquire about the identity of prophets like Nephi and Alma. This somewhat sly goodwill ambassadorship bespoke the tone of then LDS Church president David McKay, whose outreach into mainstream America and even the world at large was both prodigious and unprecedented. Nevertheless, probably because the Yovail Dancers rivaled the appeal of standard church youth programs, the Pasadena stake president shut the group down in 1964—the same year that Wilkinson appointed Handy's friend Paul Felt to head up BYU's Office of Indian Affairs.

In December 1966, Felt asked Handy to write a pageant script on Lamanite Israel to help missionary work with American Indians and smooth the pipeline of Indian students moving to BYU. Unsure whether to produce it in Salt Lake City or California, Felt

9. See Arnold H. Green, "A Survey of LDS Proselyting Efforts to the Jewish People, " BYUS 8, 4 (1968): 442–43; Kahlile B. Mehr, "Brigham Young University and Jerusalem before Semester Abroad, 1931–1968," *Religious Educator* 8, 1 (2007): 69–84; my telephone conversation with David C. Handy, May 7, 2018.

asked her to contact Gerald Ray Hall, principal of the LDS Indian seminary in Riverside. After visiting the seminary, she recommended Southern California as the site, "with emphasis on placing Indian children in non-Indian homes."[10] When the program for the pageant eventually came out, it explained that "Southern California was chosen as an ideal place for the development of the pageant, due to its large concentration of people of Indian and Mexican descent. Of prime interest is the Sherman Institute in Riverside, California—third largest federal Indian school in the nation, which also has the third largest Indian Seminary in the Church. Also, there are over 50,000 Indian people living in Los Angeles County and at least 23 Indian Reservations are found within a radius of 50 to 100 miles. 'PEOPLE OF THE BOOK' is a voice raised in their behalf!"

In July, Handy importuned Felt and his colleagues to get Elder Kimball to issue an official announcement of support for the show. Indeed, she drafted one for him to sign and send to over forty stake presidents in the region. It read, "We view with favor the Book of Mormon Pageant, 'People of the Book,' and would appreciate your full support and cooperation for this fine missionary endeavor." She conceded to Felt that she had "escalated" the pageant to "classical proportions" beyond his original expectations and that might put him on the line for its outcome. But she and her co-producer husband, George, pledged to "exert with every bit of energy of mind and body—with fasting and prayer—to make sure that this undertaking is a beautiful success. ... As I review in my mind, step by step, the marvelous chain of circumstances which have brought us to the point of creation that we are, I can only conclude, with fervent conviction, that the hand of God is in this and that He is moving on us all to bring forth quickly a significant missionary effort in behalf of Lamanite Israel."[11]

Wilkinson supported the project, warily. Since this was being billed as sponsored by BYU's Institute of American Indian Studies

10. Hall, Letter to J. Edwin Baird, Oct. 12, 1967, IAISR Papers. For early correspondence on the pageant's logistics, see these letters: Hall to Felt, Apr. 17, 1967; and Hall to Handy, May 23, 1967, IAISR Papers.

11. Quotes are from Handy, Letter to Stuart Durant, July 17, 1967; other information is from Handy, Letter to Felt, July 17, 1967, IAISR Papers.

and Research, he said that BYU must "maintain a tight control of management ... if we have several agencies of the Church meddling in it, nothing but confusion will result." Soon BYU would commit money to the pageant, raising the stakes on its success.[12]

As the content of the show evolved, so did the location. Originally they would stage it on the grounds of the church's Los Angeles Temple for four nights in the first week of September, with all tickets priced at $1.50 each. But the temple grounds could not handle the outdoor technical needs of the production. So in July the Handys moved it to an eight-night run at Farnsworth Park in Pasadena, which had a small amphitheater, good lighting, acoustics, and, most important, free rent. By the end of August, they had moved it again, this time to its final location, the Starlite Bowl in Burbank. Because that venue seated a whopping 3,800 patrons, the Handys drew down the length of the run to four nights in the first week of October.[13] By now, the total expenses, from costuming to posters, led the Institute of American Indian Studies and Research to advance the show $2,500.

Along the way, the posters dropped their original catchphrase: "Palmyra Pageant of the West Coast." That pretense did not hold water. Officially begun in 1937 as a commemorative event at the site to which Joseph Smith had been led by the angel Moroni, the Palmyra pageant now contained a cast of nearly 500 people, ages 10–70, with expected attendance for a five-performance run: 100,000. Its lead actors lip-synched the pre-recorded script on four main stages and twenty secondary stages. For years the pageant's music had simply borrowed classical pieces, but since 1957 consisted of original music by Crawford Gates, recorded by BYU choirs, the Utah Symphony, and the Tabernacle Organ, to name a few.

The music for *People of the Book*, though, would have an utterly anomalous pedigree. Young virtuoso violinist Elisabeth Waldo had toured South America, become a collector and archivist of ancient indigenous instruments from those lands, and recorded three albums of Incan-Mayan tinged music: *Maracatu*, *Rites of the*

12. Wilkinson, Memo to Felt, July 31, 1967, IAISR Papers.

13. For this pre-production history, see J. Talmage Jones, Letters to James Cullimore, Aug. 1 and 25, 1967, IAISR Papers.

Pagan, and *Realm of the Incas*, all released on the GNP Crescendo label. By the time of *People of the Book*, Waldo had created both the Studies of the Americas library-workshop and the Elisabeth Waldo Folklorico Co., consisting of twelve instrumentalists, singers, and dancers, devoted to promulgating the tri-cultural heritage of Indo-Hispanic-Afro traditions.[14] A colleague wrote of her in 1960: "She approaches her work with the reverence of an Egyptologist on the continual brink of uncovering one of the lost tombs of the Pharaohs."[15] In her soundtrack to *People of the Book,* she intended to "resurrect an audio-vision of pre-Columbian culture."[16]

Still, the Southern California Mormon Choir gently muscled its way into the soundtrack. Almost twenty years old, the choir had recorded for Capitol Records and successfully weathered an attempt by the Mormon Tabernacle Choir to forbid the use of the word "Mormon" in its name. The Tabernacle Choir's complaint—not without merit—was that the California choir was trading on the reputation of the church's bestselling "official" choir from Salt Lake City. Church president McKay said that his three-man First Presidency "does not want to do anything to lessen the ardor of the Southern California Choir, and that we are not unmindful of the services rendered as a missionary factor, but that we do not want anyone to take advantage of the name 'Mormon.'" If they continued to include the word "Mormon" in their name, they would have to disproportionately emphasize the words "Southern California."[17] In the case of *People of the Book*, of course, that did not happen, since the "Mormon" part was essential both to the show's identity and the ability of the choir to attract ticket-buyers.

As plans coalesced, the feds surprisingly allowed students from the Sherman Institute to take part. Gerald Ray Hall explained that "getting the government to agree to let [thirty to forty of]

14. See her biographical note on the *People of the Book* LP as well as "Aboriginal Music Her Love," *Van Nuys News*, Mar. 18, 1973, 30.

15. Gene Norman, Liner Notes to Elisabeth Waldo and Her Concert Orchestra, *Rites of the Pagan* (GNP 601).

16. Advertisement headed "New Indian Organization Sponsors 'People of the Book' at Weber State College," *Ogden Standard-Examiner*, Apr. 30, 1969, 30.

17. The meeting and the issues are detailed in the David O. McKay, Journal, Sept. 3, 1963, 3–7, photocopy, Special Collections, J. Willard Marriott Library, University of Utah, Salt Lake City.

our Indian students participate in this four-night pageant which involved their going to Burbank and Arcadia on school nights for practices was a miracle." An even greater miracle, Hall wrote, "was to see our students go up on stage as backward, and as awkward, and as I thought before, as undependable as they are." But their presence on stage "did lend a feeling of realness and authenticity to the program inasmuch as they represented the development of Indian Israel in a foster placement type program."[18]

To recruit dozens of both Mormon and non-Mormon Native Americans to depict the origin story of Lamanite Israel was one thing. But a unique coalition of actors, arguably the most Hollywood-savvy in Mormon history, formed the main cast. Since the script dwelt almost entirely on the original migrant family of the Book of Mormon, it had five lead roles, all men: the patriarch Lehi and the paired adversaries of, on the one hand, Nephi and Sam, and on the other, Laman and Lemuel. Because the show was being mounted in Southern California, the lead actors had strong film and television credentials.

Lehi: Gordon Jump, a character actor who had done plays, radio shows, and small roles on television and would become well-known as both the radio-station boss, "Mr. Carlson," on *WKRP in Cincinnati* and as the Maytag repairman in a long-running line of television commercials.

Nephi: Grenade Curran, who had been everything from a background dancer in *Singing in the Rain* and *Seven Brides for Seven Brothers* to a wardrobe man on *Camelot*.

Sam: French-born wrestler-turned-character actor Arthur Boyadjian (a.k.a. Mustapha Pasha). His credits included small roles in movies with Marlon Brando and Shirley Jones, television shows that included *It Takes a Thief*, *The Virginian*, *The Rogues*, *T.H.E. Cat*, and comedy specials with Jerry Lewis.

Laman: Bryce Chamberlain, who had done minor film roles, but was best-known to Mormons as the Everyman character in *Man's Search for Happiness*, the church promotional film featured at the New York World's Fair in 1964 and then transferred to filmstrips used by Mormon missionaries for more than a decade thereafter.

18. Hall, Letter to J. Edwin Baird, Oct. 12, 1967, IAISR Papers.

Nick Cravat (left) as Lemuel and Grenade Curran as Nephi in *People of the Book* (1967).

Lemuel: Nick Cravat, Burt Lancaster's sidekick and cohort since the two men began vaudevillian work together as a trapeze duo.

These five and the rest of the cast were directed by Dale White, who had played Harlow Wilson on the *Jack Benny Program* from 1955 to 1964.

There had been no casting call, as such, just word-of-mouth networking. Curran, for example, had interested Cravat in Mormonism when both men worked on the set of the Richard

Bryce Chamberlain as Laman in *People of the Book* (1967).

Brooks-directed Burt Lancaster vehicle *The Professionals*. Other *People of the Book* leads had also been fireside guests in the home of the Clingers, a quartet of Mormon sisters later widely known as the first all-girl rock group.

In the last week of September 1967, press releases appeared in various B-list newspapers, including the *Valley News* in Van Nuys, the *San Bernardino County Sun*, and the *Independent Star-News* of Pasadena, a homegrown supplement to the church's official house organ, *Church News*. The headline varied but the content was essentially verbatim. It began, "Pageantry of an ancient people, music from instruments not played for 1,500 years and imaginative dance numbers are all a part of 'People of the Book,' a production being staged Oct. 4–7 in Burbank's Starlight Bowl by Southland Mormons." The second paragraph explained who was putting it on: the BYU Institute of American Indian Studies and Research along with local stakes and missions of the LDS Church.

The third paragraph outlined the story: the "establishment of a great Pre-Columbian civilization in the Western Hemisphere." Before listing the cast and other production personnel, the press release gave the show's main come-on: "Authentic melodies and rhythms from pre-Columbian times played on actual instruments of those early times or on authentic reproductions of those instruments have been written for the pageant by Elisabeth Waldo, an outstanding composer and conductor." Then, intensifying the air of authenticity: "Miss Waldo in private life is the wife of Dr. Carl S. Dentzel, director of the Southwest Museum in Los Angeles."

Waldo's arresting music greeted the audience as the pageant began. According to the program, the opening music, "Voice from the Earth," featured "a rare Mayan bass Ocarina, made of ceramic and dating back 1500 years. Three giant conch trumpets, from the Valley of Mexico, are used in the sense of 'calling the people to hear.'" Waldo's own Folklorico Dancers lifted and turned themselves as the sounds unfolded and the narrator, Nephi, gave his opening speech, a rhyming prologue about the mysterious truth entailed in what was about to be portrayed.

The story that followed fell short of the epic to which Handy had aspired. Almost all of its six scenes depicted the lifetime of Nephi only. The dialogue quoted or paraphrased the book of First Nephi—which, of course, made it difficult to deliver, given that book's King James-era diction and hyper-formal tone. Renee Chalk Hulse, who played Nephi's wife in the pageant, recalls that because it was put on outside, all lines and underscoring were pre-recorded. "When we got to the stage the few days before we put it on, the sets were made beforehand and really beautiful costumes were put on us when we got there. … We blocked the show quickly. The lines were in the recording, so easy to mouth. It was mainly making moves and gestures big enough for the message to be seen far away." As for the sets, they "were mainly geometric risers with hardly anything but props. I remember I was barefoot on stage and glad I was because one riser was inclined and I more surefooted without shoes on it."[19] With one brief exception, the

19. Renee Hulse, Facebook message to Michael Hicks, May 31, 2018.

Festival crowd scene from *People of the Book* (1967).

vocal music belonged to the Southern California Mormon Choir. The dance music belonged to Waldo's ancient instruments.

Act 1, scene 1 ("Farewell Jerusalem") shows Lehi's family in conversation and the seizing of Laban's plates "near a tent somewhere outside Jerusalem" (Nephi, Lehi, Saria, Sarai's Handmaid, Laman, Lemuel, Sam, Zoram—servant of Laban). The scene ends with the choir singing "Shalom, Alechem."

Scene 2 ("Come Ishmael") takes place a few days later in Ishmael's home, with Lehi's sons and Zoram begging Ishmael's family to join them on their audacious trip across the ocean. Ishmael's daughters perform a dance ("Rejoicing of Israel"). The choir closes this scene as well ("Harps and Cymbals Sound").

Scene 3 ("The Tree of Life") consists entirely of a ballet interpretation of Lehi and Nephi's vision.

Scene 4 ("Trial of Faith") leaps forward to eight years after the family's exodus from Jerusalem. Lehi's embattled sons wrangle about their fate "near a cliff over-looking the sea, in Bountiful."

Scene 5 ("Blessing on the Promised Land") depicts an outdoor festival honoring Lehi's decision to leave the Old World and his success at building a decent society in the New World. Dancing abounds amid a stage crowded with all the families of the lead characters.

As an intermezzo, the choir sings "Glorious Everlasting," and a ten-minute intermission ensues.

In Scene 6 ("The Separation and the Consolation") Nephi and his family both review and preview their prophetic destiny. They reach a pinnacle of fervor as Nephi envisions the coming of Jesus, and the choir, under the rubric "Music of The Vision," sings "Behold the Lamb of God" from Handel's *Messiah*.

The sprawling "Epilogue," which begins with the opening verses of the Mormon hymn "An Angel from on High," serves as Act 2 of the whole drama. The time scale contracts and Nephite-Lamanite history unfolds in eight projected tableaux under the long soliloquy of Moroni, the benighted Nephite warrior who would one day direct Joseph Smith to uncover this age-old book. Christ appears and ministers to children, but ominous drumbeats begin to sound, apocalyptic violence follows, and Moroni envisions the delivery of his book to Joseph Smith.

Then the show's Indian placement trappings emerge in what is called the "Restoration Sequence," including the "Foster Mothers Song" and the "Dance of Learning and Doing." Stage direction from the last portion of the script reads thus: "Indians are now coming in from the back of the hall and walking up the aisles, as at beginning. They are dressed in modern clothing and are singing [Mormon hymn] 'Redeemer of Israel.'" They transition to the last two verses of "An Angel from on High." The entire cast from the show's first part flows onto the stage. "There is dance movement to form the entire group into grand finale, as emblem is raised to shine across the back of the stage. … Z I O N !"[20] This finale bespoke the real *raison d'être* of the pageant's existence.

• • •

20. The description is based on the printed program and a typescript of the script in the IAISR Papers. The latter differs from the program in some of its numbering and descriptions. It is unclear what modifications were made from the script or the program to the performance.

Gerald Ray Hall called it "one of the most fantastic and tremendous pageants I have ever seen." The general authorities who came—including Apostle LeGrand Richards—gave the show "the highest of praise," Hall said. Among the audience comments he heard were "I feel I know Laman and Lemuel and their problems better" and "I have learned more about the Book of Mormon tonight than I have learned in many years."[21]

Business manager Talmage Jones called it "successful," "meaningful," and "professional." But "from a missionary standpoint, which is what we emphasized, there should be many changes." In particular, the narrative befuddled some viewers: "Non-members in attendance report that they didn't understand much of the presentation but enjoyed the music and the dance."[22]

Milton Hunter, a church general authority and one of the most ardent champions of Lamanite-Israel, thought the narrative was "good" and "the music … intensely interesting." He noted a few inaccuracies and bristled at one detail of the show: "I don't recall Laman and Lemuel getting drunk" in the Book of Mormon. "They got angry and had murder in their hearts and did all kinds of wicked things, but I don't remember the Book of Mormon telling about them getting drunk." From a structural perspective he thought the ending diffuse and not very "exciting." "Even the presentation of the coming forth of the gospel wasn't done in a way that would thrill you very much." The ending, he wrote, should be done in "a much more vivid and dramatic way."[23]

Hearing the generally positive reactions, BYU's Academic Vice President, Robert Thomas, asked for a video tape of the show, hoping to show it to a meeting of university leaders. "If it is a really good production, this could be a general shot in the arm for our Indian programs."[24]

The Handys hoped that the show would go on. They planned to produce it in the San Diego area, even closer to the border of what they saw as the heart of Lamanite country. Like them,

21. Gerald Ray Hall, Letter to J. Edwin Baird, Oct. 12, 1967, IAISR Papers.

22. Jones, Letter to Elder James Critchlow, Oct. 16, 1967, IAISR Papers.

23. Milton R. Hunter, Letter to Brother and Sister Paul E. Felt, Oct. 17, 1967, IAISR Papers.

24. R. K. Thomas, Email to Paul Felt, Oct. 18, 1967, IAISR Papers.

Gerald Ray Hall envisioned it as an annual event in his region. Paul Felt wondered how well it would do in Utah. But, clouding these dreams, the show still owed money to BYU. Talmage Jones wrote two checks to BYU totaling $1,500, presumably from the admission proceeds. But the production still owed BYU $1,000 more. Jones proposed that, with all they had invested in the show so far, future performances could raise money to pay off the debt. Or, he asked, should they just liquidate at least some of the staging and props to clean the slate?[25]

On January 12, 1968, Mildred Handy wrote to Paul Felt that "the leading music station in Los Angeles featured Elisabeth Waldo and her orchestra live. The first half of the program was devoted entirely to 'People of the Book,' in which Elisabeth gave some great advertising for our show, the records and the Book of Mormon." Nevertheless, Handy noted that composer Truman Fisher was beginning to work with Waldo on "our new version of the show." At a recent meeting, "some very constructive ideas were put forth and all were in agreement to put every effort forward in making this the finest dramatic production ever undertaken. With God's help, we can succeed."[26]

Despite pitching the pageant hard to San Diego area stake presidents, nothing materialized. A series of three restagings along the Wasatch Front in 1969 would have to do.

But one fact hampered these reprises: almost nothing remained of the original production. Dale White would have to be replaced as director. The choreographers as well. None of the original professional actors would appear in these new performances except for Chamberlain, who was now, in effect, promoted from villain (Laman) to hero (Nephi) in the cast. The high-class amphitheater was gone. The crowds of "authentic" Indian school extras had disappeared. Even the point of the show was stripped down to a vague support for Lamanite Israel—a far cry from the overt plugging of the Indian Placement Program in the locale that had inspired it and where it seemed most viable and fitting. What

25. Jones, Letter to Felt, Dec. 1, 1967, and Jan. 8, 1968, IAISR Papers.
26. Handy, Letter to Felt, Jan. 12, 1968, IAISR Papers.

remained: Elisabeth Waldo's recorded music and Handy's script, now radically retooled.

Handy ramped up the drama in some family-conflict scenes, changing the amount, content, and tone of speakers' lines. Phrases such as "like unto" and similar King James-isms largely disappeared in the new version. The diction became less declamatory and more soap opera-ish. Consider this change in the opening confrontational scene. In the first version Laman challenges Nephi's ally Sam about the building of the transatlantic ship thus: "You have become a fool, like unto Nephi!" In the revision, Laman converses instead with his fellow skeptic and brother Lemuel and says of their *father*, "He's a fool," then adds, "we're all fools, sneaking away like thieves, hiding in the desert like animals!" Or these words of Ishmael. The first script reads: "Thy father is a great and good man, who was persecuted because he spoke boldly to people concerning their sins. And he told them things they did not want to hear, even as other Prophets have done—yea, also Jeremiah." The revision reads: "I respect your father more than any man alive. Lehi is a great man, who is persecuted because he tells people the truth—things they do not want to hear. He tells us about our sins, as Prophets have always done, even Jeremiah, who warns us also."

The three-date 1969 revival of the show began in the Highland High School auditorium in Salt Lake City, followed by a staging at Weber State University in Ogden, both in May. The final show would be at the site of the pageant's conception, Brigham Young University in Provo, that October.[27]

In the headline of its review of the work, the BYU student newspaper distilled what many had said about its previous performances: "Music Mortar Holds Book of Mormon Pageant Together."[28] Although the work combined ballet, drama, and ad hoc pageantry, the music alone was "spectacular." "Despite the weak script," it was "the sonic experience [that] made one's attendance at this production worthwhile." A full third of the review consisted of a bio note for Elisabeth Waldo—and indeed this performance's

27. "Auditions Set for BYU Drama," *Daily Herald* (Provo), Sept. 18, 1969, 2.

28. Shelby R. Seem III, "Music Mortar Holds Book of Mormon Pageant Together," *Daily Universe*, Oct. 20, 1969, 5.

Poster for the 1967 production of *People of the Book* (cut out and marked by Grenade Curran) above the program cover for the 1969 production.

Recordings Available

The beautiful musical score to "People of the Book" can be yours to enjoy at home on a stereo or monophonic long playing record. Records will be sold during intermission and after the performance.

They are offered during the pageant at a special price of $4.00 each, including tax. If you would like the record mailed to your home (50¢ extra), fill in the order blank below and mail it to:

PEOPLE OF THE BOOK
1343 Normandie Circle
Salt Lake City, Utah
Phone 355-2763 or 322-0256

POB No. 590 B.C. ☐
GNP 603 ☐ GNP 601 ☐

Monaural --------☐
Stereo ---------☐

REALM OF THE INCAS
ELISABETH WALDO
AUTHENTIC PRE-COLUMBIAN INSTRUMENTS

RITES OF THE PAGAN

GNP 603 GNP 601

☐ Enclosed is a check or money order
☐ Please send C.O.D. (C.O.D. charges will be added by post office.)

NAME ADDRESS

CITY STATE

Ad for the *People of the Book* album, alongside other Elisabeth Waldo exotica albums.

printed program hawked the LP via a detachable mail-in order form that included Waldo's two related albums: *Rites of the Pagan* and *Realm of the Incas*.

One mishap nearly shut the show down. With *People of the Book* now inside, not outside, the fog machine "engulfed the first three rows. All one could see were programs being waved frantically over the heads of the coughing." Meanwhile, the yellow backlit image of Jesus amid the fog created "the illusion of a Guru." That comment bespoke one of the deeper problems with the show: this was 1969 in the United States of America. And while that fact enhanced the reception of the "weird instruments," it threw a wet blanket over the show's pretext.

The end of the 1960s fancifully billed itself as the "dawning" of an "Age of Aquarius." Musical psychedelia reigned. New theatre reveled in extravagance and provocation. From the bead necklaces of hippiedom to the "Yaqui way of knowledge" preached in a series of bestsellers by Carlos Castaneda, the American counterculture had co-opted Native Americans not as icons of savagery but as the true prophets of a new alternative vision. With peyote rituals, nature adoration, rough-hewn couture, and geometric-symbolic artwork as conspicuous Indian traits, many white people celebrated Native Americans as *their* "nursing fathers and mothers," not vice versa. Any show whose premise was to the contrary was, for white college students at least, doomed.

A subtler reason for the collapse *People of the Book* was the rise of other, less preachy, plays about the Book of Mormon. Even on the very week that *People of the Book* premiered in Burbank, a new play premiered at BYU entitled *A Day, a Night, a Day*. Written by Doug Stewart, it centered on the hours preceding the post-resurrection arrival of Christ in the Americas. In July 1968 BYU staged *The Children of the Sun*, which dwelt on Incan beliefs that "parallel many beliefs of the Church of Jesus Christ of Latter-day Saints," the school newspaper explained. Its music was purportedly "original Incan music." In the single month of March 1971, two new plays, both derived from Book of Mormon narratives, debuted at BYU: *The Apostate*, written by Orson Scott Card, and *The Tragedy of Korihor*, written by Louise G. Hanson. A self-consciously navel-gazing "Mormon arts" movement, complete with annual festivals and a commemorative book, had begun, one in which "serious" drama rooted in Mormon narratives contended with outworn proselytizing shows, at least, in pretense, if not always in substance.

Between changing attitudes about Native Americans in the nation and changing ambitions about theatre in Mormondom, it seemed inevitable that a work like *People of the Book* would quickly be eclipsed. No further productions of it were mounted and copies of the soundtrack album gradually took their places in thrift shops and dumpsters.

• • •

The 1960s–70s saw steady growth in the population of scholarshipped Lamanites at BYU. During 1967–68, the school year of the original *People of the Book*, 135 American Indian students attended BYU. Three years later, that number had risen to 521.[29] The school's Indian education program expanded, including the faculty hiring of Bryce Chamberlain—Laman in the original *People of the Book* and Nephi in its revival. In 1971 BYU appointed Janie Thompson to organize a new singing and dancing group of Indians and Polynesians at BYU called the "Lamanite Generation."[30] And in December 1973, Spencer Kimball became the twelfth president of the Church of Jesus Christ of Latter-day Saints.

In June 1974 Kimball challenged the mission presidents of the church to step up their aid to Native Americans as a means of cultural protection. "Can we do more in the conversion of the Indians in their development and in their welfare? Let us revive our energies for them in all the places they live in the Americas and in the islands of the sea. If we wanted to be selfish, we could emphasize the fact that the Indian will be our shield and when trouble comes they can shield us from damage and harm that the pioneer brethren speak to us about."[31] Three years later, he proclaimed: "Certainly the Day of the Lamanite has arrived. And now is the time to deliver the Lamanites from their bondage. ... They must be educated, trained and brought out of obscurity into the light."[32] His attitude through the 1970s, backed by financial support, was simple: "Nothing is too good for an Indian. Nothing is too good for a good Latter-day Saint Lamanite."[33]

But "authentic" Lamanite music was part of the bondage from which Kimball wanted them delivered. Even before *People of the Book*, Kimball preached to BYU Lamanite students that they had

29. Woodruff J. Deem and Glenn V. Bird, *Ernest L. Wilkinson: Indian Advocate and University President* (Provo, Utah: n.p., 1978), 443.

30. For background to this, see John P. Livingstone, *Same Drum, Different Beat: The Story of Dale T. Tingey and American Indian Services* (Provo: BYU Religious Studies Center, 2003), 84–85.

31. Remarks at the New Mission Presidents Seminar, June 1974, excerpted in John R. Maestas and Jeff Simons, *The Lamanite*, rev. ed. (Provo, Utah: privately distributed, 1981), 372. This source, though hard to find, is the best compendium of statements on Lamanites and their destiny.

32. "The Lamanite," Regional Representatives Seminar, Apr. 1, 1977, excerpted in Maestas and Simons, *The Lamanite*, 275.

33. "Roots of Your Success Are Spiritual," BYU Indian Week address, Feb. 25, 1975, excerpted in Maestas and Simons, *The Lamanite*, 48.

to shun their indigenous expressions, whose pagan roots offended the Almighty.[34] Wilkinson felt the same, writing in a memo to Paul Felt that he had been "worried" about BYU's inclination "to perpetuate the Indian culture without improving it." Paul Felt praised Wilkinson's address to Lamanite students at that time, in which Wilkinson condemned the "incorrect tradition of their fathers." Felt believed that he, his Indian Office, BYU, and even the church "may have fallen into a trap which in effect has made our approach ... one that has also allowed , and in some cases actively encouraged, the perpetuation of a culture and a tradition which is, in the final analysis, apostate." For their culture to be "improved," they would have to "specifically eliminate some of the 'paganistic elements.'"[35] That bias quelled experimentation with "authentic" Lamanite music.

Kimball's death in 1985 dimmed the Mormon spotlight on Lamanite reclamation forever.

Meanwhile, many of those who starred in *People of the Book* went on to professionalize the church's entertainment media in conventional Hollywoodish ways. Gordon Jump appeared in a few church films, most notably as the Apostle Peter in the church's temple endowment film through most of the 1970s–80s, a film seen millions of times by temple patrons during that era. Arthur Boyadjian played roles in popular church films from *How Rare a Possession* and *Nora's Christmas Gift* to a remake of *Man's Search for Happiness*. *People of the Book* had led Bryce Chamberlain from Hollywood to BYU and thence to further Mormon exploits on stage and screen, most notably a series of one-man shows in which he played Joseph Smith, Brigham Young, and George Washington thousands of times. The afterlife of *People of the Book* resonates more in Mormon theater and film than its original incarnation could have foretold.

At the same time, in domesticating ancient "Lamanite" traditions via blending them with popular musical idioms, composer

34. See the discussion in Michael Hicks, *Mormonism and Music: A History* (Urbana: University of Illinois Press, 1989), 218–19.

35. Paul E. Felt, Memo to Ernest L. Wilkinson, Feb. 21, 1966; and Wilkinson, Memorandum to Felt, Feb. 28, 1966, both in IAISR Papers.

Elisabeth Waldo advanced a new worldwide genre known as "exotica." She gradually took her place in the pantheon of artists such as Martin Denny, Esquivel, Arthur Lyman, Les Baxter, and Yma Sumac, in whose ensemble Waldo had played. Such artists originated "pagan" music with a pop twist that made it suave, ripe enough for "space-age" lounges, yet with a whiff of antiquity that savored of "authenticity." Sleek modernity co-opted ancient instruments, just as the newly minted Book of Mormon had co-opted King James English. In each case, the message and the packaging were new, the fragments of idiom quite old. Boyadjian called Waldo's pageant music "very inspiring." Chamberlain said "that musical score was pretty much what carried [the show]."[36] Nevertheless, Mormon pageantry relinquished Waldo's Mesoamerican tropes in favor of standard Hollywood soundtracking, from the Hill Cumorah Pageant to the LDS temple endowment. Yet those tropes indelibly imprinted on the surrounding culture. Even the program for *People of the Book* had advertised Waldo's exotica albums, including, indeed, *Rites of the Pagan*. And that is where her pageant music took its lasting place—not in the productions of Mormonism but in the cultish devotions of what became known in at least some circles as "incredibly strange music."[37] In one of the more improbable bank shots of its history, Mormonism helped foster musical postmodernism. Just as Israel and Indians united comfortably in the Mormon imagination, the Waldo score to *People of the Book* fused head-butting traditions into a new alliance. The pageant faded away, but the surrealistic amalgam of its original score flourishes in the nether regions of pop esoterica, where Waldo reigns as a minor monarch.

Yet even Waldo's nascent postmodernism could not quite compete with that of *People of the Book*'s overall soundtrack. Handel? Sunday school songs? "Battle Hymn of the Republic"? All ladled onto the platter alongside Waldo's exotica? That bespoke the eclectic Mormon cosmos itself, in which, as Brigham Young explained,

36. The quotations are from interviews I conducted with Arthur Boyadjian and Bryce Chamberlain, June 8 and May 7, 2018, respectively.

37. See V. Vale and Andrea Juno, *Incredibly Strange Music, Vol. 1* (San Francisco: RE/Search Publications, 1993), as well as its sequels and recorded anthologies.

we gather and savor "truth from any source, wherever we can obtain it."[38] It is the unsettling universe where Joseph Smith walks on the banks of the Susquehanna River and John the Baptist steps up to ordain him. It is the temple pageantry where Adam and Eve flee the Garden of Eden and bump into a Protestant minister.[39] Such are the divine collisions of Latter-day Saintliness. Mormonism flings the gate wider than most churchmen's yardsticks would allow. But that is the width of the book this people are made of.

38. JD 14:197.
39. That took place in Mormon temple endowment narratives until 1988.

7 HOW TO MAKE AND UNMAKE A MORMON HYMNBOOK

For Mormons, hymnbooks sit astride two genres: standard works and commentary. They are standard works—canonized scripture—in that everyone uses the same texts and tunes as common parlance. You can quote them like scripture and everyone in the church nods and understands—at least as well as they understand scripture. But, unlike the capital-letter Standard Works, hymnbooks get massively rewritten every so often, with some hymns kept, others scrapped, and new ones adopted. Yesterday's favorites might become today's objects of scorn, while today's novelties might become tomorrow's masterworks. You could not have a church with scripture as endlessly magmatic as that. But, just so, you could not have one with hymnbooks as rock-hard as the Ten Commandments.

I have written and published about Mormon hymns and hymnbooks for over thirty-five years. Their jigsaw-puzzle complexity makes studying them seductive. Each new puzzle piece you find or fit into place beckons you to the next, beguiling you into thinking the picture will one day be complete. But here I offer a small case study. How do you go from the old to the new? Let me try to lift the curtain on this unnervingly detailed and awkward process that somehow results in a para-scriptural volume embraced, suddenly but lastingly, by millions of churchgoers. Be prepared for a parade of lists, because making lists is the lion's share of what hymnbook compilers do.

• • •

In October 1972, new LDS church president Harold B. Lee called O. Leslie Stone as an Assistant to the Twelve Apostles and in December made him managing director of a huge new Church Music Department—fifty-five members—replacing the old Church

Music Committee.[1] The department had nine "specialized areas" committees, one of which, headed by Merrill Bradshaw, was the four-member composition committee, whose job was to solicit and approve new music for use by auxiliaries and church magazines. In December, the First Presidency told Stone to have this committee "proceed in making guidelines and preparation for a new hymnal." For that task, the committee held their first meeting a week before Christmas 1973.

Bradshaw was a titan in Mormon music. The doctoral-degreed composer of symphonies, concertos, chamber works, hymns, and children's songs, stood as one of the lions at the gate of Brigham Young University's Department of Music. Feeling the weight of both history and his own intellect, he wanted the committee to review about 10,000 hymns, new and old, choose about 500 that would appeal to an international church, and have a new book ready to issue within slightly more than a year and a half.[2] But his committee members quickly brought up problems he had not thought of. The racks on the back of pews were sized for books of 400 or fewer hymns, so Bradshaw's ideal size was out. The timetable also came into question since the church would have to coordinate with Deseret Book to make sure the company's stock of current hymnbooks was depleted when the new one came out. Other questions also arose, including that of what to call the book—Bradshaw favored "hymnal." But should it be "hymn book"? "Hymnbook"? What about "Songs of Praise" (a title that some denominations were adopting to allow for many sacred songs that were not technically "hymns")? Bradshaw presented an ambitious flow chart of how the new hymnal—or "hymnbook," as they decided to call it—would progress. As they proceeded through the plan and made preliminary decisions, they could feel

1. The number comes from Michael Moody, Interview with Michael Hicks, May 27, 1987.

2. All of the information in this paragraph, as well as the flow-chart, are from the minutes and handout for the December 18 meeting of the "Hymn Book Committee" (later called the "Hymnbook Task Committee"). These and most other materials cited here were given to me by Merrill Bradshaw in 1986 or by Janet Bradshaw in 2009. I made copies and added those copies to Bradshaw's personal papers in HBLL. All documents cited herein, except as noted, are in that location. The minutes to meetings of the Hymnbook Task Committee are hereafter cited as cited "HTC Minutes."

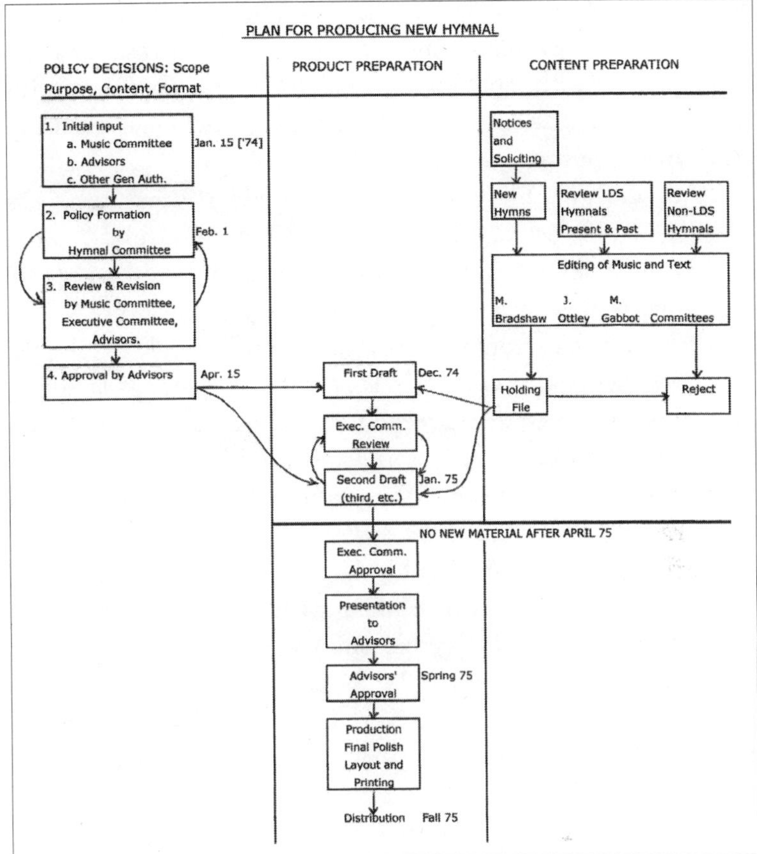

1974 flow chart for the planned new hymnbook.

momentum gathering. But eight days later, their sponsor, President Lee, suddenly died.

Stone hastily wrote to the new church president, Spencer W. Kimball, to get the project reapproved. Meanwhile, the committee began to define its vision and methods. Committee member Harold Goodman stated their mission bluntly: "We will proceed from the assumption that all hymns, present and past[,] are to be deleted from the Hymn book. Only those will be put into the new Hymn book which can be justified." To be justified meant meeting one or more of six criteria, similar to those used by hymnbook committees in the 1920s and 1940s. Two criteria were the musical quality and the "doctrinal value and poetry" of the text. Two others were the "appropriateness" and "usefulness" of the hymn for LDS services. A fifth criterion was a hymn's "traditional popularity with the Saints." And the sixth was "insistence of a general authority that a hymn must be included."

With those in mind, the committee began their ambitious weeding and harvesting of hymns. The plan was fourfold:

1. Review all hymns in the current hymnbook.

2. Review all hymns from earlier LDS song collections.

3. Review hymns from as many Protestant hymnbooks as possible.

4. Use the *Ensign*, *Church News*, and direct mailings to solicit new texts and tunes—even "experimental hymns"—from church poets and composers.[3] As the process unfolded, the committee would not only decide which hymns to include, but whether to revise any that they'd chosen.[4]

Whatever momentum they had felt as a committee, though, was tempered by the viscosity of working within a larger system. That meant that, more and more, their mission resulted in the making of lists upon lists. In April 1974, for example, their fundamental document, "Specifications and Guidelines for the Preparation of a New Hymnbook"—which they had privately called "Criteria for Sifting"—was finally approved by the Music Department advisors, Elders Mark E. Petersen and Boyd K. Packer. The fifth draft in as many months, it contained eight categories of questions to be answered.

1. Spirit: Does the hymn help members feel close to the Savior? Does it reflect the true gospel spirit?

2. Function: Is the hymn well suited for church worship services in the church and can congregations sing it with reasonable effort?

3. Doctrine: Does the hymn uphold the doctrines of the church? Is the hymn needed to extend the range of subjects in the hymnbook?

3. This term is used in the December 18, 1973, HTC Minutes. It alludes, in part, to some of the theorizing ex-officio committee member Michael Moody had done in his PhD dissertation, "Contemporary Hymnody in the Church of Jesus Christ of Latter-day Saints," University of California, 1970.

4. This matter was discussed from time to time. See especially the HTC Minutes for June 4 , 1974, and Oct. 19, 1976; also undated holograph notes by Merrill Bradshaw interleaved with the minutes.

4. Music: Is the hymn musically sound and free from undesirable connotations and associations?

5. Poetry: Is the text artistically defensible?

6. Unity: Do text and music fit together to provide a unified expression?

7. Quality: Is the hymn in its best possible form, or can it be made acceptable without excessive change?

8. Tradition: Does its meaning to church members as a whole supersede other considerations?

The list seemed ideal. But each question inherently provoked other questions. Consider these, for example:

1. What spirit constituted the "true" gospel spirit? Many styles of worship—and, indeed, personalities of members, especially converts—fed into Mormonism. Which were "truer" than others? By what criteria?

2. Regarding singability, what would constitute "*reasonable* effort" by congregations? The adjective had fostered countless debates in law. Who would gauge it in this context, given the broad range of musical training and native ability among members?

3. Who determined which "doctrines of the church" must be upheld? How much or how little, to note a bristly example, should "grace" be emphasized?

4. Was the notion of "musically sound" dependent on theoretical rules favored by theorists and professors? Meanwhile, what kinds of "connotations and associations" would be "undesirable" and by what criteria?

5. What traits would constitute "artistic defensibility" in a text?

6. Given the history of mixing and matching texts and tunes in hymnody, how "unified" an expression did any given text+tune need? How would one measure "unity" of a text and its tune?

7. Given how many text-changes might occur—especially to soften or even change doctrine in hymn texts—how much alteration would constitute "excessive"?

8. If "meaning to church members as a whole" could "supersede other considerations," of what weight should one give those "other considerations"—presumably the seven previous ones?

Current Hymn # ________ Current Title ________________

Author ________________ Composer ________________

Function: Subject:

Musical Suitability: (________________)
Whose comments

Text Suitability: (________________)
Whose comments

Committee Action: Preliminary recommendation ________ Delete ________

Response from MUSEXECO ________________

Final Action ________________ Initials ________
Hymn Committee

____
Music

____
Text

If accepted for new hymnal: Section ________________
Cross-references ________________
Indexing: Author, Composer, Alphabet, Meter, other

Form for 1970s hymnbook committee members to record their evaluations of hymns.

Such questions might seem petty or pedantic, but their consequences could weigh down the final product, or even the discussions getting there—not to mention in the give and take between the committee and their church leadership overseers, the ultimate arbiters of the book that would or would not emerge.

As the year wore on, the committee met for three to four hours every two weeks. Each committee member had his or her assignment and, after discussing it with non-committee advisors, would make recommendations to the whole group, who would then vote. All hymn reviews were both thorough and severe. When the group looked at the first fifty songs in the 1909 *Deseret Sunday*

School Song Book, for example, they thought only nine of them possibly worth including in the new book, and even then seven would need revision: "Stars of Morning, Shout for Joy," "Supplication Hymn," "Join the Children of the Lord," "Who Are These Arrayed in Light," "The Coming Day," "Missionary Hymn," and "Come with Tuneful Voices."[5]

The committee also mulled over new questions about content. Would all their choices be in all international LDS hymnbooks? They decided they should choose a core of hymns to appear in all hymnbooks and let regional committees choose the rest.[6] And what about patriotic songs like "America, the Beautiful" and "Battle Hymn of the Republic"? That latter question was quickly answered by the First Presidency: all American patriotic songs were out.[7] Questions about format also arose. The committee decided to drop the 1950 hymnbook's separation of "choral" and "congregational" hymns. They would show hymns' actual titles when those differed from first lines (e.g., "Love at Home," not "There Is Beauty All Around"). The new book would group hymns in sections (as the first LDS hymnbook had done).[8] And the book would include a far more elaborate set of indices and cross references.

After a year of assiduously reviewing hymns and policies, the committee knew they would be lucky to produce even a first draft of their hymn choices by the fall of 1975—the date they had once hoped to have the new book out. As inertia began to set in, they voted to start meeting only once a month. When fall arrived, the committee had reviewed all hymns in the 1950 book twice.[9] They voted to delete over 30 percent of its congregational hymns, 67 percent of the choir hymns, and 90 percent of the men's and women's arrangements.

The hymns they cut included old Christian favorites such as these:

---

5. Subcommittee for Congregational Music Minutes, Feb. 21 and Mar. 7, 1974.

6. HTC Minutes, Mar. 11, 1974; also Specialized Area Committees, Minutes, Apr. 30, 1974. That core of hymns would also form the content of the "simplified hymnbook," a special edition with pared-down accompaniments.

7. HTC Minutes, Sept. 10 and Nov. 12, 1974.

8. HTC Minutes, June 4, 1974.

9. HTC Minutes, Nov. 12, 1974.

> "Behold a Royal Army" because of its "militaristic approach to gospel," "'corny' text," and a melody that was "too high!" Perhaps knowing they were fighting a strong tide of tradition, the committee added, "But we would appreciate feedback, especially on the militaristic issue."
>
> "Come Thou Fount of Every Blessing" because, "even though this is a nice hymn, the imagery is too Protestant for our hymn book," the "words [were] not doctrinally sound," and the music "ends 4 times—all cadences same."
>
> "In a World Where Sorrow" ("Scatter Sunshine") because it was "too happy-go-lucky," "text is Pollyanna—shallow solutions to real problems," it had a "limited gospel message," and the "message can be said in [a] more poetical and meaningful way."
>
> "Nearer My God to Thee" because of the "over-frequent repetition of word 'God' not in L.D.S. tradition," it was "strongly Protestant in flavor," and "over sentimental."
>
> "Who's on the Lord's Side, Who?" because it was "Amateurish," had a "Jingoist attitude in [the] text," was "Self-congratulatory," and the "Music sounds like a cheap London Dance Hall tune."

But indigenous Mormon hymns were not immune. The text of "Though in the Outward Church Below"—found in the first Mormon hymnbook—"suggests false doctrine and is extremely negative." Its Mozartean music, meanwhile, is "from an opera on Freemasonry." And "Take Courage, Saints, Faint Not by the Way" earned this review: "1. Self-pity evident in text—wallows in it. 2. Not often sung. 3. We are seeking more up-to-date ways to ease the pain of suffering through congregational singing."

In October, the Twelve asked for a list of hymns the committee wanted to delete. Bradshaw agreed to do so but insisted that their list come with a detailed explanation of the committee's decisions. Before giving the fourteen reasons to cut hymns from the old book, he offered some broad principles, the chief of which were these three:

> "Very few hymns were finally recommended for deletion on the strength of a single reason. In the tabulation some hymns would be found listed in many categories."

"Some hymns are included on the list to elicit response from the Brethren to aid us in the completion of our work. We will be responsive to any guidance they wish to offer us."

"Finally, there are some hymns (2 or 3) which received little support in our committees and therefore are included on the list to see if there is support among the Brethren. If that support is absent, then deletion seems the best route."

The "categories"—more than one of which a single hymn could fall into—were these:

1. Their texts were "unsuitable." This was perhaps the catch-all for various sorts of unease the committee felt about verbal expression in the book. They actually broke unsuitability down to six types (using these exact words): doctrinal problems; excessive gloominess; secular flavor, lack of gospel association; fuzzy meaning; generally weak text construction; dated language (language so characteristic of the mannerisms of an earlier day that its significance is seriously diminished by the style of expression).
2. The hymns had a "Protestant flavor" or "revivalist style."
3. They were "dated": "no longer appropriate because of changes in church programs, emphasis, or organization."
4. They were "national anthems, state songs, etc."
5. They were "too difficult or awkward for congregational singing or family use."
6. They were "militaristic."
7. They suffered from "disuse or waning popularity."
8. They had "excessive sentimentality."
9. They were "musically inappropriate: too difficult, incompetent, not suited to words, frivolous style, etc."
10. The music or text had "uncomfortable associations": "associations may be either text or music problems with potential embarrassment."
11. "Duplications of more acceptable versions."
12. The hymn was guilty of "excessive 'preachiness' or moralizing flavor."
13. "Poor hymns for which new settings or replacements are being prepared."
14. "Bad setting of words."

Many of these reasons seemed fair, even obvious. Others were vague, especially when words like "flavor," "associations," and, of course, "excessive" came into play. Some of the specific critiques of hymn after hymn must have seemed harsh and elitist, with a tone that would not sit well with some church leaders.[10] Still, what the committee would report to the Twelve used words often far gentler than what it often used in its internal reports, which included "gloomy," "pompous," "choppy," "racist," "pantheistic" and "chauvinistic." Nevertheless, the committee could be blunt in the reasons they gave to the Twelve. More than one hymn they called "musically embarrassing to the church."

As we saw, their putdown of "Who's on The Lord's Side, Who?" was particularly savage. Since some of the deleted hymns might still have "historical value," the committee proposed they could be published in a separate book that would "tell things about our past." Meanwhile, their reasons for *keeping* hymns were far less colorful: "beloved," "useful," "appropriate," "standard," "favorite," and so forth.

With so many old hymns out, the committee hoped to put as many as 175 new hymns in, but without making the new book any longer than its predecessor. By mid-1975 they had gathered more than 3,000 potential hymns to be added to the book, as well as about 2,000 more texts without music for possible use. The gathering included Protestant favorites—especially Christmas and Thanksgiving songs; international and ethnic hymns, from the Japanese "My Jesus, As Thou Wilt" to the so-called Omaha Tribal Prayer ("Father, a Needy One Before Thee Stands");[11] and newly written LDS texts and tunes, especially sacrament hymns and others that specifically treated LDS themes (priesthood, prophets, fast day, tithing, and so on). Bradshaw summed up the latter submissions this way: "a lot of very good things, a lot of mediocre things, and a lot of very bad things. With that many being submitted you could expect quite a few clinkers. And we got them." The committee played through every single potential hymn to add, and for months they discussed and voted on all of them. According

10. Tellingly, on the back of the folder containing the draft of the committee's report to the Twelve, Bradshaw made a list of President Kimball's six favorite hymns—none of which they proposed to delete.

11. These two in particular were discussed in HTC Minutes, Aug. 21, 1976.

PROPOSED DISPOSITION OF THE M RIALS IN THE PRESENT HYMNBOOK

Hymn #	Title	keep	delete	comments
1	Come Rejoice	x		Good strong hymn. Some minor text revisions suggested
2	Abide with me; tis	x		Well-loved hymn. Minor text revision suggested
3	A mighty Fortress	x		Luthers mighty hymn of the reformation
4	All Creatures of	x		Great Hymn of praise
5	As Swiftly my Days		x	Protestant Spirit and Doctrine
6	Beautiful Zion for		x	not used any more, dated style, excessive range , local view of Zion
7	Behold a Royal Army		x*	Militaristic aspect is offensive to some
8	God Our Father,Hear	x		Very useful Sacrament Hymn
9	In Hymns of Praise	x		A good hymn for many occasions
10	Christ the Lord is	x		Good Easter hymn
11	Come all Ye Saints		X	Words and Music do not match
12	Come all ye Saints		x*	Words and music do not fit; new music needed
13	Come Come Ye Saints	x		One of our greatest hymns
14	Come Follow Me	x		Limit the number of verses to three or four, see recommended text changes
15	Come Go With Me		x	Text refers to Utah gathering, Music too elaborate, text not "worldwide"
16	Come Hail the Cause		x	Text now obsolete: MIA no longer exists.
17	Come Let us Anew	x		See recommended Text changes. Good newyear's message.
18	Come Ye Disconsolate		x	Non-LDS text in both Doctrine and Spirit; not used much
19	Come Along, Come Along		x	No unified message, tricky music, not used anymore
20	Come O Thou King of	x		Bro Pratt's greatest hymn. Put all the verses between the staves
21	Think Not When you		x	seldom, if ever, sung; "gathering" message not current or appropriate
22	Come Unto Jesus	X		We ought to change the notated rhythm to the way we all sing it
23	Come Ye Children of	x		We suggest some minor minor musical revisions
24	Behold thy Sons and	x		A very good hymn that deserves to be used more than it is.
25	Come We that Love	x		See recommended text revision for verse 2
26	Dear to the Heart	x*		Often prolonged when sung, but the Saints like to sing it; Lost sheep story useful
27	Do what is Right	x		Some minor musical revisions suggested
28	The Lord be With us	x		A good closing hymn that would be used if it were properly labeled
29	Come Ye Thankful	x		Dignified and robust; we would like to add a third verse if possible
30	Earth with Her ten	x		Beautiful Hymn; some minor text revision might be considered

First page of 1977 chart assessing hymns in the then-current hymnbook.

to Bradshaw, only one apostle made requests: Elder Thomas S. Monson, who asked that they include the German hymn "Sehet, ihr Völker" and the evangelical favorite, "How Great Thou Art." Church music committees had been resisting the latter song for years. And when it eventually made it into the hymnbook, Bradshaw said, "I can't even bring myself to sing [it]." The German hymn was, he felt, "a very good hymn" that he wanted to include. "I was hoping [Monson] would settle for 50%."[12]

Another year passed and they still had not completed a first draft. New questions surfaced at every meeting. There had always been ad hoc extraneous inquiries to contend with—such as this one: "Deseret Book sent a method for playing hymns on the harmonica to find out how it would fit into our plans and programs. Brother [Michael] Moody will reply, saying that although it may have value as a social instrument, we would not want to include it as a part of our program at the present time."[13] At the same time, dozens of ad

12. Merrill Bradshaw, Interview with Michael Hicks, Aug. 11, 1986.
13. Church Music Executive Committee, Minutes, May 14, 1974.

hoc questions from the general church membership arrived—some oddly offbeat, including one that proposed deleting all hymns by composer George Careless, a Mormon master of the nineteenth century. But as the self-imposed deadline approached, more and more weighty in-house questions set in. Consider just a few.

Questions of internationality, for instance. Who was going to translate the hymns for other countries? Could core hymns have the same numbers in all international printings, whose content would otherwise be varied? Publication issues also kept cropping up. Who would handle copyrights and how? Royalties? What about proofing and editing? Typeface and fonts? Thickness of the paper? Color of the cover? Were such questions supposed to be addressed by this committee? If not, by whom?

What about the keys of hymns? Some, old and new, needed lowering for congregations to sing them, as we saw, especially if congregations would sing the melodies in unison (rather than parts, common among Mormons for decades). But that would necessitate a drop in the "brightness" of a hymn. This process of, in effect, "remastering" the hymns would become enormous, involving recommending, debating, and voting on key changes for every hymn in the book.

Much discussion over the months grew from this question: Should hymns be sung in first person singular or plural—or even second—person? "We" was fine for general principles of the gospel, they decided, but "I" for "testimony-type ideas." Meanwhile, changing "You can make the pathway bright" to "I can make the pathway bright"? That "indicates smugness."

Should the committee field-test new hymns to see if Mormons liked and would sing them? If so, how? Some committee members questioned the "validity" of the results, presumably on aesthetic grounds. The best approach, they came to feel, was to invite small groups of people to sing the new hymns for the committee. These people would come from varied backgrounds, musical and otherwise. They would sing hymns with no names of composers or lyricists attached to the hymns. They would then rank them.

Finally, question of authority, access, and logistics for the committee's findings kept arising. Even when a draft seemed ready to present to the brethren, how would they do that—cassettes? And how would they introduce this new hymnbook to the church at large, especially since it would appear first only in English and international versions would vary?[14]

The slow pace also stemmed from knots in the administrative process. These led the committee in September 1976 to make a new list: six categories of questions about authority and protocol, not to be directly posed, but to consider in all deliberations:

1. What kind of direct communication should exist between this committee and Stone, managing director of the Church Music Department? Does Stone understand our rationale and all of our activities?
2. On a specialized project such as the hymnbook, should the "expert," who has been selected because of his expertise with hymns and music, be allowed to sit and communicate with those higher up in the administration?
3. Exactly what authority does this committee have in relation to decisions made on the new hymnbook? What responsibility?
4. What is the role of this committee in the new hymnbook project? Will the committee be able to defend their work and rationale to those in decision-making positions?
5. What is the role of this committee in relation to Correlation and the new hymnbook? Deseret Press and the new hymnbook? Editing Department and the new hymnbook?
6. Concerning our role with Correlation, how will they react to our suggested Protestant hymns being included in the new hymnbook?

Perhaps predictably, the Correlation Committee, flexing its administrative muscles, wanted to overturn the hymnbook committee's decisions. (Some general authorities also intervened. Elder Ezra Taft Benson, in particular, lobbied hard to get the patriotic songs back in.) In October 1976, the hymnbook committee learned that eleven hymns they had voted to delete were being put back in and three they voted to keep were being thrown out. The committee came up with three ways to respond to being overruled: "Acquiesce" (let the brethren's decision stand without argument),

14. These questions are raised in 1976 HTC Minutes of Aug. 21, Sept. 12, and Oct. 19; see also Michael Moody, Memorandum to A. Theodore Tuttle, Mar. 8. 1974.

"Fuss" (let the brethren know why the committee disagreed, but eventually acquiesce if a few changes could be made), and "Fight" ("strongly disagree with their decision, and be prepared to back up the disagreement with specific reasons and rationale"). Regarding the fourteen hymns on which they had been overruled, the committee voted to "acquiesce" on four, "fuss" on four, and "fight" on six. Here is the breakdown:

Correlation had reversed the committee's decision to delete "All Hail the Glorious Day," "Arise, O Glorious Zion," and "Cast Thy Burden Upon the Lord." One member of the Correlation Committee insisted they also keep the deleted hymn "Go, Ye Messengers of Glory," because the book needed missionary hymns. The committee acquiesced.

Correlation's reversals on these hymns, though, gained a "fuss" rating from the hymnbook committee (their comments in parentheses): "Come All Ye Sons of God" ("poor arrangement and 'gather-to-Zion' text outdated"); "Dear to the Heart of the Shepherd" ("good message, but so overly sentimental"); "For Our Devotions, Father" ("bad syllable breaks, rhythm; very weak hymn"); and "God of Our Fathers, Known of Old" (one of two settings, the other better, and "we need space in the hymnbook for new material").

Finally, the committee voted to "fight" over these ones: "Arise, My Soul Arise" (only one Correlation member supported it and "it is a bad hymn musically, and the text is not LDS"); "Before Thee, Lord, I Bow My Head" ("terrible text—bad word choice, bad word breaks" but "the Brethren put it back in"—"we will point out to [them] how difficult it is to work with"); "Come All Ye Sons of Zion" ("we *must* replace [this song] with something better, that does the same job"); and "Great God Attend, While Zion Sleeps" ("words just aren't LDS"). Additionally, the committee had voted to *keep* "Come Let Us Sing an Evening Hymn," "Father in Heaven," and "Break Forth, O Beauteous Heavenly Light" (a Bach setting of a Reformation favorite), but Correlation deleted all three. "Fight."[15]

15. HTC Minutes, Oct. 19, 1976.

As 1977 opened, the project hit its biggest obstacle. In February the First Presidency divided the all-church Melchizedek Priesthood Executive Committee into two smaller committees, one of which, headed by Elder Gordon B. Hinckley, had three subcommittees, one of which, headed by Elder Dean L. Larsen, would oversee church publications, including music. Upon his appointment to oversee the hymnbook, Hinckley immediately asked, according to Bradshaw, "Who authorized this?"[16] He directed Larsen to find out the status of the hymnbook project begun more than three years earlier. Within a week, Michael Moody, secretary of the Church Music Department and ex-officio member of the Hymnbook Task Committee, prepared a ten-point explanatory memo called "Why A New Hymnbook." In short, these were the points:

1. The church had spread internationally and some hymns, especially about "gathering" to Zion, did not work as they used to.
2. Many hymns had fallen out of favor or, indeed, had never caught on.
3. The church had increasingly "gained its own identity," which argued for discarding many old-line Protestant hymns.
4. Some hymn texts needed editing for doctrine and style.
5. The church needed more hymns on "new areas of emphasis" (e.g., the family).
6. Some keys needed to be lowered to encourage congregational singing.
7. The ordering of hymns in the old book was "haphazard."
8. A new English hymnbook would help supply new hymns for hymnbooks in other lands.
9. *New* hymns "will speak to members of the Church today, and will serve as a contribution from this generation, to be added to the legacy of hymns from the past."
10. "We need millennial hymns to prepare the Saints to welcome the Savior when he comes."

The committee also prepared a new, detailed breakdown of their first draft, explaining which old hymns they wanted to discard or revise and which new ones they wanted to include. By month's end, Larsen told Moody that the First Presidency and Council of the Twelve seemed ready to scrap the "major revision"

16. Bradshaw Interview.

the committee had prepared and "take an entirely different direction," probably consisting of "minor modifications" of the 1950 hymnbook. Moody told the committee members they should collate everything they had done and prepare to be released. "So, we submitted [our draft] and the committee was released. That was the response—at least that's the way it looked. We never really knew why we were released."

The wife of one of the advisors to the music committee said that the hymnbook team "had a really bad spirit." Bradshaw felt that impression arose from the committee's often "unguarded" comments, which, as we have seen, could be testy. Bradshaw characterized at least some of them more as "facetious." But he worried that serious deliberations about his church's hymnody might be "impossible for anyone to be anything but Pollyanna and survive."[17]

A year and a half later, the Twelve reauthorized the project and called the committee back together. For a few weeks they began meeting again as the "Reactivated Hymnbook Task Committee," re-reviewing their earlier drafts and answering a list of thirty-one questions posed to them about their plans. Herewith are some of Bradshaw's answers. Number of verses for each hymn? No more than four. Chord symbols with the hymns? No. "It encourages people to get by with less than adequate musical training in preparing themselves to serve the Kingdom musically." The color of the book? Several colors would be best, to allow wards and stakes to adapt to color schemes in their buildings. There were larger questions too, especially about what values should rule in the choices they made. Bradshaw was emphatic: "Every compromise with excellence will return to haunt us a thousand times." Within weeks they submitted essentially the same plans as they had before. They received no reply.

For the next five years the church's publication committee focused on new editions of LDS scriptures: the LDS Bible appeared in 1979 and a new triple combination in 1982. In 1983, ten years to the day from the original hymnbook assignment by President

17. Ibid.

Lee, the First Presidency told Moody to revive the project.[18] He was not to work with any of the previous committee's members, just the current members of the Church Music Department. He and they held closely to the previous committee's principles and decisions about format and even repertoire, foregoing any new hymn submissions. But field-testing hymns became the dominant decider. Singability and popularity trumped artistic or intellectual standards. Many of the hymns the earlier committee had cut were back. And the international breadth of this hymnbook fell far short of the ideals of the 1970s committee. Perhaps the most telling statement about the new criteria came from Elder Hugh Pinnock, this project's general authority advisor, who articulated the official attitude both committees had fought: the men and women who produced this hymnal, Pinnock said, had "only one disability: they knew too much about music."

"Bad spirit" or not, the previous committee had had an aestheticist tilt. The new directive for constructing a hymnbook was to make it a *revision* of the old one, not a *new* one. This revision would require professionals to cede more ground to popular tastes. The new committee, though, did use the previous committee's work as a template, if not a foundation on which to build this revision. The previous committee had taken almost four years to end up with its "final" collation. The new committee took about two and a half years to move from first meeting to the books arriving in the racks of Mormon pews. What they submitted was "virtually unchanged" from the earlier committee's draft, said Moody.[19] Still, he and his colleagues did decide not to be so "dramatic" in its choices to keep or remove hymns. The direction was that hymns be, according to Moody, "singable and memorable, and that the hymnbook was to be a hymnbook for all members of the church and not musicians." Their advisers told the committee to "put away our prejudices as musicians and sense the real preferences and needs of the membership of the church."

The push and pull of styles in the resulting book may be seen

18. The "ten years to the day" and some of the of the information in this paragraph comes from Moody Interview.

19. This and the quotes that follow it are from Moody Interview.

in two hymns, one new and the other old: "Because I Have Been Given Much" and "If You Could Hie to Kolob." The former, a tuneful modern anthem about charity, was popular but raised some eyebrows for its easy, quasi-pop style. Nevertheless, its charm was irresistible, it made the final cut, and became one of the most avidly sung pieces in the book. At the same time, "Kolob" was on the previous committee's scrap heap, both for its antiquated, esoteric text and its cloying, bouncy tune. But its doctrinal uniqueness and Mormon-specific cosmology made it hard to jettison. Moody said that substituting Ralph Vaughan-Williams's austere modal tune "Kingsfold" for Joseph Daynes's jaunty original as the setting for "Kolob" was one of his proudest achievements in the revised book.

When the new hymnbook was published in 1985—exactly 150 years after Emma Smith's original volume—Moody wrote a letter of thanks and consolation to Bradshaw. Moody said that he'd never been told why the earlier version had been scrapped but that the timing of this version was right: "There were too many factors that fell into place to have it otherwise." The earlier committee's work was "a necessary foundation and preparation for the eventuality." Bradshaw praised Moody's successful midwifing of the new hymnbook and wrote that, "knowing a little ... of the pressures, politics, and emotions that are involved in getting such a project finished, approved, and published, I consider the final product to be little short of a miracle."[20]

"Pressures, politics, and emotions"—not sufficient for the making of a new hymnbook, to be sure, but necessary. To dismantle a standard work and build a new one in its place disrupts a whole culture of worship. One then has to face some bedrock questions of human experience: what to salvage and what to throw away. Tracy Cannon, in explaining the decisions that shaped the 1948 hymnbook, wrote that to be criticized for their decisions "goes without saying." "It is a long way, I fear, from the dignity of [the great English hymns] to the triviality of some of the music we sing. ... and it may be that our people will never, as a whole, find the same appeal in them that we musicians do." So their task in

20. Michael Moody, Letter to Merrill Bradshaw, Dec. 31, 1985; Merrill Bradshaw, Letter to Michael Moody, Jan. 8, 1986.

unmaking the 1927 hymnbook to make the 1948 hymnbook was to "step forward, without being altogether too drastic." Because "we cannot make transitions to a higher plane of expression very fast in a democratic body of people."[21] But even a slow transition to that higher plane is worth its share of acquiescing, fussing, and even a little fighting.

21. Tracy Y. Cannon, Letter to G. W. Richards, Oct. 19, 1945, in Church Music General Files, CHL.

III

8 ELDER PRICE SUPERSTAR

I'll never forget the first time I heard my mother swear. I was in my thirties and had finally decided to talk to her about her second husband, whom she'd married when I was eleven, divorced two years later, and about whom we never spoke. One day, I said to her, "So tell me what was going on in that marriage." She bit her lip, paused, then said, "It was really shitty." And that was it. This woman from whose mouth I'd never heard a "hell" or a "damn," a woman who read her *Daily Light* devotional every morning, listened all day to Christian radio, and kept a pocket-size New Testament in her glove compartment, had now, deliberately and with great care, spoken a word I could never imagine escaping her lips. It was one of the great initiations in my life: with one word I suddenly understood how deeply something must have hurt her. And the tumblers of her life turned for me. Why? Because what she said was exactly the right wrong word.

The Book of Mormon, the musical, is a very public, late-breaking initiation for the LDS Church whose ranks I'd joined a dozen years before that experience with Mom. And, like that experience, the swearing in *The Book of Mormon* is what starts the illumination. Because if we know nothing else as Mormons, it's that we live and die by language—the right kind, the wrong kind, God's or the devil's, truth or falsehood, praise or sacrilege, the sacred and the profane. Yet if we know nothing else as adult humans (thanks, Mom), it's that sometimes one can only truly understand our species—animal and divine—when one kind of language bleeds into another.

And so here is this noisy, heartfelt, touching, gawdy, and weirdly illuminating patchwork of tenderness and blasphemy that dares to go by the name of that most Mormon book, The Book of Mormon. This musical is to Mormonism what Bernstein's *Mass* was to Catholicism, a wildly exploitative trope on the faith's core liturgy—though, in this case, without the brilliance of Bernstein. He, after all, knew not only the classical repertoire intimately (think of the *Young People's Concerts* or the *Omnibus* series on TV), but Broadway (think of *On the Town* and, of course, *West Side Story*). The makers of *The Book of Mormon* weren't raised on Broadway and don't even pretend to understand it. But they understand perfectly the trans-generic pop into which Broadway has been mutating for decades. They were raised on the music of breakfast commercials, *Nick at Nite* theme songs, Top Forty radio, and, of course, the second wave of Disney animated movie musicals, from *The Little Mermaid* to *Beauty and the Beast* to *Aladdin* to (especially) *The Lion King*, which *The Book of Mormon* explicitly and implicitly cites and paraphrases. It's those Disney cartoon songfests that not only resurrected Disney's fortunes but helped keep Broadway in the black—the Broadway that keeps reverse-engineering Disney-esque formulas into ticket sales.

More to the point, the makers of *The Book of Mormon* understand Mormon pop culture. If their show's songs sound painfully piecemeal and derivative, that's what perfectly attunes them to Mormon commercial music: road shows, pageants, Primary songs, *Saturday's Warrior*, Stadium of Fire, Young Ambassadors, Pearl Award-winning albums, etc. What *The Book of Mormon* may lack in Broadway tradition it more than makes up for in Mormon resonance: even without the words, the show would feel like a Mormon musical.

But there are words. That's what will vex Mormon viewers the most. If the music is leftover casserole, the lyrics range in flavor from cotton candy to excrement—a hyper-sweet-and-hyper-sour confection spooned up for almost two hours. Latter-day Saints will love the sweet and hate the sour, of course. But if they're anything like the Mormons checkerboarded on the new Times Square "I'm a Mormon" billboard, they will differ on which is which and why.

The show's plot forms a convenient scaffold for the songs: two mismatched missionaries—one a lithe seminary honor student pre-anointed for success, the other a chunky sci-fi fan trying to please his father—are paired and sent to the blood fields of

Uganda. These two, Elder Price and Elder Cunningham, face, on the one hand, a district full of hapless (and baptism-less) elders and, on the other, a village full of foul-mouthed, myth-addicted natives, who are trapped in the cyclic fear of warlords and AIDS. In time, a daunted Elder Price leaves for a dream mission in Orlando (more Disney) and Elder Cunningham (a.k.a. Arnold) takes over, inventing doctrine to meet the villagers' needs but refute their traditions. A penitent Elder Price eventually returns to help, a tide of baptisms ensues, and the villagers create their own Arnold-based Mormon history pageant to perform in front of the mission president. Mortified, the president chastises the elders and releases them for disgracing the church. But the elders refuse to go home: the Lord has called them to Africa, they say, they're helping people, and they've resolved that doing good—doctrine be damned—is the better part of Latter-day Sainthood. And, oh yes, Elder Price recognizes that Elder Cunningham is the real spiritual stud.

The opening songs are the easiest to swallow. "Hello!"—which reimagines *Bye Bye Birdie*'s "Telephone Hour" via the *Brady Bunch* theme—could reasonably be piped into Times Square as the soundtrack for the Mormon billboard. (Its young Mormon, EFY-style diction reaches its apex in the line "Eternal life is super fun.") Next, "Two By Two" parades the (apparently all-male) Mormon missionary "army" through a seeming tribute to TV game show themes and the title song to *Car 54, Where Are You?* With well-conceived poetic license, the missionaries receive all their assignments (companionships and destinations) as a group at the missionary training center—one of the breaches of fact that have been jeered by faith-defenders who attack the show's "inaccuracy," as if imagination were a sin in the art of fiction.

The third and sixth songs sketch the character of the main companions. "You and Me (But Mostly Me)," sung by Elder Price, satirizes his radical self-esteem and, by extension, Mormon narcissism en masse, that dark sidebar of quasi-Greatest Generation sermonizing in the 1970s–80s ("God has held you youth in reserve till this time in history") as well as the standard Primary song, "I Am a Child of God" (whose verses and chorus use the words "I," "me," and "my" fifteen times—but never the words "you" or "your"). "I Am Here for You" is Elder Cunningham's response, a plea for emotional intimacy with the Quixote to whom he's been consigned to play Sancho Panza.

As Joseph Campbell was fond of reminding us, every initiation to a higher consciousness must include an ordeal that takes us through the underworld. For the elders in *The Book of Mormon*—and certainly for Mormon viewers—the show provides what I'd call *ordeal overkill*: a trilogy of mini-descents strategically placed throughout the musical. The first comes soon after Elders Price and Cunningham arrive and the villagers dance and chant their infectious song "Hasa Diga Eebowai," a phrase whose meaning—the ultimate epithet toward God—conveys their default response to current updates of biblical motifs: plagues (now summarized in AIDS), miraculous healing (with the rape of babies as some Ugandans' imagined cure), and circumcision (now of females, not as covenant but as victimization). What jangles in listeners' ears most, though, may not be the singers "cursing God" through profanity, but the musical setting: a mix of jubilant Disney-ethnic styles, equal parts "Under the Sea" (from *Little Mermaid*) and "I Just Can't Wait to Be King" (from *Lion King*).

The elders meet their district of fellow missionaries, who launch into the show's vaudevillian comic gem. "Turn It Off" typifies the comedic style that is one of the Judeo-Christian (But Mostly Judeo) tradition's great gifts to the world: it doesn't mock, it just elbows. In this song Elder McKinley explains a "nifty little Mormon trick": "When you start to get confused because of thoughts in your head, don't feel those feelings! Hold them in instead." Some of the other elders give sad (though cheerily delivered) soliloquies about family abuse and personal neglect to which the rest give the antidote for feeling less than gleeful: "Turn it off!" (or as BYU religion professor Reed Benson used to put it, "Snuff it out!"). When Elder McKinley confesses to fleeting gay fantasies, misunderstandings start to fly as the music (and lighting and choreography) channel-surf their way into a mugging Bugs Bunny-ish promenade (as in "Overture, curtain, lights ..."), which melts into a chorus-line of elders in red-sequined vests. It's the sort of scene that invites laughter then compels it, as tear-jerking tragedy hardens into the steely resolve of nineteen-year old missionaries—then cracks.

Soon the preaching begins. "All-American Prophet" fuses *Music-Man*-meets-*Elmer-Gantry* stump preaching and infomercial pitch-man schtick—a cheery confession that the American industries of proselyting and advertising form a single conglomerate. As Elder Price spins his tale of Mormon origins, his cultural myopia constricts both to the recent past ("Let me take you back to biblical times: 1823"), Malibu looks (Joseph is "the blonde-haired, blue-eyed voice of God"), and homeland geography ("He didn't come from the Middle East like those other holy men. No, God's favorite prophet was All-American!"). Meanwhile, in an upstage backlit tableau, Joseph Smith (who has, we're told, "a little Donny Osmond flair") receives the plates from Moroni on the condition he not show them to anyone, despite the doubt that will create. Moroni explains, "This is sort of what God is going for." (Such was the explanation when I as a non-Mormon in 1973 first asked friends about the plates' whereabouts: if we had the plates, they said, you wouldn't need faith.) When Joseph dies in another tableau near the song's end, he laments he couldn't show the plates to prove he was telling the truth—till the light dawns in him and he says to God, "I guess that's kinda what you were going for."

As in the Garden of Eden, it is not until a female voice enters the world of testosterone that something truly interesting happens. Here, it arrives in the first (and only) solo sung by a woman, the young villager named Nabulungi (the role for which Nikki James rightly won a Tony Award). In "Sal Tlay Ka Siti" (i.e., "Salt Lake City") she fantasizes about how life would be in the promised land of "Ooh-tah," a place where "the warlords are friendly" and "flies don't bite your eyeballs," a heaven she can have "if I only follow that white boy." The most relentlessly serious song in the entire show, "Sal Tlay Ka Siti" draws the audience into a vision of plenty that most theatre-goers long since have taken for granted: "a Red Cross on every corner with all the flour you can eat," "vitamin injections by the case," and "people [who] are open-minded and don't care who you've been." Still, she sings, "all I hope is that when I find it, I'm able to fit in." It's a stock pop ballad, yes. But if there were a machine that manufactured compassion, this is what it would sound like. And you'll understand why I choke up every time I hear the final lines: "I'm on way—soon life won't be so shitty. Now salvation has a name: Sal Tlay Ka Siti."

When it comes time for Elder Arnold Cunningham to take up the mantle of the runaway Elder Price, he updates the catch-phrase "What would Jesus do?" into "What *did* Jesus do?" then answers with a cliché from the 2010 campaign: Jesus "manned up." Arnold's solo "Man Up" offers a hard rock soliloquy (with hints of the *Greatest American Hero* TV theme) in which he gins up his courage with muttering that ranges from gender stereotypes (Jesus didn't "scream like a girl") to bodily fluid jokes ("I'm gonna man up all over myself"). Along the way, he metamorphoses from a kind of dancing teddy bear to a Motown exec wearing shades—but one who can improvise bizarre doctrine to solve tribal problems (leading to the stuttering chorus "You're making things up again, Arnold!")

And then, the second descent into the underworld. It happens when the now-confessional Elder Price goes through a "Spooky Mormon Hell Dream," whose minor-key distorted guitar lines and growling background chorus present a Black Sabbath-style parody of the (creepy) doctrine of James the Apostle: "For whosoever shall keep the whole law, and yet offend in one point, he is guilty of all." A quasi-Homeric catalogue of wicked characters appears, announcing themselves and reviewing their crimes to the next condemned man, Elder Price. Hitler: "I started a war, and killed millions of Jews!" Genghis Khan: "I slaughtered the Chinese!" Jeffrey Dahmer: "I stabbed a guy and [bleeped] his corpse!" In his self-flagellatory state, Elder Price answers: "You think that's bad? I broke rule 72!" The grandly produced spectacle ends with one more nod to *A Chorus Line*, the perfect Broadway source for a parade in the Plutonian realm.

"Spooky Mormon Hell Dream" provides the underworld from which a transformed Elder Price climbs back, resurrected into heroic stature (and voice). His solo "I Believe" is the unquestioned showstopper, a pseudo-Articles of Faith in which "line upon line" Elder Price lays out a credo of blasé truisms ("I believe that God has a plan for all of us") answered by jarring untenabilities, which culminate in "I believe that the Garden of Eden was in Jackson County, Missouri," the ultimate "all-American" revisionism that Joseph Smith espoused. Price's personal branding of the Mormon message is now clear: sense be damned, belief has power. He moves from the scrapyard of his theology to pillaresque affirmation, telling a gun-belted warlord (before he dances with him): "I believe that Satan has a hold on you. I believe that the Lord God has sent me here. And I believe that in 1978 God changed his mind about black people." This is one of the more glorious moments in recent theater: howling at absurdity as the lightbulb of epiphany flicks on. Elder Price's mantra becomes: "a Mormon just believes" ("dang it!"). And our Thirteenth Article of Faith confirms it: "We believe all things," it says, with no exceptions offered.

Still, it's not so much the content as the assertion. One thinks of Norfolk's question to Thomas More in *Man for All Seasons*: "You'll forfeit all you've got … for a theory?" To which More replies: "Why, it's a theory, yes. … But what matters to me is not whether it's true or not but that I believe it to be true, or rather, not that I *believe* it, but that *I* believe it." For More, as for Elder Price, narcissism matures into faith. As if to validate that transformation in "I Believe," each chorus begins by setting the words "I am a Mormon" to the five notes of the opening fanfare for the Hill Cumorah Pageant, the annual commemoration of Joseph excavating the plates.

His "new song" works. Villagers want to be baptized, including Nabulungi, with whom Elder Cunningham performs an innuendo-filled soul duet in the tradition of Marvin Gaye and Tammi Terrell, Peaches and Herb, and the Lionel Richie and Diana Ross of "Endless Love." If the music is unmemorable, the concept works, nicely showing off the patina of eros that sometimes sticks to ordinances chaste men perform on chaste women. The song, which trumps the "boys club" feel of the mission home, may seem crude in its pseudo-sexual teasing. But it reminds us that spiritual transactions carried out bodily between genders often feel like flirtation. (One may discern the physical-spiritual nexus in the phrase "the laying on of hands for the gift of the Holy Ghost." And, let's face it, the term "missionary position" had to come from somewhere.)

A flood of baptisms leads to the pseudo-national anthem "I Am Africa"—the "We Are the World" of the show. The elders surrender to their success and one-by-one declare not that "I am a Mormon" (as earlier) or "I am a Latter-day Saint" (which comes later), but simply "I am Africa," each missionary self-identifying with that continent's weather, landscape, people, and animals (including "the noble Lion King"). Though one of the most heartfelt songs in the show, it gets plenty of laughs. The scene suggests that atonement for decades of Mormon race discrimination might be recompensed by adolescent bravado. The missionaries' spiritual imperialism jars with Nabulungi's yearning—she wonders how she'll fit in, while they simply gobble up the terrain ("Africans are African, but we are Africa"—with the latter two syllables separated from the "A" to make it sound like a cognate of "frickin'"). The Book of Mormon (the book) contains a subplot in which white people turn dark and vice versa; *The Book of Mormon* has the same subplot, now transposed to East Africa. It's even more awkward now than in 1830.

The skyrocketing baptismal stats lead to the final ordeal—for the audience more than any of the characters: "Joseph Smith, American Moses," a Mormon history pageant that torques itself into a quasi-reprise of "Hasa Diga Eebowai" tangled with "Making Things Up Again." Performed for the mission president by the villagers, the cute tribal beatitude in music, dance, and costume almost instantly twists into a messy disgorgement of the villagers' magic world view, now boxed and tied up with Arnold's well-meant lies. We (and the president) are forced to undergo surreal clashes of imagery, most of them gynecological or gastrointestinal (though all in one-syllable words). God stops Joseph Smith from raping a baby and gives him a frog as a substitute; God curses Brigham Young by turning his nose into a clitoris; a plague of dysentery fells Joseph (as if the chanted scatology of its description would not have done it more quickly); etc. The viewer can't "turn it off," must endure it to the bittersweet end. It is a catharsis that is to *The Book of Mormon* what the meltdown of the celebrant is to Bernstein's *Mass*—a soliloquy whose refrain is "How easily things get broken." Here, though, the language continually dances with obscenity. The effect on the audience is almost chiropractic.

So what, in the end, amid their seeming contempt, do the villagers prize in the hopelessly vulgarized Book of Mormon? Hope. The book is a doorstop against warlords and a doorway to a promised land where all their day-to-day pain will be soothed. Isn't that enough?

And that becomes the real Mormon message in the show. All creeds collapse into personal feelings. But Jesus was a behaviorist. I like to think of Jimmy in David Mamet's production of *The Untouchables*. Whenever a need arises, top G-man Elliott Ness quotes the law-enforcement handbook. To which Jimmy always asks, "But what are you prepared to *do*?" That's what lovers (and haters) of religiosity have to keep asking themselves, not just "What would Jesus do?" but "What are you prepared to do?" And not even "What did Jesus do?" as Elder Cunningham asked, but "What have you done?" I think of another cinematic scene, this one from *One Flew Over the Cuckoo's Nest*. In this scene Randall McMurphy bets his fellow psych-ward patients/inmates that he can pull the marble bathroom fixture off the floor, throw it through the window, and free them all. They laugh and jeer him on. He grabs the fixture's sides, pulls and pulls until, out of breath, his face flushed like a beet, he gives up. As they mock him, he glares at them and says, "But I tried, didn't I? ... At least I did that."

The makers of this musical celebrate Mormons because, dang it, at least they try—and indeed try to do something that, as Elder Price says at the outset, will "blow God's freakin' mind." To do that, one has to move—as the musical's finale does—from "I am a Mormon" or "I am Africa" to "I am a Latter-day Saint," with "latter-day" not meaning "pre-apocalyptic" but "the day after this one." "The only latter-day that matters is tomorrow," the finale exhorts. Pray and work for that day, it says, that "full of joy and all-the-things-that-matter day." It's the gospel ("good news") restored indeed. The implicit message is: (1) the Old Testament is now, (2) the New Testament is tomorrow, and (3) The Book of Mormon—the show or, especially, its namesake—should be a hinge from one to the other. "We are still Latter-day Saints, all of us," Elder Price explains (after the elders have refused to go home in disgrace), "even if we change some things, or we break the rules, or we have complete doubt that God exists. We can still all work together and make this our paradise planet." Or, to put it as Joseph Smith so memorably did: "If we go to hell, we will turn the devils out of doors and make a heaven out of it."

As on most construction sites, language can be initiatory. But as I learned from my mom, profanity sometimes cuts a path to a truth you couldn't arrive at without it. She taught me—involuntarily, I'm sure—that sometimes cursing is the most honest speech, even though the ordeal of it can be severe. Questions arise, like a stinking Lazarus from the tomb. Can one be that honest? Can profanity be sanctified by the imagination if it's to help people to a higher consciousness? Is there an audible line between the primal and the celestial? And there are the more practical questions: What is the relevance of fastidious truth-telling that doesn't save good people? (Think of Oskar Schindler.) And what is the value of propriety if it is its own reward? (Think of Jesus.)

I think that most Latter-day Saints, especially the ones on the billboard, are learning that truth (big "T" or little "t") is more than accuracy and niceness. It is, rather, what this musical so ferociously asserts about its alleged targets: "They tried, didn't they? At least they did that." Some Mormons feel stung by the show. But *The Book of Mormon* scolds no one so much as those who dismiss Mormon zeal. So I savor this public ordeal-fest, however gritty it feels on the tongue. Because, I believe, this is sort of what God is going for.

9 SPENCER KIMBALL'S RECORD COLLECTION

I should keep a journal. If I did I could look up what year this happened. Or exactly why I had driven to Ed's house and knocked on his door. Or what time it was when he phoned me up weeks later to make his offer. But it all happened. I've got the proof on my shelves. Well, some of it, anyway.

Ed Kimball lived up in the foothills behind the Provo temple, a few blocks north of what they call "Indian Hills," with names of Native American tribes on block after block of street signs. Fitting, I thought, as I headed up the shaded gravel driveway of this son of the twelfth president of the Church of Jesus Christ of Latter-day Saints. If William J. Clinton was our country's first black president, as we used to say, Spencer W. Kimball was our church's first Indian president. An Arizona desert-raised son of a missionary to over twenty nations of Native Americans—"Lamanites," in Mormon parlance—Kimball had focused his vision on these indigenous peoples more than any Mormon apostle before or since. As president of the church, he'd move thousands of Native Americans off the reservations for schooling, deepen the bank accounts that funded Lamanite scholarships at BYU, and generally jack up the top-level rhetoric about white Mormons' duty to those with browner skin.

Ed, Spencer's third son, had co-written with his nephew the whizbang biography of Spencer that knocked us flat in 1977 for its candid, full-blooded look at a sitting church president's life to that point. Is this how biographies would be written in the church now? We wondered. (The answer was … sort of, sometimes, maybe.) When I went to Ed's house, I asked him questions about his dad and music and specifically if there was anything in Spencer's diaries about Jay Welch's firing from the Tabernacle Choir.

He graciously looked up some dates for me. Not much there. When I asked about the couple hundred LPs on the shelf near where we sat, Ed told me that, yes, those were his dad's. Could I look through them? I asked. Sure, he said. Did he want to sell any of them? No, but if I wanted any of them, I could have them.

Now, I'd been collecting records since I was nine. By this point in my life, records seemed to wash up on my shore from the strangest places. But this was the unlikeliest: the record collection of one of my heroes, samples free for the taking. Still, the historian in me—along with a dime's worth of tact—made me focus on the content of the collection, what it might reveal about its owner, and be sparing about what I grabbed up.

Many of the records were gifts to Spencer. The usual, expected "official" gifts, of course: records by the Tabernacle Choir, the Mormon Youth Symphony and Chorus, M.I.A. conference choirs, temple pageant casts, and so forth. Most of these LPs were still sealed and had a note on them gifting them to President Kimball. There were also gifts from ad hoc Mormon choirs I'd not heard of: The Mormon Expo Choir, the Detroit Mormon Concert Choir, the Indianapolis 4th Ward Choir, etc.

But many other gift records came from Native American soloists and groups, inscribed by their makers with love and thanks and all else one might expect from citizens of a Mormon nation of tribes that lionized Kimball. These I gingerly started to pull off the shelf to take home, though I had impure motives. I'd sold some limited-pressing Native American records on eBay, including one I saw here in better condition, and thought I might put some (read: all) of these up for auction, too.

I saw a few international records—Mexican mariachi bands, Russian Orthodox church music, Greek dance records, British organ recitals. There was classical, mostly "Best of"-type collections, *25 Most Beloved Melodies*, and the 1941 *Music Lovers Chest of Records* set. There was even some pop, ranging from Jim Reeves to ELO to Gene Cotton to Simon and Garfunkel to Bob Dylan. In all fairness, Ed assured me, some of these probably got stuck on the shelves by grandchildren.

I asked him about his dad's listening habits. While working

at his desk at home, Ed said, Spencer liked to listen to Hawaiian music. Before becoming president of the church at the end of 1973, Spencer "went to the symphony with some regularity." But after he took the church's top post, that stopped. Too busy. What was the main thing that governed Spencer's record-buying habits? "He was thrifty," Ed said. That was why two-thirds to three-fourths of the records in his collection were gifts.

Besides the Lamanite records, I took one or two others and headed out to the car. I shouted thanks to Ed from my window as I drove away.

I did sell that one record I'd sold before on eBay. Most of the others I crammed into the "LDS" corner of my collection, a fat row of LPs between a three-high shelf and a two-drawer file cabinet.

A few weeks later the phone rang, and it was Ed. "How would you feel about just taking all of Dad's records?" he asked.

"Hmm." I said. My heart raced in two directions: I loved the thought of getting this collection, but didn't love the thought of having it. Because (a) I wasn't an archive or storage facility, (b) there wasn't much of musical interest in these discs, and (c) I didn't know the provenance of some of the more interesting records. My greed and savvy both kicked into gear.

"I'd take them on the condition that you understand most of them will end up at the D.I.," I said. ("The D.I." is how Mormons refer to Deseret Industries, the Mormon equivalent of Goodwill or the Salvation Army.) I explained my reasons for wanting to get them but not keep many, how I'd sort them, and such.

"That's okay," he said. He could use the room. And they weren't being used. Like most people, he'd shifted to FM and CDs when he listened to music at all. So these footwide black vinyl discs were just trinkets of a life and relationship from which he had much more intimate and more usable trinkets already.

I drove to his house, parked my red '93 Taurus close to the front door, and knocked. He let me in, and we started looking for boxes to pack up the records. When we'd filled a few boxes, he said, "There're more records downstairs." We walked into his basement, and the first thing that caught my eye was the tall bookshelf of binders: all of Spencer Kimball's looseleaf diaries. I wanted nothing so much as to spend the rest of the day—the rest of the month—leafing through them and taking notes. But I was on a mission. And besides, though you wouldn't think this of me, I was bashful. "Those are his diaries, huh?" was all I said. "Yes," he said. And that was that.

He asked me if I wanted an old Dictaphone his dad had used, but I didn't. Too clunky. Then he showed me what turned out to be the treasure. Second-hand treasure, that is. Two boxes filled with 12-inch classical albums—78rpm albums, that is, sets of several discs each, bound into an actual hinged album to yield, say, a single symphony. "Those were my brother Spencer's," Ed said. "But when he moved back east to go to school they were too heavy and breakable to take with him. So he left them with Dad."

Now I thought I was getting somewhere. They were all classical and fit better with what I thought a prophet should be soaking up. "Did your dad listen to them?"

"Some of them. You can tell the ones he liked by looking inside the front cover. This one, for example, was one of his favorites." He handed me the 1950 five-disc Victor album of Pierre Monteux conducting the San Francisco Symphony in the Franck Symphony in D Minor—one of my favorite pieces when I was in high school. I opened the cover and saw the inscription on the left, written in black ballpoint:

Spencer L. Kimball
839 Simpson Ave
Salt Lake City

In red pencil someone had crossed out the street address and written a "W" over the "L." "That's how Dad showed which ones he was claiming for himself," Ed said. "He crossed out the address and wrote his middle initial over my brother's."

After flipping through all the albums in these boxes, I carried them and the other boxes out to the car, putting half in the trunk and half in the back seat. I thanked Ed again, then drove home. When I got there, my wife, Pam, was home and I told her all about what had just happened. Then I started to sort through the records.

Even before I'd picked up the discs at Ed's, I knew the three

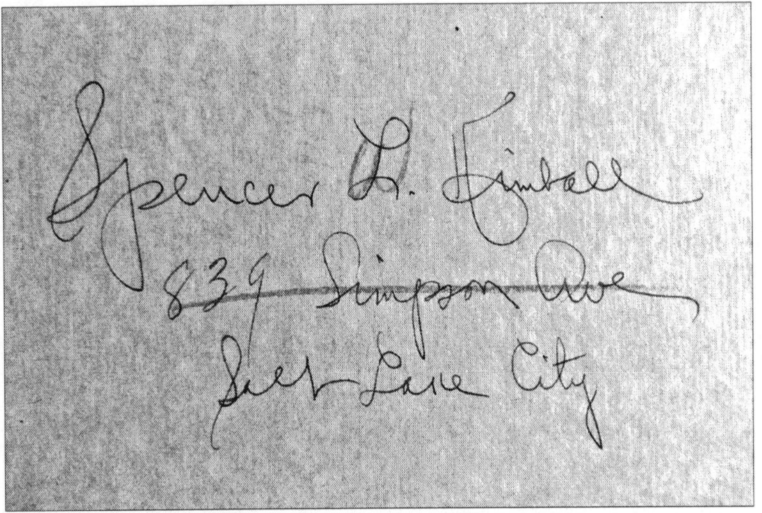

How Spencer W. Kimball adopted his namesake son's albums.

categories: records I wanted to keep, ones I wanted to give to the BYU library, and ones I was hauling to the D.I. I worked quickly and within a couple of hours I had the basic sorting done.

There were only a few of this new batch that I wanted to keep: a Mötley Crüe album (obviously a grandkid stray), Dylan's *Nashville Skyline*, a few more LDS artists and pageant soundtracks for my Mormon music corner, and, no surprise, the Franck. I picked out a batch of records I thought might make a nice mini-archive in BYU Special Collections: unusual records owned by a church president, which included the other re-initialed albums and a couple of one-off 7-inch field recordings of tribal singing, presumably given to him by a missionary or Lamanite admirer. All the rest: the D.I.

A few days after my donation, I was in the D.I.—I used to go at least once every day back then—and saw that these records had just come out and were in the racks. Two women with British accents were admiring one dark blue box set from the batch, the 1975 BYU centennial four-disc *Sounds of a Century* set of speeches. This set only rarely appeared at the D.I., and I knew from this one's condition and a couple of distinctive marks that it was indeed the one I'd brought from Kimball's shelf, the complimentary copy BYU had given him.

I had to say something. "I know this sounds weird and you'll probably think I'm making this up, but I know for a fact that that copy you're holding belonged to President Kimball."

Their eyes widened, and before they could say more than "Really?" I told them the whole story and how I knew this was his personal copy. They both said that this was a treasure they would love to take back to England. Cost? One dollar.

"If you want, I can write you a certificate of authenticity and sign it so you have something to back you up." One of the women found a grocery receipt in her purse and I wrote my ad hoc certificate on the other side of it. They thanked me over and over, and I thought maybe I should just stay around for awhile and tell people when they pick up a Kimball record. But the impulse quickly passed and I drove home.

As for the BYU records, I found out later that they didn't all stay together, as I'd hoped. The titles got processed like any other donations, duplicates probably got sold off or given away, including the initialed 78s. The Lamanite 7-inchers are in Special Collections, but you have to know their names to find them. And, truth be told, who knows if Pres. Kimball listened to them at all, let alone liked them? From some of his sermons, I'm pretty sure he thought Lamanite music was as savage as, well, the Book of Mormon Lamanites.

As for the ones I kept, understand the situation: all of my 7000+ records stand in eighty-some shelf cubicles, or perch on top of the shelves, or lean against walls, or sit in bins in an oblong room above our garage, a mini-warehouse that also holds stereo components, rock posters, art prints, books on cartooning and Persian rugs, my large Annette Funicello collection, hundreds of rare and bargain basement pop CDs, dozens of horror DVDs, and VHS tapes of B-movies and interviews with poets, cassette mix tapes I made for my wife's old aerobics class, binders full of movie stills and promo photos and postcards, file drawers stuffed with book contracts and folders of articles I'll probably never read again, piles of mailing supplies, and, stuck in spaces here and there, autographed pictures

The cover of one of Kimball's favorite classical albums.

of everyone from Joey Bishop to Anna Nicole Smith. Amid all that, the record collection—and my memory—has swallowed up the few Kimball records I stowed there.

There are just two things in plain view in this room that remind me of President Kimball. One is that Franck album, which sits at the front of a thick group of about eighty albums leaning crosswise on another long stretch of about two hundred sitting on top of a pressboard shelf. The cover is one of the real works of art in the room: a flag-draped rifle bayonet in front of a ghoulish hand reaching up from a pool of blood inside a flame tongue rising from a burnt-out cityscape. It's quite extraordinary: a semi-kitschy outtake from the Nazis' "Forbidden Art" hall of shame. It reminds me of that mongrel post-war era when both

The all-purpose box I cherish.

a cheery Apostle Kimball and post-Holocaust dread flourished side by side in this country.

The other, far gentler, mark of his presence is not a record at all. It's one of the boxes I carried his records home in. Ed and I had scrounged around in the basement till he asked me if this one would be okay: a large, lidded cardboard cube covered with color photographs of sky and clouds. A gift shop oddity from the 1970s, I'd say. A tourist-class disposable prop. It's breezy and chic. It's the flip side of the Franck.

I've used the box for years to haul toys from floor to floor or to stow books for Mormon research or, now, to hold up my cassette deck because the cord that runs from it to my Denon receiver isn't long enough for the deck to sit on the floor, where I'd prefer it to be. I'm looking at the box right now, a firm but hollow foundation for an outdated technology I still insist on using. Though partly cloudy, the box shines, beams from wherever it sits. And it has sat in every room in our house over the years since I got it from Ed's house. Where will it be in a month? I don't know. And that, I guess, is the continuing revelation of it, this portable, smiling souvenir of a prophet.

10 MAKING BOOK ON THE TABERNACLE CHOIR

I've written eight books, the best known of which is probably the one I wrote about the Mormon Tabernacle Choir. In some ways, what you are reading now recounts the making of that book. But my title is a fairly sophomoric word play: making a book is not the same as "making book." Making book is gambling. Placing a bet. Although, to be fair, making *a* book is also a bet. And usually a bad bet at that. You bet time, tears, money, even relationships, hoping that what you make with your brain and fingers will pay off in—something. Not clear what. Bragging rights? Small-time fame? Certainly not dollars-per-hour. The payoff is probably something like this: a satisfying piece of work, the "pleasure of the text," as Roland Barthes would call it. And maybe a few nerdy friends acquired by that pleasure.

Writing Mormon history is a special kind of gambling, though. With one eye on your fellowship and the other on the page, you wonder, how honest can I be? What reprisals might dog my disclosures or interpretations? If I work for the church, can I keep my day job? Not to mention, can I keep my Sunday school job?

• • •

How did I get into this gamble? Blame Andrés Segovia. I was a self-taught classical guitarist in high school. I played Bach and Sor and lots of Anonymouses, even wrote a few pieces, including "Modified Baroque Guitar Study no. 1" with my better guitarist friend, David Tamres. At the same time, I played folk guitar in my Pentecostal church group. I spent every evening with that group, strumming and smiling in the budding Jesus Freak tradition at our coffee house or in one of the halfway houses we ran for alcoholics. But after newspaper ads said that the classical guitar demigod Andrés Segovia was performing at De Anza College in Santa Clara, I sneaked out and went to the concert. I couldn't tell my fellow Jesus Freaks because I knew they would find this too worldly. Gospel music was the only true music, they felt, the only kind God listened to and endorsed.

Then I encountered Mormonism, its doctrine of eternal progress, its "Pursuit of Excellence" program for young adults, the musical sophistication of its Tabernacle Choir, and so much more that suited my artistic impulses and pursuits. I felt a kinship I'd lacked in my Pentecostal circles. I realized that evangelical Christianity was only a bus stop on the way to my new home. Mormonism was Christian, sure. But I'd had Christian. This was bigger. Eternal progress. Potential godhood of all humans. Truth from every source, all "gathered into one great whole." And a history that was more American than I was. Mormonism was to my Bible-thumping faith what Segovia was to my Jesus songs. I loved them both, but come on.

I joined the church, and after three years I was giving talks on the history of sacred music to small living room gatherings of Mormon adults. I learned the music of new Mormon heroes like Merrill Bradshaw, with whom I soon began to study at Brigham Young University. I joined the fledgling Mormon arts movement, subscribed to *Sunstone*, and drank up all the usual fare of the would-be Mormon intelligentsia. Then, attending graduate school in music composition at the University of Illinois, I began to study the music of Nauvoo in my off hours.

My studies broadened, and soon I had not only a stack of plump file folders on church music but had published a few articles about Mormon arts, aesthetics, and such—part of the portfolio that in 1985 got me hired as a music professor at my alma mater BYU.

Enter the person who triggered my career as an author of books: Judy McCulloh from, of all places, the University of Illinois Press. As a new faculty member at BYU, I was on the make, trying to get on whatever conference programs I could. I had made it onto one for the Sonneck Society (now Society for American Music) in Boulder, Colorado, and in February 1986 got an unsolicited letter from Judy asking to see a copy of my paper, "Brigham Young as a

Musical Entrepreneur." "As you surely know," she wrote, "Illinois is a leading publisher of Mormon studies—though to date we haven't had that much occasion to deal with Mormon music. I would like to read your article myself and then pass it along to our editor who handles the Mormon list."[1]

I fired back a reply, with previous articles of mine enclosed, "which suggest the sort of work I have been doing in Mormon music history. … I have thought from time to time that a book on Mormon musical life in the nineteenth century would be a useful contribution to both American music studies and Mormon studies. Since the U of I Press has capitalized on both those markets, I wonder if you might entertain a proposal for such a work."

She wrote back: "I'm delighted at your suggestion of writing a book on Mormon musical life in the nineteenth century. When can you send us a manuscript? As you point out, such a work would be of great interest for both our Mormon studies list and our Music in American Life series. … Why just the nineteenth century? Is there enough to be said to fill a whole book? Was there something in Mormon (musical) history that would make 1900 or thereabouts a natural break?" She recommended some readings and scholars to consult and awaited my submission.

I was happy but shaking in my boots. I had nothing on the twentieth century in this field or even on music in Utah and had no idea how much I could get. But I hastily improvised a list of chapters and descriptions of each, then sent it to her with the proposed title, "Mormon Music: A History." I forecast the audiences the book would have, assured her of its academic bona fides, and generally bragged my way into her good graces.

Within three months she sent me readers' responses. The usual mix of positive, snippy, encouraging, head-scratchy, and head-patting. Overall, I got the go ahead. Write the book.

I'd spent years making notes on early church music, spent the next eight months drifting in and out of libraries and union catalogs, lounging in bed with a yellow pad and a No. 2 pencil, stacking notecards and scrap paper around my office, and

1. This letter, as with all others cited herein, except as noted, are in my personal files.

sometimes just sitting in a slump with a glazed look letting the Rolodex of questions in my head flip in circles till it stopped at the right entry. I was a rank novice—no, I was worse than that. I was an untrained and untested bag of anxiety, brooding and jittery, trying to squeeze my way into the New Mormon History, while the church's Historical Department was slamming shut its file drawers in the wake of Mark Hofmann's forgeries, the Tanners' relentless Xeroxing of gee-whiz documents, and the stamping out of Leonard Arrington's in-house tribe of transcribers and historiographic utopians.

But I was writing about music, I thought: how bad could it be? Music, the church's stock in trade, with the Tabernacle Choir its most attractive window dressing for all of the century that had elapsed so far. I hunkered down in the Historical Department as much as I could, requested everything from trifles to bedrock, spooled through more microfilms than any human should suffer, and typed notes into a weird Brother portable word processor that spit ink letters onto the page and buzzed loudly every time you hit "return." But the department turned down my list of requests for office files, project files, minutes of meetings, and everything that could reveal how the church ran music in the twentieth century. So, I kept searching, finding the odd non-restricted collection of cartons full of half-sorted documents—memos, letters, handouts, and policy statements.

I constructed a little cathedral of prose in my best Jacques-Barzun-fueled academese. Along the way, my wife got to know the book's awkward bedside manner: I hunched up in bed for how many dozens of nights next to her with pages spread on the bed, lit by a weak nightstand lamp. You shouldn't have to earn sainthood that way, but fortunately she already had her degree in that. I was still working on mine.

On August 20, 1987, I had a full draft that I sent to … the Church Music Division. Any comments? I asked. I spent the next five months waiting for a reply. While you're waiting to hear back from your church/employer, you hear voices. They emanate from what any church is at heart: a guilt factory. The writer's handbook we used at BYU contained this epigraph by Sloan Wilson: "A writer's job is sticking his neck out."[2] I've written—and lived—by that thought for forty years. But when you're writing your employer's history—well, no one has a neck that long. So the accusing voices buzz through your mind.

On January 22, 1988, the reply came from Michael Moody, head of church music. He commended me for the "scope and depth" of a "thorough, authoritative, and well written" book with a "candid, informal style [that] creates interest where other writers lose their audience." He cited other readers to the same effect. Then the big breath-draw: "Although I think most of the manuscript is excellent and acceptable, I'm disappointed that, in an obvious attempt at objectivity, you have sometimes been critical, unfair, and even inaccurate about certain personalities and events. Because history is an art rather than a science, the point of view you choose to take colors the history. One reviewer felt that your negativism hurts the scholarly aspects of the work. 'It makes him look biased, not smarter.'" This did not bother Moody so much, he said, because "the work has a very limited audience." But any breaches or innuendo would be "perpetuated and magnified through the years." To adjust my vision, he enclosed a copy of Elder Boyd K. Packer's condescending talk to historians, "The Mantle Is Far, Far Greater Than the Intellect," which, of course, I, like other Mormon scholars, knew quite well. I didn't read it again.

Moody also enclosed the marked manuscript. One anonymous reader's annotation set the tone for many of the critiques: "I feel he is angry about something and wants to include every facet of Church music as he 'acts out' his feelings." I actually wasn't angry about anything, though I felt I might soon be coaxed in that direction.

One reader hated how the Introduction began:

> This may be a foolhardy book. The topic is at once vague, audacious, and terribly necessary.
>
> Vague because of the problem of isolating "Mormon music." If a book said it was to treat "Methodist music," one would probably assume that meant Methodist liturgical music—hymns—since that is the only music overtly peculiar to Methodists. Conversely, if a book

2. Quoted in John R. Trimble, *Writing with Style: Conversations on the Art of Writing* (Englewood Cliffs, New Jersey: Prentice–Hall, 1975), 25.

> professed to treat "Catholic music," one might justifiably be confused, since the Roman Catholic church has been the preserver and parent of a huge repertory of great music, much of which has sounded far outside the cathedral walls. While the field of "Methodist music" seems rather narrow, that of "Catholic music" is impossibly vast.

Another annotation: "Too superficial; (unnecessarily) raises a problem + then doesn't take it far enough." So, I cut those paragraphs, although I knew I'd really miss the first one for its shapeliness and verve.

Some reviewers also chided this statement: "Mormonism has grown from a disreputable adjunct to frontier revivalism to a small, self-contained nation in the Rocky Mountains and thence to a trans-cultural brotherhood of faith, authority, zealotry, and communion." One reader wrote: "Why grind this ax here?" I had no idea what the ax was. Later, I noted that "Mormons can make a big seller out of even the most trenchantly bitter speculations on themselves." A great line. Or so I thought. "More 'ax-grinding,'" the reader said: "keep the text objective + dispassionate." Again with the ax. I didn't even own one. Plus, I always spell axe with an "e."

Dozens of annotations littered the pages. I had quoted Brigham Young saying that some Latter-day Saints were dancing "like niggers." That had to go. Even the completely unrelated "niggardliness" got flagged. My use of the word "gentile" should be changed to "non-Mormon." Many other pleas for word-softening: change "chagrined" to "disappointed." Change "often inaccurate" to "sometimes inaccurate." "These chapters give special attention to administrative postures and policies toward music," I had written, "while not neglecting the frequently poignant clash of personalities among musicians and priesthood authorities." A reader crossed out "frequently poignant" and inserted the word "some" before "musicians." I also had written this sentence: "Students of Mormonism generally need to see how musical values strive with doctrine and how musicians struggle with priesthood." Moody changed the last three words to "serve under the priesthood," adding this annotation: "My experience is that this is a false generalization—only a strong-willed minority struggle."

Unfortunately, jokes flew right over some readers' heads. When I quoted Alexander Schreiner, longtime Tabernacle organist, describing over-sweet church music as an "all-day succor," one reader corrected it to "sucker." Schreiner was witty, yes, but this "correction" was hilarious.

As a kid scholar on the church's payroll, I agreed to follow most "suggestions." But with some I dug my heels in. Maybe the biggest was when my reviewers asked that I remove my reference to the First Presidency toasting singer Adelina Patti with champagne, as President Wilford Woodruff had recorded in his own journal. For my readers this was "misleading" and a blow to the church's reputation for abstinence from alcohol. But I felt a reader needed to know how important it was for the First Presidency to reach out to this famous singer on her own terms. Here was a case where I would not bend—and one that would foster later criticisms of the book's final draft.

More serious than those "image" issues were readers' challenges to my well-documented facts and doctrinal summaries—especially over the Adam-God doctrine. For example, I quoted the hymn "Sons of Michael, He Approaches," whose second line reads, "Rise, the Eternal Father greet." The doctrine behind that, of course, was Brigham Young's fairly consistent teaching that Adam was the *spiritual* as well as temporal father of all humankind. In my text I'd written that the archangel Michael "in Latter-day Saint theology was identified with both Adam and the Father in the Godhead." The church readers' critique of that statement was fairly stern: "tres tres misleading. Let the reader draw his own conclusion from the text. I choose to think of Adam as the Eternal Father of the human race, but not the Father in the Godhead." They flagged my statement and changed it to say merely that Michael "in Latter-day Saint theology is identified as Adam." But stacks of sermons from Brigham Young say what I'd said.

Then I used the "Sons of Michael" text again, commenting that "There was theological retrenchment as well: the church having rejected Brigham Young's old theory that Adam (i.e., Michael the archangel) was in fact God the Father, the venerable hymn text was changed"—"Rise, the Eternal Father greet" became "Rise, the

Ancient Father greet" in the 1927 hymnbook. My readers rewrote my statement thus: "There was theological clarification as well: misinterpretation of Brigham Young's statement that Adam (i.e., Michael the archangel) was 'our Father and our God' caused a change in the venerable hymn." They added a marginal note that reflected the anti-historicism of latter-day orthodoxy: "B. Young was misinterpreted. He never meant that Adam was God the Father Eloheim [sic]." Which, of course, is correct: God the Father was Michael, not Elohim. Needless to say, I declined to shade the past to soothe uninformed readers. I left my sentences intact.

The biggest complaint, though, was that I had used documents dated after 1969. Which I did. I used open collections from the 1970s that—Moody later realized—had been left open without his approval. So, he said, I must remove everything in my book that relied on these sources, as well as minutes given to me by the chairman of a committee from the 1970s. The problem with his request was: I'm an American. I think things should be open. And the 1970s represented exactly the Watergate era that buttressed my ideas about disclosure. While I never purloined anything, I could not unsee (or untranscribe) documents the Historical Department had handed me. Especially the ones that told vivid stories or yielded perfect quotes.

At the end of my manuscript, an anonymous writer handwrote this apt distillation: "This is an amazing, excellent piece of research, clearly biased toward a view of history that focuses on confrontation and controversy. As such, it is not a history of Mormon music, but of certain sociological aspects of music in the Mormon culture." That comment made me change the title. I kept the subtitle but changed the front end to "Mormonism and Music." Because the reader was right. The book was about Mormonism via music. Not music via Mormonism.

Five days after I got Moody's letter and the marked-up, Post-it noted manuscript, I wrote back. I copy here the latter half of my reply, because it is a mini-manifesto of my Mormon scholarship then and now:

> Last week in our high priests group we were studying the material in lesson six of the Melchizedek Priesthood Personal Study Guide.

> On one page the manual rhetorically asks, "Is telling only part of the truth bearing false witness?"
>
> Everyone except myself answered yes. I explained that we often conceal our true feelings or judgments for the sake of others' feelings. And Elder Packer's statement, which you have often cited to me, came to mind: "That which is true is not always expedient." I really believe this. And I hope you realize that I frequently restrained myself in the book from telling stories that would be true, and many readers would find interesting, but served no good purpose to tell.
>
> But the priesthood manual suggests a necessary complement to Elder Packer's maxim: that which is expedient is not always true. There are several events and statements—chronicled and preserved in open files—that you would like me to conceal in the book for the sake of expediency, but that clearly would mislead my readers about how certain decisions were influenced, and how certain policies evolved. Were I to take your advice in a number of cases, I believe I would indeed be "bearing false witness."
>
> Years ago, a Sunday school teacher [Hugh Nibley] made a remark I haven't forgotten. He said, "The church has always wanted to put its best foot forward. But the question has always been, which is the best foot?" If anything, my book is a chronicle of how church music has moved forward—and sometimes, perhaps, moved backward—as we struggle to decide which is our best foot. In writing my book I have tried to reveal and conceal events according to the constraints of my conscience, bearing in mind Elder [Dallin H.] Oaks's counsel that we "pursue our search for truth with the tools of honest and objective scholarship and sincere and respectful religious faith, in the mixture dictated by the personal choice each of us is privileged to make in this blessed and free land" (*Ensign*, October 1987, p. 69, emphasis added). This personal choice will differ from person to person, of course. Understanding this, I respect your differences with me on a number of issues and hope you will continue to do the same in return.

I revised the book manuscript pretty quickly and sent the revision back to Moody, who replied on April 21, 1988. He thanked me for the new draft and for my efforts to "accommodate our concerns." But some problems remained for at least some readers. "They are mostly picky and of little consequence, but there are some that are felt to be very important and probably need to be fixed up." He again affirmed that I had "earnestly tried to be sensitive in fulfilling our initial trust" but noted that "there are some who feel strongly that there still remain some negative overtones." Then a subtle warning: since access to materials in the church's historical department are "affected by how these things are used and perceived on the open market," I needed to take the criticisms seriously—"even though you may be justified in everything you have written."

He included a list of nine readers' comments, mostly testy, the harshest of which were these three:

> "He is to be commended [but] we should counsel him not to publish some things. The negative references add nothing to his book; it will be a better book without them. Nor do they add anything to the Church. In fact, they reflect poorly on the Church."

> "I find the tone is sometimes too critical. Some things may be true, but they put leaders and Church musicians in a bad light and give the non-LDS reader an incomplete perspective."

> "There are things of a sensitive nature we thought he would not say … he hasn't kept his trust with us."

Moody later told me over the telephone that a few church leaders were discussing firing me from BYU if this book was published as I'd written it.

The problem was that, because I came into Mormonism out of personal conflict—remember Andrés Segovia—and was emotionally drawn to the conflicts within Mormonism's tragic history, I felt bound to the Book of Mormon's adage, "For it must needs be, that there is an opposition in all things." Or, as Joseph Smith himself said, "It is by proving contraries that truth is made manifest." Maybe *I* was the opposition, passing out the contraries like leaflets. I had not been raised in the church and been soaked in its stock phrases. I came with my own stock phrases from Protestantism, rooted, like early Mormonism itself, in protest. And I'd found *new* stock phrases independently in the language of my new heroes, including the man for whom my university had been named. Understand: I not only had read *Teachings of the Prophet Joseph Smith* before reading the Book of Mormon, I had read *Dialogue: A Journal of Mormon Thought* before reading *A Marvelous Work and a*

Wonder or even *Meet the Mormons*. I knew that the Mormon history I wrote would never be the handbook-driven, defensive, often faux-ameliorative writing that most lifelong members had been raised in. So there I was, standing on the platform of my upbringing and diving into the history of a people not my own by birth.

I came to realize that I was telling a new story made of old stories. And when you are telling the old stories in ways that differ from the people holding the keys to the files, you are in trouble. My tone was not the prevailing churchy tone, devout as I was. Ken Burns noted that what we routinely call "war" is actually "murdering large groups of people."[3] The first term is orthodox and, oddly, benign. The "murdering" phrase is the candid, "negative" one. In my books I lean toward the latter, because it feels more like truth. Call me a Protestant Mormon.

• • •

So, you write a book, it gets published, hits the shelves, and the slow dirge begins. Checking at stores nearby to see who's carrying it. Waiting months, even years for reviews. Having friends tell you they'd read it and liked it. For most people, I discovered, reading a book takes half as long as I take writing one. Who's to blame for that, I don't know. Maybe both: I write too fast and people read too slow. The best place I found my book on the shelves, though, was the Church Museum of History and Art. That was my book's certificate of clemency. How could the church censure me for a book they were selling? Although reason seldom rules in churches, especially this one, I felt safer. The second-best bookstore that carried it was Stanford's. That meant I was, as Dobie Gray used to sing, "in with the 'in' crowd." I was riding the Mormon intelligentsia horse with feet in both stirrups.

Reviews were great. A couple of awards kicked in. I was glad about all this. But for all the hassle, I didn't want to write another book about Mormon anything. My next book was *Sixties Rock: Garage, Psychedelic, and Other Satisfactions*. The one after that was *Henry Cowell: Bohemian*. A few articles on Mormon topics spilled out of me in the 1990s, but my heart resided on other authorial

3. From his course on the *MasterClass* site.

planets. If anyone wanted another Hicks book on Mormon stuff, they'd have to wring it out of me. I couldn't bear the thought of skulking in archives for yet another project like that first one. "Passion is no ordinary word," Graham Parker growls in his song of that name. And if you don't have it for a subject, run away.

Still, if you once had the passion, you never know when it might come back.

That's what happened to me on the night of November 25, 2012. I was thumbing through file folders and kept finding pages of notes on the Mormon Tabernacle Choir, quotes and paraphrases from journals, newspapers, letters, and minutes of meetings. Suddenly the thought dropped into my head, "With just the material I have in these files, I think I could write a better book on the Tab Choir than anyone else." I knew I'd need more, of course, if I wanted a sturdy, thoroughgoing book. But I had the mother lode sitting in steel drawers in my office above the garage.

At the same time, times had changed—metamorphosed, really. The world of research's axis had tilted 180 degrees since my earlier book on Mormon music. At least nine things had radically shifted, seven of which I'll speak somewhat about. First, BYU had not only received two major collections of papers from former Tabernacle Choir conductors, they also had papers from important personnel in the choir's orbit. And these archives I could get into just by walking across the quad. Second, the church had gotten oral histories from several people in recent years that threw klieg lights on the choir's workings, from the stage to the backrooms. Tougher to get those histories, but they existed and I'm tenacious. Third, photocopies of the papers of President David O. McKay, who led the church through the choir's Golden Age were now at the University of Utah, with the door to accessing them flung wide open. His papers revealed the dickerings of top leadership over its biggest public relations—better known as "missionary"—efforts. Fourth, some strong scholarly articles and dissertations on the choir had appeared since the 1980s. Fifth, Google had torched much of the need for old-time heroics like card-catalog searches, letter-writing campaigns, Union Catalog lookups, etc. What once took weeks now sometimes took seconds. Sixth: I was a proven commodity in this scholarly world. Awards, subventions, and good reviews had greased the proverbial rails for me, the ones that had been sticky as tar when I first went down them. Seventh: email.

The other two things I don't want to say much about may be the most important. One is that scans of documents could now be shared from person to person electronically. The second, which rides on the handlebars of the first, is that I had friends in high places, the meaning of which to scholars is "generous friends who have access to stuff you need."

I wanted to interview members of the choir, maybe a lot of them. But that thought was quickly blown out like a candle by the choir management itself. A member I wrote to requesting an interview replied with the statement, "As it is Choir policy that any correspondence such as this be reviewed by our Choir office, I have forwarded your letter to them." Exchanges with choir management convinced me that this was Don Quixote-ville. I worked with a few former members and avoided current ones out of respect. And dismay.

Meanwhile, I'd already decided up front I was not going to interview any of the living conductors of the choir. I'd learned from interviewing in the past that the subject will lobby for favors: they gave you an interview, so you have to treat them well in return. Mutual back-scratching. I didn't want that. And the conductors had given hundreds of pages of interviews and oral history that left me awash in their autobiographic material. Meanwhile, although I'm tempted to say more about my weak expectations of candor from Mormon company men, I try to, as the song says, "yield not to temptation." I read later that George Orwell and Christopher Hitchens had the same non-fraternization policy. Orwell: "I won't have lunch with X or Y because I'm going to write about him soon, and I'm sure I'm going to find he's really quite nice, and, therefore, I don't want the corrupting effect of an acquaintanceship or friendship. I'd rather keep clean and keep pure."[4] I was already perilously close to being friends with all the living Tab Choir conductors. That was enough.

4. As quoted admiringly by Hitchens on C-Span *Booknotes,* Oct. 17, 1993, www.booknotes.org/Watch/51559-1/Christopher-Hitchens (accessed July 9, 2019).

Now, given the constraints handed out like candy by the church and the perhaps more profligate constraints I'd tied myself up with, I knew this: my research on the choir would be like putting together a puzzle, except that I had to get each piece via a scavenger hunt where all the houses are in different neighborhoods and the house with the most pieces is Fort Knox.

Then came the question of readership. I checked with Laurie Matheson of the University of Illinois Press to see if they had first rights of refusal for this manuscript. I thought the book might have "legs" elsewhere, maybe at a non-academic press. "I'm working on a book to be titled *The Mormon Tabernacle Choir: A Biography*," I wrote her. "This is a somewhat important book in this domain, I'd say, and one for which I'm an apt author. (I'd been urged by friends to write it for several years, begged off, and now finally have taken up the challenge.) I expect to take about two years till a suitable manuscript for review is ready." We determined U of I Press had first rights and Laurie said, "This is a very exciting project, and one we certainly would relish publishing." With that nudge, I started telling people about the book and decided I'd keep a running chronicle of its progress on my Facebook page.

Friends offline, though, could readily sense something was afoot. One ran into me in a hallway and asked me if I was working on something. I told him I was writing this book on the Tabernacle Choir. He said, "I could tell." I guess I get a vaguely anointed look when I'm writing. I don't know how much that's a Mormon thing or just a general defect of authors. But I do suspect that writing a book on Mormon history while you're getting a day-job paycheck from the church in question sends you into a deeper trance than most historians fall into. You know you're trying to make something great for which the odds are you'll get busted.

I ran into another friend in the public library. He asked me what my latest project was, I told him, and he said, "That's a great topic. The book almost writes itself." Spoiler alert: never say that to an author. But in truth I *was* getting some fine pages out. Heady, gossipy, fussily musicological, brimming with unobserved facts, but humane and even a bit visionary—at least so it seemed to me in my middle-aged imagination. By February 11, 2013, it did seem as though the book were writing itself. I'd already gotten fifty decent pages of manuscript—and that was only two-thirds of the Evan Stephens-as-conductor years (1890–1916).

Meanwhile, getting out of my files and getting into bigger ones turned out to be less drudgery than I'd thought. Especially at the Church History Library. Getting access to papers from *Music and the Spoken Word* announcer—and apostle—Richard L. Evans was a minor coup and a major boon. Abundant insights, untold tales of why and how certain things happened with the choir from the late 1950s through 1971 (Evans's death). I gasped over and over as I sifted through the musty delight of papers piled in cartons and dusted with actual soot, not to mention slaving over a dark, literally cranky machine we call a microfilm viewer.

Who could resist the charm of eleven large boxes of fan letters Richard L. Evans got from the 1930s through the 1960s, all string-tied in plump bundles like love letters? Most of the letters asked for a copy of Evans's latest radio message. Some just fawned over Richard. Others told personal stories of how his message had moved the writer. Still others asked for advice, à la Dear Abby. The whirligig of addresses on the letters was fun in itself:

> Richard Evans, Tabernacle, KSL
> Richard L. Evans, Mormon Church
> Richard Ellis, Salt Lake City

and lots addressed to

> Richard L. Evans, Mormon Temple

He was such a celebrity, almost any address would do.

On April 7, 2013, I culled all the Tabernacle Choir references from David McKay's complete diaries of the 1950s through 1960s. I took pages and pages of notes. I took photographs too, iPhone shots of almost 200 crucial pages of the First Presidency discussing the choir, its tours, repertoire, and broadcasts. It felt so breathtaking to walk into those meetings through their minutes. After five and a half uninterrupted hours with the papers, I left the library, got into my car, turned the key, and the radio started playing the Youngbloods' "Get Together." When I heard the opening words, "Love is but a song we sing / Fear's the way we die," I started to cry and didn't stop till well after the song ended. Here, swooping in on the angelic airways, had come the summation of so much I'd felt and lived.

Throughout the whole process of research, I didn't expect to get choked up and sob so much as I did. One reason for that was the humanity I kept bumping up against. Here's one case: a well-respected long-term Tabernacle organist was weary after more than two decades in the loft and needed to devote more time to his more-than-full-time church school administrative duties. He wrote a letter of resignation to the LDS First Presidency. They wrote him back accepting the resignation and thanking him for the "spirit" in which his letter was written. I thought: that's the response? No thanks for his superb work as an organist in conferences, broadcasts, funerals, pageants, etc., for twenty-one years? Thanks only for the grace with which he took his exit?

Then I ran across a letter that that organist wrote to a friend after receiving the presidential reply. I saw that we were on the same wavelength, that we've both lived a long time in the world of church music (LDS and otherwise). "The only thing that rather hurts," he wrote, "perhaps more than anything else, is that in accepting my resignation, the Presidency stated that they appreciated very much the spirit of my letter, but said not one word of appreciation of my many years of work as an organist. And you know how many years we have worked for nothing and how many more for practically nothing and how many hours of extra service we have given without words of appreciation."[5] Again, my eyes welled up.

And then there was flying over the landscape of a decades-long deterioration. Not only of what the choir's broadcasts once were, but of the whole era of radio as the visionary acoustic-realm in which America congregated each day and night. Then, too, was the lapse in seriousness of the language we once shared as Americans qua Mormons. Case in point: in one broadcast Richard L. Evans announces an organ medley not as "Mormon hymns," or "Latter-day Saint hymns," or "LDS hymns," but as "hymns of the

5. Tracy Y. Cannon, Letter to Edward P. Kimball, May 13, 1930, Tracy L. Cannon Papers, CHL.

valleys of the inland West." We were all Americans, then, tied to the land, even in our art.

My throat knotted up again and again when I surveyed the wondrous crosstalk of musical idioms we used to hear in our church's semi-annual general conferences. In one typical Saturday in the early 1970s, the Tabernacle Choir sang six hymns (two with the congregation) and six other full-scale pieces by the likes of Mozart, Fauré, and Randall Thompson. The next day's morning session had three hymns (one with congregation) and five other pieces by Handel, Purcell, Mendelssohn, et al. The afternoon session had one hymn (with the congregation) and three other pieces (including, again, Mendelssohn, and Gounod—you can guess which one). So, the choir sang fourteen bona fide choral works in two days, alongside a mere six (non-congregational) hymns (some of them arranged). That pursuit of non-formulaic musical excellence was one of the things that drew me into the church as a young convert. That is the musical church I recall joining. Now I kept thinking of Robert Frost's "The Oven Bird," whose ending lines are: "The question that he frames in all but words / Is what to make of a diminished thing."

Meanwhile, there is the flip side of that "writing itself" coin. A reader might not realize how enormous the work was to arrive at even a seemingly perfunctory passage such as this:

> Year after year in the mid- to late-1960s memos circulated about adjusting the heater for warmth, fixing the noise the heating system made during recordings. increasing the lighting for the choir, patching leaks in the basement ceiling, changing the lettering on the granite panels outside the Tabernacle, and installing: air conditioning, new carpet, a teleprompter at the pulpit, warning lights on restrooms (to tell occupants the broadcast was about to begin), a trophy case (for Gold Records and other awards), bulletin boards, equipment cases for visiting orchestras, pay telephones, bigger cupboards, and more drinking fountains.

Imagine how many memos one has to read to craft that single sentence.

Still, historians know that when you are laying down prose like steel tracks, day after day, sometimes you get handed a golden spike. That happened more than once, as when I offhandedly got a trove of inside documentation on the Orchestra at Temple Square, Telarc, the American Federation of Musicians (Local 104), and why the Tabernacle Choir had to create its own record label. Fascinating, sometimes half-crazy, and often utterly predictable contests of will. I reveled in all such documents that got handed to me by, I have to say it, amazing grace.

• • •

By July, 2013, I was adding endnotes to some chapters. It had been a long time since I'd done that sort of intellectual masonry. I'd forgotten how taxing yet satisfying it felt to cement your sources—in this particular month, sources dealing with the Tabernacle Choir's October–November 1911 East Coast tour that was constructed around the controversial American Land and Irrigation Exposition. Nerdily blissful.

A handful of weeks later, I posted this on Facebook:

> I am shocked and delighted to say that by the end of next week, barring cataclysm, I will have a complete, decent draft of "The Mormon Tabernacle Choir: A Biography" in my hands (and desktops and flash drives). Shocked that this has gushed out of my brain and fingers so fluidly—although, honestly, for months I've been focused on the task like a laser in an old James Bond film. Delighted because this morning the ending laid itself out in my mind so elegantly that I see not just the light at the end of the tunnel, but the scenery onto which the tunnel opens.
>
> The draft still has lots of what I call "expansion joints," spots where I know I will bring in more material that I have on the shelf. And I'm still slapping down endnotes like a roofer with his nailgun. But the joists, rafters, and all the other housing metaphors you can think of—even the kitchen sink—are in place. Oh, a basement, too, though I try to visit it only now and then.

At 1:41 on the morning of August 11, 2013, I wrote the final line of my Tabernacle Choir book. There were some sentences leading up to that last line that were only sketched. And I knew I would keep inserting new passages throughout the whole work. More endnotes and revisions galore awaited me. But anyone who writes knows there are various "completions." For me, this was the first one that felt like it.

In the coming weeks, I took a quick inventory of all the sources cited in the endnotes of my new book. To give a sense of the research, here is the count, arranged by types of sources, from highest to lowest number used; except where noted, each source (e.g., diary) may have been cited numerous unspecified times:

Books and pamphlets: 89 (many of these are published diaries)
Newspaper articles (1820s through the present): 80
Unpublished letters: 71
Magazine articles (scholarly and popular): 43
Unpublished Choir minutes: 39 different dates cited
Miscellaneous unpublished documents: 24 (e.g., internal reports, surveys)
Websites: 19
Oral Histories: 12 (just one of these, for example, by Jerold Ottley, is cited dozens of times)
Dissertations and theses: 9
Unpublished journals and diaries: 9 (one, the David O. McKay diary, has fourteen separate citations)
Letters and emails to me: 4
Interviews with me: 3

How many more sources were consulted, used in some way, but *not* overtly cited? I have no idea.

My friend and colleague Heidi Reed proofed the manuscript. With her annotations in hand, I gathered more endnotes, added a few words and sentences here and there, and readied the book to send to the press for the next round of readings. Heidi heartened me with her synoptic comments, which included these: "After reading some of the swings back and forth between the pendulum of populist and classical repertoire [you chronicle], I have come to believe that the Choir is itself a technology of sorts, that is neither good or ill, but serves those who are at its head, generally the ecclesiastical leaders, not the musical directors. … Instead of being made up of such and such repertoire on such and such date, the story is made up of who was choosing the repertoire, and why, and the pressures felt from all around."

The press got good anonymous readers for the book. Many suggestions made sense, many not so much. But they yielded my favorite quote on any book manuscript I've sent to a press. An anonymous Mormon historian complained that my "occasional over-dependence on particular facts is a bit distressing." Other comments made me chuckle. "So why did [Evan] Stephens want to go to Wales when he hadn't wanted to go to St. Louis? Can you give more context/perspective on what his motivations actually were?" I didn't reply in writing to that one. But in my head I replied: "If you don't know why someone would prefer Wales to St. Louis, why are you getting paid to judge anyone's book?"

One reader liked the manuscript a lot, except for two paragraphs in the Introduction—shades of my first book—which he hated so much he said he'd wanted to stop reading right there. He wrote me a fussy single-spaced page on how I could address the problems: he blasted the paragraphs' premises, speculated on ways to create a better context for my assertions, proposed insertions that would clarify my meaning, refuted some key sentences, suggested an alternative interpretation I hadn't considered, and even corrected my spelling of one name. I thought for a couple of hours about his critique, tinkered with ways to respond, jotted some notes in the margins, then rolled up my sleeves and got to work: I cut those two paragraphs.

On May 2, 2014, I sent a revised manuscript and complete set of photographs to the press. Copyediting lasted through July. In time, with page proofs finally in hand, I started to index. After two weeks, the final entry: "Barnum, P. T." Something about that seemed deliciously divine, a sign from above that I'd grasped the essence of this jumbo, ultra-talented, American spectacle we call the Mormon Tabernacle Choir.

That October I learned that my book would be lead title in the UIP spring catalogue. And the blurbs were terrific, lofty praise from sources more diverse than I'd ever dreamt of. On the cover, my name would be above the choir's. The press said this was to display that this is *Michael Hicks's* biography of the choir. So I got top billing, a first for me as an author. The book launched at the annual meeting of the American Choral Directors Association, coincidentally being held in Salt Lake City in February 2015. Then I was chosen for the press's one-hour book signing at Book-Expo America at the end of that May in New York City. The press paid to get the book displayed on counters and "New Releases" tables at Barnes & Noble, the greatest benefit of which was that I learned about the backroom negotiations that yield spots in those hallowed vistas in big stores.

Most of the reviews made me blush. My favorite was Alex Beam's in the *Wall Street Journal.*[6] His talent and the high-profile venue itself made it shine. But the line that meant the most to me was simply this: "Mormon history written by Mormons can be pretty dry, but Mr. Hicks, a professor of music at Brigham Young University, is funkier than your average saint." In coming months, scholarly journals weighed in, with some occasionally glorious summations that matched the book's blurbs in their warmth. I'd quote more of my favorite passages from positive reviews, but for your sakes I'll dwell on the most entertaining reviews, which are always the negative.

The first bad review, if one can call it that, was from Deseret Book. On February 20, 2015, I got this email message from the press via its Utah sales manager: "Apparently the Deseret bookstore has canceled its initial order of 240 copies for two reasons: (1) There is an 'official' biography of the MTC coming soon. (2) There is information in the book which the Church doesn't approve of." I felt bad for the press, of course. Deseret's first rationale was a lie, of course. I knew that because I know the field and its players better than anyone. To the second rationale, I responded, "There is information in the book which I don't approve of, either." When I shared the news with one of the book's informants, he replied, "Not that you needed it, but your book just got instant credibility."

The second bad review came in a ten-minute telephone call on March 5, 2015, from former choir conductor Richard Condie's elderly son Bob. He was primed to gripe at me about "inaccuracies" on his father in my book. I asked him where he got the book and he said that—although "I would never buy that book!"—photocopies

6. Alex Beam, "The Singing Saints," *Wall Street Journal*, Apr. 10, 2015.

of four pages were sent to him from a source that he refused to disclose. I pressed him until he claimed it was "a professor on the east coast." He angrily disputed my account of how Richard had been released from his conductorship and the bitterness he felt about it, even though my account was taken directly from Richard's oral history. Bob also fought me about the Grammys. He said he had a letter from an attorney for the church in which the church agreed that the choir's Grammy and its gold and platinum record awards all belonged to *Condie* and that at the Condie family's request the church would change all references in its printed and online materials accordingly. I just paused for a moment, speechless. "Oh, nothing to say to that, huh? Cat got your tongue?" We went back and forth for a few more minutes until he said, "Shit, I'm just gonna call the head of that music department out there and complain to them about you." All this confirmed some of what I'd said about Richard. Nastiness doesn't fall far from the tree.

Another bad review appeared on *Goodreads*. Its author, a frequent reviewer for the *Deseret News*, wrote, "My review [for the newspaper] on this book pointed out the author's negative bias toward the LDS church, so it was never published. Needless to say, I was unimpressed with this book and the many inferences the author took." She gave it one star—the same as she'd given to *War and Peace*. And to *Moby Dick*.[7]

Finally, the offhand bad reviews from inside the choir, whispered to me on the sly, came in two types. One was that mine was the most read book that no one would admit to reading, a popular title that got passed around a lot, but always by hands soaked in guilt. The other was that I was being called "a tool of the enemy," the latter term being an old-timey nickname for Lucifer himself.

Again, I dwell on the snotty quotes not because they vex me or because they dominate the field, but because they're more fun. And I realize that that's the problem my readers back at the Church Music Department had tried to ward me away from in the 1980s: fun. Which is a shame, because in this transitory world,

7. Elizabeth Reid posted this on *Goodreads* on April 14, 2015 (screen shot in my files). As of this writing, she has removed it—though she retains her slams on Tolstoy and Melville.

coated with soot and footnotes, fun is the truest form of divinity I know. "Rejoice," God says over and over. Don't forget that.

Which brings me back to my title. "Making book." I hedged my bets on the Tabernacle Choir book based on what I'd learned from *Mormonism and Music*. What I'd learned, mostly, was "stay out of Dodge." If you try to work with most any administration, they'll instinctively slam the door on your ambitions and suck the juice from your prose. So, make book by making a book, a real book, your own book. "Let the consequence follow," as we sing, and "battle for freedom in spirit and might." Because when you're making book on this kind of a race, you soon learn you're also the horse and the jockey.

I've now done my bit for Mormon musical history. What I have left are boxes full of files and a thimble full of interest. Did my gamble on this Tabernacle Choir book pay off? If God is the bookie and heft the payoff, then yes. We finally all got the kind of book the choir deserves. If I got to write my own blurb, it might be this: "Here is America's book on America's choir." In the book's wake, I also got my future epitaph from the *Wall Street Journal*: "Funkier than your average saint." The best news: I escaped church prosecution, which always lurks around the corner of the historian's desk. I kept my job at BYU, until I was ready to walk away from it in 2020, after thirty-five years in its murky trenches. Sadly, there are two words I've never gotten from the church or the choir or its members or its bosses, two words I indisputably earned: "Thank you." No matter. The betting on this race is now closed.

INDEX

Note: in the text, variant spellings or punctuations of the same titles sometimes appear (as they did originally), but are not listed separately here. Also, first lines of hymns sometimes function as, or overlap with, titles. For example, the *first line* of what was originally titled "Hosanna to God and the Lamb" almost immediately became its *title*, "The Spirit of God Like a Fire Is Burning"; "Love at Home" became known by the title "There Is Beauty All Around," its first line, although it is usually published under its actual title. Many such overlaps and divergences among titles and first lines exist. I chose not to list more than one version for any given hymn or song in this index. —MH

#

25 Most Beloved Melodies, 188

3-Ds, The, 121–22

44 Old Time Mormon and Far West Songs, 108–09

A

A Day, a Night, a Day, 149

Abel, Elijah, 75

Abraham, 41

Adam and Eve, 91–92

Adam–God doctrine, 203–04

Adam-ondi-Ahman, 3, 56

Adamless Eden, An, 91

Adamson, J. H., 110

African Band, The, 78

AIDS, 180

Aladdin, 178

alcohol, 14

"All Hail the Glorious Day," 168

"All Is Well," 62

"Amazing Grace," 25, 46

America, the Beautiful," 161

American Choral Directors Association, 216–17

American Federation of Musicians, 214

"American Star," 63–65

Amos and Andy, 96

Apostate, The, 149

"Arise, My Soul Arise," 168

"Arise, O Glorious Zion," 168

Arrington, Leonard, 200

Articles of Faith, 182–83

Artisan Sound Recorders, 129

"Auld Lang Syne," 4

Axis: Bold As Love, 122

B

"Babylon Is Fallen," 79
Bach, J. S., 197
Bad Men Ballads, 117–18
Badmen and Heroes, 118
Badmen, The, 118–19, 121, 125
Ballads and Songs from Utah, 115
Barlow, Milt G., 86–87
Barnes & Noble, 217
Barnum, P. T., 216
Barthes, Roland, 197
"Battle Hymn of the Republic," 105, 129, 152, 161
"Battle of [the] River Raisin," 8–10
Beam, Alex, 27
Beauty and the Beast, 178
"Because I Have Been Given Much," 172
Beesley, Ebenezer, 20, 63, 80, 85
Beethoven, Ludwig van, 5–6, 12, 23
"Before Thee, Lord, I Bow My Head," 168
"Behold a Royal Army," 162
"Behold how brightly breaks the morning," 75
Benson, Ezra Taft, 167
Benson, Reed, 180
Bernstein, Leonard, 105, 177–78, 184
binder's volumes, 3, 5, 22–23
Bishop, Joey, 193
Bitter End, The, 103
Black Sabbath, 182
Blackface and Music, 96
Blind Tom (Thomas Bethune), 88
"Blue Blood Colored Coons,"
Book of Commandments, 27
Book of Mormon (musical), 98, 177–86
Book-Expo America, 217
Boston Tea Party, 73
Boyadjian, Arthur, 138, 151–52
Boyé, Alex, 98
Bradshaw, Merrill, 156, 198; hymnbook and, 162, 165, 169–70, 172
Brady Bunch, The, 179
Brand, Oscar, 119
Brando, Marlon, 138
"Break Forth, O Beauteous Heavenly Light," 168
Briegel, George, 108–09
Brigham Young University, 121, 129, 191; Indian–Lamanite programs of, 132–36, 144–45, 149–51; library, 8, 133–34, 208; performances at, 146–48; professors, 120, 156, 198, 219
"Brighter Days in Store," 124
Brimhall, George, 21
Brooks, Richard, 139–40
Brown, Dick, 88
Browne, Raymond, 95
Bugs Bunny, 180
Bullock, Thomas, 17–18, 57
Bureau of Indian Affairs, 132
Burr, Charles, 107, 110–12, 115–20
Bye Bye Birdie, 179

C

Cain, 73, 100
Camelot, 129, 138
Campbell, Joseph, 180
"Campfire Meeting, The," 124
"Camptown Races," 108, 116
Cannon, Tracy, 172–73
Capitol Records, 121
Car 54, Where Are You? 179

Card, Orson Scott, 149
Careless, George, 85, 166
Carmer, Carl, 120, 122, 127, 128
Carthage Jail, 12, 16–22, 48, 63, 73
Cash, Johnny, 117
"Cast Thy Burden Upon the Lord," 168
Chamberlain, Bryce, 138, 145, 150, 151
Chapin, Schuyler, 111
Cheney, Thomas, 111–16, 118, 120, 122, 127
Children of the Sun, The, 149
Chopin, Frédéric, 88
Chorus Line, A, 182
Christmas, Robert, 112–13, 119
Christy's Minstrels, 79
Church Museum of History and Art, 207
Church Music Committee, 21, 155–56
Church Music Department, 155, 218
Church Music Division, 200
Church News, 133, 140, 158
Church of England, 57
civil rights, 124–25
Civil War, 80, 87
Clayton, William, 62
Clingers, The, 140
Clinton, Bill, 187
Coles, George, 16
Columbia Broadcasting System (CBS), 104
Columbia Records Legacy Series, 103–07, 115–18, 120, 128
"Come, All Ye Sons of God," 168
"Come, All Ye Sons of Zion," 168
"Come, Come Ye saints," 62, 109–10, 114, 124
"Come Let Us Sing an Evening Hymn," 168
"Come with Tuneful Voices," 161
"Come Thou Fount of Every Blessing," 44, 162
"Coming Day, The," 161
compact discs, 189, 192
Condie, Richard, 104–05, 111, 115, 217–18
Confederacy, The, 105, 117, 128
Contributor, 21
Coon Chicken Inn, 96
Cooperman, Jeannette, 76
Corbyn, Sheridan, 84–85
Cornwall, Spencer, 21, 97
Cotton, Gene, 188
"Cracovian Maid, The," 75
Cravat, Nick, 139–40
cross, 40–41
Curious George, vii
Curran, Grenade, 138–39
Curtain, The, 81

D

Daily Light, 177
Daniels, William, 16–17
Daughters of the Utah Pioneers, 107
Davidson, Levette J., 108–09
Davis, Dick, 122
"Day Is Past and Gone, The," 3
Daynes, Joseph, 68–69, 88–89, 172
De Anza College, 198
"Dear to the Heart of the Shepherd," 168
Deseret Book, 125, 156, 217

Deseret Industries, 189, 191–92
Deseret Minstrels, 93
Deseret News, 19, 20, 78, 218; minstrel shows and, 80, 81, 83, 85, 88–90, 91
Deseret Sunday School Songs, 160–61
Detroit Mormon Concert Choir, 188
Dialogue: A Journal of Mormon Thought, 126, 206
Dickinson, Emily, vii
Disney, 178, 180
"Dixie," 79–80
Doctrine and Covenants, 27–28, 29–30, 32
Donizetti, Gaetano, 88
"Don't Marry the Mormon Boys," 113
"Duane Street," 16, 62–63
Dunbar, William C., 80
Duprez and Benedict's (minstrels), 85
Dylan, Bob, 106, 188, 191

E

"Echo Canyon Song," 109, 114, 124
Electric Light Orchestra, 188
Elektra Records, 118
Elliott, Ramblin' Jack, 103–04, 119
Elmer Gantry, 181
Emmett, Dan, 79
Ensign, 21, 158, 205
Especially for Youth (EFY), 179
Essentials in Church History, 22
Ethiopian, 76, 78, 81, 83, 87, 88, 90
Evans, David, 106
Evans, Richard L., 119, 211–13
Evening and the Morning Star, The, 27, 55–57
exotica, 152

F

Facebook, 214
Farm Boy and the Angel, The, 127
"Father in Heaven," 168
Fauré, Gabriel, 213
Felt, Paul, 134–35, 145, 151
Fife, Austin and Alma, 108–10, 117–18
First Presidency, 132, 156, 169, 211–12
Fisher, Truman, 145
Folk Music Worldwide, 12
Footlights, 85–86
"For Our Devotions, Father," 168
Fort Knox, 210
Foster, Stephen, 11, 23, 78–79
Franck, César, 190–91, 193–94
Frost, Robert, 213
Frye, Northrop, 73–74
Funicello, Annette, 192

G

gambling, 197
Gates, Crawford, 136
"Gather Round the Camp Fire, Brethren," 110
Gaye, Marvin, 183
"Gentle Annie," 79
Germany, 31
"Get Together," 211–12
Gibbs, George, 4–5
"Glorious Things of Thee Are Spoken," 3, 4
"Go, Ye Messengers of Glory," 168
"God of Our Fathers, Known of Old," 168
"God spake the word and time began," 36
Goodman, Harold, 157–58

Goodreads, 218
Goodwill Industries, 189
Google, 208
Gounod, Charles, 213
grace, 44–46
Grammy Awards, 104–05, 218
Grant, Heber J., 21
Gray, Dobie, 207
"Great God Attend, While Zion Sleeps," 168
"Great was the day, the joy was great," 40
Greatest American Hero, 182
Grover, Thomas, 30

H

Hafen, Leroy and Ann, 120–22
Haight, David, 22
Hall, Gerald Ray, 135, 137–38, 144
Hamilton Wood Type Foundry, 122–23
"Handcart Song, The," 109, 114, 124
Handel, George Frideric, 105, 129, 143, 152, 213
Handy, Mildred, 134–36, 141, 144–46
Hanson, Louise G., 149
"Hard Times Come Again No More," 108, 109, 114, 121
"Hark, Listen to the Trumpeters," 3
Harris, W. T., 83
"Have Courage, My Boy, to Say No," 110
Haverley, Jack, 92–94, 100
Hawai'i, 189
"He dies, the friend of sinners dies," 37
Hendrix, Jimi, 122–23
Henry Cowell: Bohemian, 207
Hewlett, Lester, 105–07, 111–15, 119
Highland High School, 146
Hill Cumorah Pageant, 136, 152, 183
Hilton, L. M., 109–10, 113, 119
Hinckley, Gordon B., 169
Historical Department of the Church, 200, 204
History of the Church, 17–19, 22, 29
Hitchens, Christopher, 209
Hofmann, E. T. A., 14
Hofmann, Mark, 200
"Home on the Range," 108
"Home, Sweet Home," 76
Homer, 182
Hosanna shout, 58
"How Great Thou Art," 165
How Rare a Possession, 151
Howe, E. D., 54–55
Howells, Rulon, 106
Hubbard, Lester, 108–09, 110–11, 115
Hulse, Renee Chalk, 141
"Humors of Glen," 64–65
Hunter, Milton, 144
Hyde, Orson, 31
Hyers Sisters, 87–88
Hymnbook (1985), 22, 155–73
Hymnbook, Manchester, 16, 20, 30–36, 39
Hymnbooks, early Mormon, 25–51

I

"I Am a Child of God," 179–80
"I Am a Mormon" campaign, 178
"If You Could Hie to Kolob," 172
Improvement Era, 21, 125
"Indian Hunter, The," 4

Indian Placement Program, 132, 145

Indiana University Press, 110

Indianapolis 4th Ward Choir, 188

Indians, American. *See* Native Americans

Institute of American Indian Studies and Research, 133, 135–36, 140

International Music Industry Conference, 128

Irish Melodies, 12

Irish Uprising, 128

"Iron Horse, The," 121

It Takes a Thief, 138

"I've Been Working on the Railroad," 108

J

Jack Benny Program, 139

James (apostle), 182

Jazz Singer, The, 96

Jesus, 16, 186; blood of, 41–44

Jesus freaks, 197–98

"Jesus, Once of Humble Birth," 39

"Jesus, the name that charms our fears," 37

John Fitzgerald Kennedy . . . As We Remember Him, 125, 128

John the Baptist, 153

Johnson, Benjamin, 4–5, 23, 48

Johnston, Col. Albert Sidney, 78

"Johnston's Army Song," 124

"Join the Children of the Lord," 161

Jolson, Al, 96

Jones, Shirley, 138

Jones, Talmage, 144–45

"Joseph Smith's First Prayer," 119, 120

Journal of American Folklore, 108

Jump, Gordon, 138, 151

Juvenile Instructor, 20

K

Kennedy, John F., 121, 125–26

Kimball, Edward, 187–90, 195

Kimball, Heber C., 47–48, 99

Kimball, Prescendia L., 57

Kimball, Spencer Levan, 190

Kimball, Spencer W., 132, 135, 150–51, 157, 187–93

"Kingsfold," 172

Kirtland Revelation Book, 56

Kirtland Temple, 56, 58, 65–66

Kirtland, 36

Krehbiel, Clayton, 119

KSL radio, 110

L

Lamanite Generation, 150

Lamanites, 10, 129–33, 149–51. *See also* Native Americans

Lancaster, Burt, 139–40

Larsen, Dean L., 160–70

Latter-day Saints' Psalmody, 71

Lay, Hark, 75

Lee, Alexander, 11

Lee, Harold B., 155, 157, 170–71

"Let all the saints their hearts prepare," 37

Lewis, Jerry, 138

Liberty Jail, 7–8

Library of Congress, 109

Lieberson, Goddard, 105–07, 113, 117, 120–21, 128

Lincoln, Abraham, 14

Linda di Chamounix, 88
Lion King, The, 178, 180
Liszt, Franz, 88
Little Mermaid, The, 178, 180
longing, 14
"Lonsdale," 69
Love at Home," 79, 161
"Lucy Long," 80
Lyon, Laurence, 126

M

Mace, Wandle, 4
Madsen, Carol Cornwall, 21
Madsen, Florence, 21
Mamet, David, 185
Man for All Seasons, A, 183
Man's Search for Happiness, 138, 151
Maracatu, 136
mariachi, 188
marriage, 47–48
Marvelous Work and a Wonder, A, 206–07
Mass (Bernstein), 178, 184
Matheson, Laurie, ix, 210
McClure, John, 111
McCreery, John, 63
McCulloh, Judy, 198–99
McCurdy, Ed, 119
McKay, David O., 105–06, 124–25, 134, 137; papers of, 208, 211
McNaughton, John Hugh, 79
Meet the Mormons, 207
Melchizedek Priesthood Committee, 169
Mendelssohn, Felix, 213
Messenger and Advocate, 57, 63
Messiah, 105, 143
meters, musical, 62–63
Mexico, 121, 125
Millennial Star, 49
"Missionary Hymn," 161
Mississippi River, 76
Moby Dick, 218
Monson, Thomas, 165
Monteux, Pierre, 189
Montgomery, James, 15
Moody, Michael, 165, 169–72, 201–06
Moore, Thomas, 11–12
More, Thomas, 183
Mormon, The (newspaper), 122, 128
"Mormon Army Song," 114
"Mormon Battalion Song," 114, 124
"Mormon Coon, The," 95–96
Mormon Country, 111
Mormon Creed, 76–77, 84
Mormon Expo Choir, 188
Mormon Folk Ballads, 121–22
Mormon History Association, 126
"Mormon Love Serenade," 114
Mormon Pioneers, The, 103–28
Mormon Songs from the Rocky Mountains, 127
Mormon Story, The, 106
Mormon Tabernacle Choir, 20, 97, 187, 188, 198; *Mormon Pioneers* album and, 104–06,
113–14, 119
Mormon Tabernacle Choir: A Biography, The, vii, 199–207
Mormon Youth Symphony and Chorus, 188
Mormonism and Music: A History, vii, 199–207

"Morning Breaks, the Shadows Flee, The," 39
Moroni, vii
"Moroni's Lamentation," 56
Mötley Crüe, 191
Motown, 182
Mozart, W. A., 213
"Muhlenberg," 67
Murphy and Mack's (minstrels), 84–85
Music and Prejudice, 11
Music and the Spoken Word, 211
Music Lover's Chest of Records, 188
Music Man, The, 181
Mutual Improvement Association, 21, 188
"My Heart's Experience," 60–61
"My Jesus, As Though Wilt," 164
My Life's Review, 4
"My Skiff Is by the Shore," 76

N

"Nae Luck Around the House," 4
Naisbitt, H. W., 21
Native Americans, 8–10, 149; boarding schools for, 132, 137–38; and Kimball, Spencer, 187–88; Mormon indenture of, 131; seminaries for, 134–35, and Wilkinson, Ernest L., 132–33, 151. *See also* Lamanites
Nauvoo, 30, 33, 99, 198
"Nearer My God to Thee," 162
"negro's eleventh commandment," 76–77
Nibley, Hugh, 205
Nick at Nite, 178
"Nigger's Lament," 80
Nora's Christmas Gift, 151
"Northfield," 67
"Now Let Us Rejoice," 55–56, 66

O

"O how happy are they," 43
"O My Father," 119
Oaks, Dallin H., 205
Octoroon, The, 80–81
Office of Indian Affairs (BYU), 134
Ogden Junction, 90
"Oh Babylon, Oh Babylon!" 109
"Oh Susanna," 108
Omaha Tribal Prayer, 164
Omnibus (Bernstein), 178
"On the Road to California," 114, 124
On the Town, 178
"Once I Lived in Cottonwood," 113, 124
One Flew Over the Cuckoo's Nest, 185
opera, 10–11
Orchestra at Temple Square, 214
Original Georgia Minstrels, 89–90
Orwell, George, 209
Osmond, Donny, 181
"O Thou in whose presence my soul takes delight," 37–39
"Our Mountain Home," 114, 120
"Oven Bird, The," 213
"Ox Team Trail, The," 114, 124

P

Packer, Boyd K., 158, 201, 205
Page, John E., 31
Panic of 1873, 90
Parker, Graham, 208
Parker, Wallace, 129
Paskman, Dailey, 96–97

Patten, David W., 58

Patti, Adelina, 203

Paul (apostle), 54

Peaches and Herb, 183

Pearl Awards, 178

Pentecostalism, 197–98

People of the Book: cast, 138–40; music, 136–37; production, 135–36; promotion, 140–41; scenes, 142–43; script, 146

Petersen, Mark E., 158

Phelps, Sally, 36

Phelps, W. W., 79–80; hymnbooks and, 27–28, 36, 37–38; "Spirit of God" and, 55–61, 64, 66

Pinnock, Hugh, 171

Pioneer Songs, 107–09, 115

"Plunged in a gulf of dark despair" 45

polygamy, 47

"Poor Wayfaring Man of Grief" 15–22, 62–63, 115, 119, 122

"Praise to the Man," 119

Pratt, Parley, 56; hymnbooks and, 29–30, 32, 34, 39, 49

Primary Tune Book, 70–71

Professionals, The, 140

Proust, Marcel, 23–24

psychedelia, 130, 148–49

Purcell, Henry, 213

Purdy, Scott, and Fostelle (minstrels), 85–86, 90

Pursuit of Excellence program, 198

Pyper, George D., 21

R

Raines, T. W., 117–18

Realm of the Incas, 137, 148

record collecting, 188–91

"Redeemer of Israel," 4, 37–39

Reed, Heidi, 215

Reeves, Jim, 188

Relief Society, 45–47

Rentz-Santley Female Minstrels, 90–92

Reorganized Church of Jesus Christ of Latter Day Saints, 49

Reynolds, Alice, 21

Reynolds, George, 86

Richards, LeGrand, 144

Richards, William, 16–17, 18, 32

Richie, Lionel, 183

Rigdon, Sidney, 25–26, 27, 58

Rites of the Pagan, 136–37, 148, 152

Roberts, B. H., 19

Robertson, Leroy, 115–16

Robinson, Ebenezer, 33–34

Rogers, David W., 28, 30

Rogues, The, 138

romanticism, 14

"Root Hog or Die," 124

"Rose that All Are Praising, The" 107

Ross, Diana, 183

Russian Orthodoxy, 188

Ryman, Add, 94–95

S

Sacred Harp, 62

Saints of Sage and Saddle, 110

Salt Lake Mastodon Minstrels, 93

Salt Lake Minstrels, 81–83, 86

Salt Lake Social Hall, 78

Salt Lake Theatre, 80, 83–93

Salt Lake Times, 89

Salt Lake Tribune, 85, 93, 97

Salvation Army, 189
Sambo, 81, 96
San Francisco Symphony, 190
Sandburg, Carl, 120
Saturday's Warrior, 178
"Scatter Sunshine," 162
Schreiner, Alexander, 203
Schubert, Franz, 23
"Seagulls and Crickets," 109, 114, 124
"Sego Lily," 109
Segovia, Andres, 197–98, 206
"Sehet ihr Völker," 165
Seven Brides for Seven Brothers, 138
Sherman Institute, 135, 137
Shindler, Oskar, 186
Simon and Garfunkel, 188
Singing in the Rain, 138
Sixties Rock: Garage, Psychedelic, and Other Satisfactions, 207
Smith, Anna Nicole, 193
Smith, Asael, 76–77
Smith, Emma, 25, 27–50, 172
Smith, George A., 4, 17–18, 75
Smith, George Albert, 132
Smith, Henry Clay, 95
Smith, Hyrum, 16–22, 30
Smith, Joseph Fielding, 22
Smith, Joseph III, 8, 49
Smith, Joseph, 58, 73, 75, 76, 136, 151; hymnbooks and, 25, 27, 29–30, 32, 34, 41; songs
associated with, 3–24
Smith, William, 3, 77
Smithsonian Institution, 109
Snow, Eliza, 71, 78–79
Snow, Eunice B., 4
Snow, Lorenzo, 32
"Soldier's Dream, The," 11–13, 14
"Soldier's Tear, The," 10–13
Songs of American Railroading, 117
Songs of Our Soil, 117
Songs of the Mormons, 127
Songs of the Mormons and Songs of the West, 109
Songs of the North and South, 115–16
songs of Zion, 55–56
Sonneck Society, 198
"Sons of Michael, He Approaches," 203–04
Sor, Fernando, 197
Sorrels, Rosalie, 115
Sounds of a Century, 191
Source Book, 108–09
Southern California Mormon Choir, 137, 142
Spaeth, Sigmund, 14
Spencer, William Robert, 5
"Spirit of God Like a Fire Is Burning, The," 3–4, 119; importance, 53–54; music, 61–71, text, 54–61
"St. George and the Dragon," 113, 121
Stadium of Fire, 178
Standard Works, 155
"Star-Spangled Banner, The," 63
Starbound Records, 103
Starlite Bowl, 129
"Stars of Morning, Shout for Joy," 161
Stegner, Wallace, 111
Stephens, Evan, 216
Stewart, Doug, 149
Stone, O. Leslie, 155–56
Stories of Latter-day Saint Hymns, 21
Stories of Our Mormon Hymns, 21

Sun Records, 117
Sunstone, 198
"Supplication Hymn," 161
Swain, Joseph, 37
Swanee Singers, 97

T

"Take Courage, Saints, Faint Not by the Way," 162
Tamres, David, 197
Tanner, Jerald and Sandra, 200
Taylor, John, 16–22, 32, 63, 107, 122
Teachings of the Prophet Joseph Smith, 206
Telarc, 214
temple endowment, 153
Terrell, Tammi, 183
Thalberg, Irving, 88
Theater Comique and Bowery, 86
"The Lord into his garden comes," 37
"There is a fountain fill'd with blood," 42
"There Is a Land of Pure Delight," 36
"There Is a Land the Lord Will Bless," 36
"There's a feast of fat things for the righteous preparing," 36
"There's a Power in the Sun," 36
"This Is the Place," 114, 124
Thomas, Robert K., 144
Thompson, Marilyn (Mom), 177
Thompson, Randall, 213
"Though in the Outward Church Below,"
"Through All the World Below," 36
Times and Seasons, 33–34
"Tittery-irie-ay," 113, 124
tongues, speaking (or singing) in, 54–57
Tony Awards, 181
Towne, Jacob, 76–77
Tragedy of Korihor, The, 149
"Trumpet, The," 67
Tullidge, John, 85, 88
Twelve Apostles, 47–48, 132, 155, 162, 179

U

Uganda, 178–79
Uncle Tom's Cabin, 80
Union, The, 105, 117, 128
University of Illinois Press, 198–99
University of Utah, 110, 115, 208
"Unknown Grave, The," 115
Untouchables, The, 185
"Upper California, The," 107, 114
Utah Humanities Review, 108
Utah Musical Bouquet, 68–69, 71
Utah Musical Times, 89
Utah Reformation, 78
Utah State Centennial Commission, 108
Utah Symphony, 136

V

vaudeville, 96, 139
Vaughan-Williams, Ralph, 172
Virginian, The, 138

W

"Wait for the Wagon," 114
Waldo, Elisabeth, 136–37, 141–42, 145–48, 152
Walker Opera House, 92
Wall Street Journal, 217

War and Peace, 218
War of 1812, 10, 72
Washington, George, 151
Wasser, Alan, 122
"Waste Not, Want Not," 113, 124
Watergate, 204
Watts, Isaac, 37
"We Are the World," 184
"We Gather Together," 65–66
Weber State University, 146
Welch, Jay, 187
West Side Story, 178
Western Folklore, 108, 110
"What's the Use of Repining?" 110
"When Joseph His Brethren Beheld," 4
"When restless on my bed I lie," 37
White, Dale, 139, 145
Whitney, Elizabeth Ann, 56–57
Whitney, Helen Mar, 75–76
Whitney, Newell, 48
"Who Are These Arrayed in Light" 161
"Who's on the Lord's Side, Who?" 162, 164
"Whoa! Ha! Buck and Jerry Boy," 109, 113, 121, 124
"Wife, Children, and Friends," 5–7, 14, 23
Wilkinson, Ernest, 132–33, 135–36, 151
Wilson, Billy, 89–90
Wilson, Sloan, 200–01
"With joy we meditate the grace," 45
WKRP in Cincinnati, 138
Women of the West, 117
Woodruff, Wilford, 17–19, 78, 203
Word of Wisdom, 14
Work, Henry Clay, 79
Wright, Jay, 110

Y

"Yankee Doodle," 116
Young Ambassadors, 178
Young People's Concerts, 178
Young, Ann Eliza Webb, 53
Young, Brigham, 23, 53, 58, 108, 151, 152–53; Adam–God doctrine of, 203; *Book of Mormon* musical and, 184; hymnbooks and, 28, 30, 32–34; Native Americans and, 131–32; race and, 77, 78–79, 82–83, 86, 202; Smith, Emma, and, 47–48
Youngbloods, The, 211–12
Yovail Dancers, 134

Z

"Zack, the Mormon Engineer," 109, 114, 116, 124, 127
Zion's Camp, 3, 75